THE TAILORS'

Classical and Infallible

TEXT BOOK of CUTTING

All Garments

...WORN BY...

Men, Women and Children,

...BY...

The MOST WONDERFUL

Road - to - Fortune, Perfected

AND Unapproachable

SYSTEMS,

FORMING

A Complete Standard Encyclopædia

OF

The Whole Art and Science of Tailors'

Cutting to Fit Properly.

British Library Cataloguing-in-Publication Data
A catalogue record for this book is available from the
British Library

PREFACE.

HITHERTO no Classical and Infallible Text Book of Cutting has been brought out. In days gone by, a few individuals thought that Dr. Wampen's Work occupied such a position ; but the majority of mankind found it to be anything but classical and infallible, and hence a vacant field has still remained to be filled, as the imitations of our Works and other execrences have amounted to very little and gone very little or no length toward occupying the position. This Work is designed as an attempt to fill not only the vacancy, but the role of being the first really Classical Work ever issued on the Art and Science of Cutting in the true sense of the word, and we hope and trust—and have faith—that it will do so.

THE PUBLISHERS.

The Art and Science of Cutting

TAILORING has been frequently looked upon by the ignorant and foppish as contemptible and unmanly. But that it is not so, but is both a Science and an Art of the very highest order and origin, there cannot be the slightest doubt; as it is based upon the very same foundation as all other sciences and arts.

SCIENCE.

Science means, 'That which we know deductively or inductively.' It is a combination of laws and principles, in their perfect relationship to each other, forming a system. Deductively, we have the conclusion, with the facts producing it so presented that only the separate facts are manifest; while inductively, both the facts and their results are at the same time clearly evident. According to the principles of deduction, "all things agreeing with the same thing, must agree also with one another." According to that of induction, "in the same substances and same circumstances, from the same causes the same results will follow."

Science was for a long period clad in antiquated technical phraseology, causing it to be difficult and repulsive to the popular mind, and requiring for its comprehension a wider field of preparatory study than it was within the power of many to attain. Thus the beauty and simplicity of natural laws remained a sealed book to the majority of readers ; and the writers had to charge a high price for their works from the limited demand for them.

By the ancients, science was divided into seven classes—arithmetic, geometry, astronomy, grammar, rhetoric, logic, and music. In modern times its classifications have become multiplied. By one, however, it has been divided into three classes : subjective, as existing in the mind ; objective, as embodied in truths; and speculative, as in practical science.

We have abstract science, and absolute science ; the former being the knowledge of principles and their combined results, and the latter pertaining to the reason of principles.

Also we have mental science, which pertains to inorganic bodies, or the laws of the body ; natural science, pertaining to the three great divisions of the natural world, called the animal, vegetable, and mineral kingdoms; and pure science, the component parts of which are self-evident facts, as mathematics, etc.

Many of the branches of science, especially of natural science, being connected with the cutter's art, it will be necessary to give a short resume of those which have a special bearing npon the subject under consideration, beginning with

GRAVITATION.

Every connected mass of atoms of matter has a certain point or axis about which all other parts are balanced or have equilibrium, which point is called its centre of gravity. Every one of these atoms is subject to the force of gravity, or weight, all of which forces are parallel to each other, equal, and act in the same direction, their effect being the same as if it were a single force applied to a single point; this point is the centre of gravity. By this point the mass may be lifted; or, if supported on it (that is, the weight counteracted) then the mass or body is at rest. This point has always a certain position in any given body, and therefore the part may be known about which, in every position, the mass will have equilibrium. Be it noticed that this, the scientific idea of balance, is very different from the notions abroad in the tailoring profession for so many years. Now, though it may be said that the centre of gravity will be exactly in the centre of an exactly square piece of wood, this may, on being tested, prove not to be the case, for part of this wood may when growing have faced the sun, and another part not have done so; hence the former part will be more dense than the latter, and the centre of gravity therefore not be where theory would point out as its position. If we place a stick across the finger, the part where it balances on the finger will be the centre of gravity. In a ring, the centre of gravity does not exist in the ring itself, but in the centre part where the particles of which it is constituted would balance.

Diagram 1.

If we take a painter's palette, and let it hang freely by the edge in its longest direction, and then drop a plummet with a line, the centre of gravity will be in the line which touches the surface of the palette, and on this line it will balance. Turn it sideways, let it hang freely, and again drop the plummet and line, which will bisect the other line, and on this line the centre of gravity will be found to exist, as the palette will balance. Hence, then,

as it is found to be in both of these lines, the centre
of gravity desired to be known is at the point where
they cross each other.

Diagram 2.

Geometrically to find the centre of gravity of a
triangle a c e, draw a line from a to b, and from c to
d, bisecting the opposite sides ; and as it will balance on either of the two lines, the centre of gravity
is in both the lines at point f, where they intersect.
Thus, a f equal two-thirds a b ; therefore a line from
one angle, bisecting the opposite side, having measured off from the angular point a distance of two-
thirds of its length, gives the centre of gravity of a
triangle. Having given this mode of finding the
centre of gravity of a triangle, a pyramid constructed in the form of so many triangles may
have its centre of gravity easily proven.

Diagram 3.

From our knowledge of the pyramidical form, we
perceive that the centre of gravity lies low, and the
broader the basis the more firmly will a body stand.
If we attempt to overturn any substance in the form
of a pyramid, we find that its centre of gravity has
to be lifted considerably, and also the whole mass of
which it is composed. According to the breadth of
the base of the body, compared with the height of
the centre of gravity above it, will be the rise of
the centre of gravity—which will be easily compre-
hended by noticing the direction of the sweep cast
by point s from the top of the plumb line.

Dia. 3 represents a pyramid in which, from the
breadth of the base, the centre of gravity is low,
which may be considered supported on the plummet
line. Now if this had to be turned over, so as to be
supported on the part s, the centre of gravity would
describe the part of the circle shown by the dotted

line drawn from the top of the plummet line by the point s, as s is the part on which it would rest in turning, called the centre of motion. The greater the distance the centre of gravity, as shown by the plumb line, is from s, the further will the centre of gravity be from the top of the circle it moves in, in

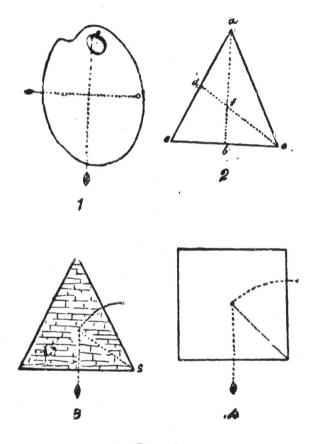

PLATE 1.

turning over, and the resistance nearly equal to the whole weight. The line marked by the plummet is called the line of direction of centre.

Diagram

In this figure the base is also broad, and therefore

firm, from the centre of gravity having to be considerably raised before the body can be overturned. In
Diagrams 5 and 6,
The commencing path of the circle, described by
the centre of gravity, is not so perpendicular, or

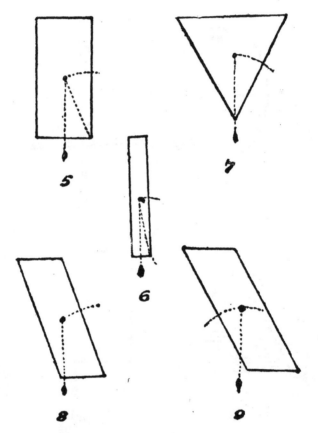

upward, as in the former figures, and therefore they
are less steady on their basis.
Diagram 7.
In this figure, from its narrow base and the high
position of the centre of gravity, the slightest movement would make it fall, as the motion described by

the dotted sweep line must be descending, and cannot be any other.

Diagram 8.

A figure of this form and position is unstable on

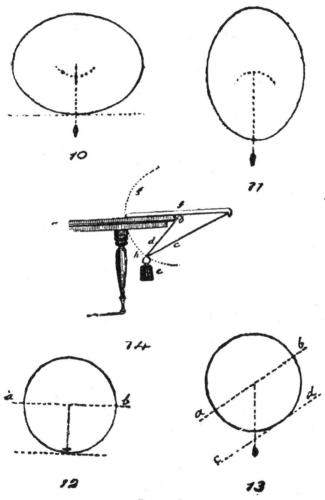

10

11

14

12   13

PLATE 3.

the one side, and more stable on the other, for the
sustaining base is actually narrowed; the line of
direction falling within the angle from the centre of
gravity to the corner of the base, the body is still

supported, but if moved over at the right side the centre of gravity would be lowered and the body soon fall. In

Diagram 9

The line of direction falls beyond the base, and therefore the object must fall.

Diagram 10

Is an oval body which, when on a plane and moved, the centre of gravity will describe a curve like that of a pendulum, returning to its former position, but not turning over.

Diagram 11

Is also an oval figure on one end, and if moved either on one side or another, as the motion of centre of gravity is downwards (see curve in its centre) it will fall.

Diagram 12.

A globe or ball, when on a level plane, is supported on a single point ; but as in every position the centre of gravity would be the same distance from the sustaining point, it has no tendency to move. When it is moved the centre describes the straight line a b. The equilibrium in this case, receives the term indifferent, as it makes no attempt, on being moved, to return to its former position, or move from that in which we place it.

Diagram 13.

If a ball or globe be placed on an inclined plane and rolls down, then the centre of gravity will have an oblique motion, as in the line c d.

Diagram 14.

Place a walking-stick on the edge of a table, a b, so that it would fall if left to itself ; attach to it a weight e by a cord d ; place a rod c against one end of the stick and the top of the weight, which rod must be of such a length as to push the weight a little underneath the edge of the table, and the whole will rest steadily in their positions; because the cord being out of the vertical, no lateral motion can be given to the weight withcut raising the centre of gravity of the system. The stick, in falling, must turn round the edge of the table; in so doing it will describe the dotted part of the circle g, lifting the centre of gravity in the arc h; and as the weight is heavier than the stick, this is against the laws of gravity, hence an equilibrium is preserved.

HUMAN EQUILIBRIUM, EQUIPOISE OR BALANCE.

In the human body, the centre of gravity must be directly above the points of support, which are the feet. If, therefore, we take a load on our back, we bend forward, so that the centre of gravity may be above the point of support; or in taking a weight in our arms, we lean backward. If we wish to stand very firmly, we widen the base by placing our feet at a greater distance and turning out the toes. Walking on wooden legs or stilts requires practice, so as to preserve an equilibrium in an unstable position.

On looking at the ancient statue of Hercules, the feet are seen to be turned out, giving an appearance of strength and firmness. In that of Mercury, where swiftness is the object to be personified, the feet are nearly straight. and the toes only touch the ground.

When we walk up a hill we lean forward, and in descending lean backward, from the necessity of preserving the centre of gravity in its right position; short persons also lean backward, as if proud of the incumbrance on their bones, and light-fronted, and heavy-backed men forward.

The human position is therefore determined by the law of mechanics called gravitation, which means that the weight is attracted to a certain line or point termed centre or axis of gravity, on which it rests, or to which it gravitates by reason of nature's law of attraction. The bulk and weight of a straight figure is proportionally divided on either side of the centre of revolution, or axis, when the body is at rest; though the law of attraction does not prevent the figure from forcibly assuming other attitudes, so long as the strength of the system will not give way. The bulk of a crooked figure is distributed disproportionally on either side the centre of gravity or attraction, yet in such a manner that the weight on the one side will counterbalance the weight on the other. And thus, whilst the form is constituted and determined by the local bulk or weight, the position is governed by the law of attraction, called gravitation —which, plainly speaking, means balance.

THE MECHANISM OF THE HUMAN FRAME.

WHEN treating of human mechanics and anthroposophy, we should not call it anatomy; and in treating of anatomy or anthropotomy, we should not call it anthropometry; for when the nature and structure has been already found, it is not anatomy, but anthroposophy; and when not found, and certain means suggested or adopted to find out the structure, it is geometry, anthropotomy, dissection or anatomy, and not anthropometry. 'Anthropos,' a man; 'metron,' a measure, has no meaning in connection with suggested means of finding out the structure of a human body.

By examining minutely the structure of many insects, we discover that they are provided with formations for the purpose of fulfilling the destiny of their peculiar conditions; that their saws, rasps, gimlets, needles, lancets, spades, hooks, hinges, awls, pincers, and other tools, afford lessons in which man may profitably learn the best construction of such implements.

In that most admirable of mechanisms, the human frame, we have surprising examples of economy of material, combining lightness, force, firmness, elasticity, leverage, hinges, joints, sockets, motion, resistance, security and grace; so that its description becomes an appropriate section of this work. In comparing the ingenious contrivances of talented engineers with the perfection of the framework of organised beings, we cannot but mark with reverential awe the difference between the works of man and the Creator of all nature.

The most lofty portion of the human frame is technically called the cranium, a word derived from the Greek, signifying 'helmet,' but it is better known as the skull. The form of this part is that of an arch, the best to give strength, whilst the tenacity of its material is so great as to resist shocks in all directions.

When the living principle early acts in the germ of the future human form, the covering of the brain is but a flexible, tenacious substance which progressively shoots out bone, like delicate icy crystallisation of water, until the whole becomes so many scales bound together by a membrane. The edges overlie each other, and the whole is soft and elastic in early infancy. Gradually, as years approach to teens, the bone hardens, and processes form for dovetailing it neatly and compactly together, which seams or joinings are called sutures. During the thoughtlessness and mishaps of youth these joinings are not perfected; and thus, when an unlucky blow is received, its effects are dispersed at the edges of the sutures, and the vibrations being checked, the injury is comparatively harmless. As maturity creeps on, and consequently caution and power, these minute but strong dovtailings become thoroughly and firmly knit, and the whole a hard case of bone.

On looking at the mature skull, it presents to our view first the frontal or bones of the forehead, that continue backward to the sutures, which may be felt on the crown and sides of the rounding of the head. From this, and comprising the principal part of the sides, top and back of the head, are the 'parietal,' or wall bones. Below the last-named are the 'occipital,' or back of the head bone; in it is the hole through which passes the continuation of the brain into the spinal bone. The 'sphenoid,' or wedge bones, lie behind the orbits of the eyes. and touch the frontal and temporal, or temple bones— which latter contain and protect the organs of hearing, and overlie the parietal bone, being joined to it by what is termed a 'squamous' or scaly suture.

The bone of the skull consists of two layers or tables, the one external, the other internal, separated by a spongy substance, resembling in form the cells of a marrow bone, unequally spread, called the 'diploe'; this and the outer covering, the scalp and the hair, by their elasticity aid in deadening the effects of a blow.

The outer dovetailed table is fibrous and tough, thus admirably suited to resist the blows to which its position exposes it; while the inner table, called 'tabula vitrea,' or the glassy table, against which the delicate brain contacts, is smooth, dense, and brittle. This latter quality would render the little projections in dovetailing easy to be snapped; therefore, with that wondrous adaptation to every circumstance, the edges of the joinings are laid in contact. In the operations of man, tough wood is dovetailed ; but the edges of china or glass that have to be in contact are merely laid together.

When a man receives a blow on the head it may cause such vibrations throughout the brain as to deprive him of sense of motion, and a severe blow usually fractures and indents the part struck. A blow from a sharp instrument may cut into the brain itself and not render the person insensible, while a blow with less force, but received from a broader surface, being resisted by the arched bone of the head, usually cracks the bone at an opposite part to that struck. This bears a similitude to the piers of a bridge being cracked and thrust out when not strong enough to bear the weight at the crown of the arch. The utility and power of the arch in the erection of dwellings seems to have been known early in the history of the world, as it has been discovered in the buildings of the buried city of Nineveh.

Nature protects the brain of man, the seat of glorious mind, that has to direct us in our duties as to the present and the future, in the hard, bony arched case we have just described.

Let us, for a moment, glance at but one case, to see the necessity for such a beautful strong covering. A youth received a blow, given by his tutor, on the head, with a ruler ; this caused a slight depression of the skull, which, pressing on the brain, caused the promising youth to fall into deplorable idiocy. A few miserable years thus passed away, when a skilful medical man, undertaking the case, by an operation removed the pressure, and at once restored the patient.

The lower jaw has a hinge-joint that permits of

two motions, the greatest being in the perpendicular
direction, and the lesser in the lateral. The one is
for cutting ; the other for grinding.

The first teeth are small, to adapt them to the
mouth ; when these fall out they are replaced by
others suitable to the enlargement of the frame; and
finally, in maturity, the teeth of "wisdom" complete
the set. Some are formed like wedges and chisels,
others for tearing and grinding, all being covered
by a beautiful enamel, so much prized by all.

Next to the head in importance is the function of
sensation ; and as important as the brain itself, to
the continuation of life, is the spinal marrow. Some
physiologists call it the prolongation of the brain ;
while others think that the brain is a continuation
of the spinal cord, rearing up and spreading out like
the branches of a tree.

In the grand framework of the human body, not
only is powerful protection afforded by the formation
of the spinal bony column for the nervous matter
which fills its cavity, but while it sustains the head,
and bends to the motions of the body, it is also the
connection of the higher and lower parts of the
skeleton

Behind the bones that keep the body erect, a spinal
process projects, from which the common name given
to the column, of 'the spine,' is derived; the separate
bones of which it consists are called vertebræ.
In form the spine resembles an italic *f*, the lower
end tapering off ; joining this root part it curves in-
ward, and the bones of the vertebræ are here largest, and, somewhat like the stem of a tree, decrease
upward. Twenty-four distinct bones constitute the
two movable vertebræ. The part designated the
root is composed of a triangular-shaped bone called
'os sacrum,' and another 'os coccygis,' which, being

in four pieces, and from resemblance, are frequently termed false vertebræ.

The bones are nearly cylindrical, with a perforation behind for the spinal marrow, and have the projecting spinal process referred to, as well as two at the top and two at the bottom of each vertebræ.

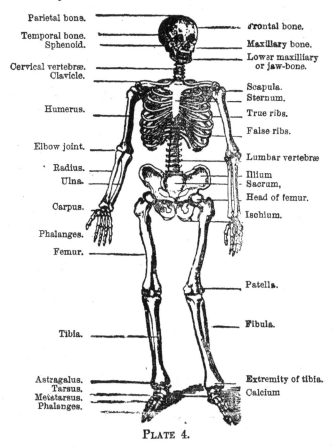

Parietal bone.
Temporal bone.
Sphenoid.
Cervical vertebræ.
Clavicle.
Humerus.
Elbow joint.
Radius.
Ulna.
Carpus.
Phalanges.
Femur.
Tibia.
Astragalus.
Tarsus.
Metatarsus.
Phalanges.

Frontal bone.
Maxillary bone.
Lower maxillary or jaw-bone.
Scapula.
Sternum.
True ribs.
False ribs.
Lumbar vertebræ
Illium
Sacrum,
Head of femur.
Ischium.
Patella.
Fibula.
Extremity of tibia.
Calcium

PLATE 4.

The first five large vertebræ are called 'lumbar'—that is, pertaining to the loins; above which are twelve, called the 'dorsal' or back vertebræ, to which are fastened the ribs, forming, with the breast bone, the part called the 'thorax'; the seven piled on the last-named are called 'cervical,' or belonging

to the neck. These curve first in a forward direction,
and then recede in the upper back part of the head,
giving that graceful form so admirable in the neck.
The highest but one of these, from a remarkable
bony process it possesses, is named the 'vertebræ
dentata'; and the topmost one, that immediately
supports the head, the 'atlas'—and justly so, as it
bears upon it the individual world the mind creates.
From the ideas that form the links of the mental
chain, organised beings recognise themselves from
each other; when it is broken, the living mass of
matter is in that pitiable state of confusion called
insanity; and when annihilated by the flight of the
imperishable soul of wit and wisdom, there is dark-
ness and vacuity and death.

Having piled up this wonderful column from the
foundation, let us now see how inimitably it is
adapted to the purpose of its design. Beyond that
of protection to the life-constituting cord of matter,
it has to possess elasticity to prevent any jar upon
the brain, and therefore to let the head be borne
with the ease of carriage-springs; it has to be flexible, that the body may move in all directions; firm,
to support the upright position of the body—a fulcrum to the muscles and a prop to the ribs; and it
has to possess strength, that weights may be borne
on the shoulders and back. It is related of Topham
that he lifted by his shoulders three hogsheads of
water, weighing 1,836lbs.! Wonderful, then, is the
mechanism of this column! First, we may note the
manner the head is placed on the spine. There are
two prominences at that part of the skull called occi-
put, that are received into corresponding cavities of
the atlas; by this the head can move in the manner
it does when we nod, but the atlas-bone turns horizontally round the tooth-like process of the next

bone, the vertebræ dentata, and thus the head moves
from side to side; therefore there is an up-and-down
and a rotatory motion effected by these two bodies.
But as these motions are limited, and man requires
more, the flexibility of the spine comes to our assis-
tance, and thus we can freely move the head in all
directions. Now, as the joint of the head and spine
is not quite in the centre of the bottom of skull, the
head, unsupported, would drop forward ; to prevent
which, in the living subject there is a strong ligament which comes from the cervical vertebræ, and
is fastened to the bottom part of the skull. When
in a sitting position, and when sleep overcomes us,
the muscles relax, and the head drops forward.

The contrivance to give elasticity to the spine
consists of a soft, firm and elastic substance, about
half as bulky as the vertebræ itself, that is inserted
between each vertebræ; this in some parts is thicker
before than behind, so that when we stoop forward
it is compressed, and the surfaces of the bones ot
the vertebræ become more parallel to each other
than before, and no opening between takes place ;
then, when the pressure is relieved, the elasticity,
like a spring, sends the body again into an erect
position ; while any danger that might arise from a
shock at the lower part is removed by this body of
elastic substance, which prevents the hard and unyielding bone, which resembles a strong irregular
ring or double rings (or double arches), from being
in contact.

The spinal column is accurately described as a
chain, from its firmness and flexibility. The number
of joints gives it the pliancy it possesses, which is
greater in the loins, being more required in that
part than in the back, where firmness is necessary,
and greatest of all in the neck, on which has to move

that part containing the organs of sight. Then, to preserve uninjured the spinal marrow, and yet to allow the free movements of the parts containing it, the processes and projections of the vertebræ so lock into and overlap each other as to securely prevent the slightest derangement of the bones, and the free unharmed continuation of the delicate cord. Though we may bend the back to a great extent either backward or forward, yet its many links prevent any part from being over-strained. We know that if we give considerable inclination to a cane, that although on the whole there is a great bend, yet each individual part is only bent to a small extent. To add still further to the compactness of the elasticity, a ligamentous substance joins the root of the spinous processes to each other. In fact, the whole is really stronger than if a solid column of bone had been inserted—so perfect and far-seeing is the design of the Great Architect of the human race.

The contortionists who exhibit their feats in various places rarely injure their spines, and diseases of that part are rare, excepting those brought on by a false and pernicious system of education. Keeping the body too long in an upright position, and not allowing free scope to the excess of animal spirits in the young, is an outrage on the highest laws, frequently retaliated by a distortion of that graceful portion of the body.

Forming a powerful bony elastic exterior to a hollow interior is accomplished by the ribs attached to the spine The ribs are long, curved, flattened, narrow bones attached to the back of the spine, or that part called the dorsal vertebræ, and their transverse processes being joined in front by an elastic cartilage affixed to the sternum or breast bone. They are twelve in number. The uppermost seven are called the true ribs; and the lowermost five, the cartilages of which do not reach the sternum, are named the false ribs. A great security to these bones arises from their not being straight, but hanging downwards like the lower part of the sunshades ladies used to affix to their bonnets. But there is another advantage; in the action of filling the lungs with air, the ribs rise up and enlarge the space for the reception of the breath, while the great elasticity of the cartilage and this important action also gives way to any sudden blow. This could not be so well effected if, instead of the cartilage, there had been a bony joint. In stooping forward, or on one side, the elastic substance readily yields and recovers itself by its spring. The muscles which have their origin in the ribs, and their insertion into the bones of the arm, afford an example of action and reaction, being equal and contrary. When the ribs are fixed, these muscles move the arms; and when the arms are fixed by resting on a chair or other object, they move the ribs. This is seen in fits of asthma, difficulty or shortness of breathing. As age advances the cartilage becomes bony, and hence less suitable . for violent exertions of the respiratory organs. This should lead us to be tender to our friends who have reached the evening of life; and truly are those men philanthropists who would provide ease and comfort, after a certain age, for those who have unprofitably to themselves spent the energy of their prime in labour for others.

The shoulder-joint, by which we can exert great strength, and which has such freedom of action, is formed by a round head of the shoulder-bone, called the 'humerus,' which is placed in a shallow cup of the bladebone or scapula, together forming a ball-and-socket joint. There are two strong bony projections above and behind which keep it in place, and the ends of the bones are enclosed by a thick strong membrane, so that dislocation is provided against. The two objects of strength and extent of motion are thus carefully secured; and, to add to the latter, the shoulder blade, holding the round head of the arm-bone, slides about itself upon the hollow of the chest—held, however, within bounds by a strong trace to the breast bone.

The 'clavicle' or collar-bone is of a slightly arched form, attached to the breast-bone or blade-bone in a very shallow cavity. It is of great strength, and, from its situation, liable to accidents. Resting on it, and on the bed of muscles near, great burdens are borne in the industrial occupations of man.

At the upper part of the chest is the bladebone, giving the mechanist an example of lightness combined with strength. When the wheelwright desires to give the best form to his work, he makes the felloe, the spokes and nave strong, and bends the spokes inwards in a manner termed 'dishing'; and thus it is that the bladebone is constructed, slightly arched, with its principal strength at the edges and spines, and other parts thin and light. This simple and incomparable mode of construction is found generally in animals possessed of bony framework.

Joined by a hinge joint at the elbow is the arm-bone or humerus to the 'ulna' or forearm-bone and 'radius': their motion here is only backward and forward, being restrained by strong ligaments from a lateral motion; thus it is a mere hinge, and can only be considered as a lever, as the muscles that move this part are very long and much slanted, and have to act near the fulcrum or centre of motion. They have consequently to be very strong. In fact, it is calculated that the muscles of the shoulder-joint, when lifting a man upon the hand, puts forth a force of 2,000lbs. But what is lost in leverage power of the arm is gained in velocity; thus in rapidity of action we make up for the sacrifice of power. How lost should we find ourselves were the muscles different—formed for giving only immense strength, and accompanied with slowness of motion; we then could not speedily protect ourselves by quickly raising the hand, and from thousands of our present engagements and employments we should find ourselves excluded — as for example, sewing sixty stitches per minute.

The wrist and hand is divided into four bones that form the joint with the arm or radius; the first four are joined to other four, and these constitute the wrist. From this part forward proceed five, that may be felt at the back of the hand; joined to these are the three in succession of each finger and the two forming the thumb. The turning round of the hand and wrist is effected through the radius-bone of the arm revolving round the ulna—and of course the hand with it, without the wrist-joint moving. It is clear that this important part derives its name from its power of motion in radii or circles. Not only is power of minute motion given by the number of small bones in the hand and wrist, also the many shocks to which it is subject are deadened ere reaching the higher parts of the arm. There is at the wrist-joint a strong tyre passing round it, with which the tendons that proceed from the arms for the movement of the fingers are swathed together. Were this not the case, we should have a hand about as shapeless as a hoof, and not much more useful, whereas now we not only have grace and elegance through this arrangement, but we have also strength with united motion, and delicacy with partial motion, as of the fingers alone, instead of weakness. The mechanism of the hand is worthy of careful study and deep reflection, as one of the principal sources of man's pre-eminence in creaticn, aided by reason, and of one man's pre-eminence over another; and it also displays in distinct characters the marvellousness of the works of the Supreme Mechanic.

In physical laws, the nearer a weight is to the fulcrum, the greater the amount that can be carried; as from experience we know we can sustain a weight on the arm near the joint that we could not hold in the hand of the outstretched arm. If a 2lb. weight were placed 1in. from the fulcrum of the joint, and then moved to the centre of the hand, and say the distance it is removed is 15in., then to find the force with which the weight will press downwards the distance must be multiplied by the weight. In this example the force exercised will be twice 15lbs.

To support the spinal column and affix the two columns of locomotion (the legs), there is a broad, light and hollow bone called the pelvis. The two haunches or hips are large, and where no strength could accrue from its presence the bony substance is omitted; they present a broad surface, and are so placed as to form an inverted arch, that form conveying the greatest strength with economy of material. In the hollow is received the lower part of the viscera. At the upper edge of the pelvis is firmly joined that part of the spinal column named sacrum. Powerful muscles are attached to the bone, at the lower portion of which two large projectors support the back when in a sitting position. The bones are connected by cartilaginous surfaces and large ligaments so strongly that the whole must be destroyed before a part will yield.

The hip joint is an admirable adaptation of the

ball-and-socket joint; a large rounded head-part of the thigh fits into a deep cup of the haunch, and is prevented from slipping out by thick, strong rising edges around the cavity. From the head of the ball, at the lower part of the cup and around its edges, are cartilages and ligaments that give security to the joint and resist any force likely to displace the bone, while at the same time it allows a free motion to the foot and ample range to the various actions of the leg.

In the thigh bone the rounded head stands off from the shaft, and the projection is so placed that the strength and weight are thrown upon the shaft. The thigh bone bends forward in an arched manner, and has knobs, to which are attached the powerful muscles of the leg ; on the fore part of the bone the action of the muscles is great, and the curve of these bones gives a strength which they would not possess if straight.

The knee joint is composed of three bones, curious in their arrangement, at the same time perfect for the purposes intended. At this end of the thigh bone the termination appears of a rounded ball form, resting on a shallow cup, and implies no strength from the manner in which it is placed ; but to make up for this there are two strong lateral ligaments, and an immense ligamentous rope within the cavity of the joint. It is a singular property of the ligaments of the inside of the knees that they increase in strength the greater the strain that is put upon them. The duties thrown upon the ligaments in this part cause the great elasticity of limb so often called into use in violent, quick exercise, such as we have referred to elsewhere, and is another of those arrangements so inimitably suited to give advantage to man's position in the scale of organised beings.

The large muscles óf the front of the thigh are fixed to the leg below the knee, and in their passage have to pass over where the joint of the knee exists. Before they arrive there they are contracted into a tendon, and become inserted into the bony structure in front of the joint; this part is called the patella or knee-pan, and is a valuable protection to the joint. By this arrangement a mechanical advantage is gained, from the centre of motion being increased in distance from the pulling power.

1 he bones of the leg much resemble those of the arm ; the largest is called the 'tibia,' leg or pipe, and the smaller the 'fibula' or 'brace' ; they are angular, as a preservation against knocks, and present a considernble surface for the attachment of the various muscles. A large flat portion of the tibia is covered only by skin, and is named the shin.

Between the two bones of the leg joint named, which project at each side to form the ankle, is received the great articulating bone of the foot cailed 'astragalus.' When the foot is raised this joint is fixed, and as the body comes down the support is thus firm and steady to bear the super-incumbent weight. The tendons are tied down by a ligament passing over them, as at the wrist; were this not the case, the foot would be more in the shape of an elephant's, and although the tendon would have greater power to draw up the toe on which it acts, yet its velocity of movement would be less. One of tendons passes along a grove under the bony projection of the inner ankle, exactly as we would place ropes over a pulley.

In the foot there are twenty-six bones ; of these, seven comprise the 'tarsus,' a part that reaches from the heel to the middle of the foot. By projecting backwards it forms a powerful lever, on which the muscles of the back of the leg, terminating in the achilles tendon, act by lifting up the body and throwing its weight on the ball of the toes. Where the muscles of the calf are naturally small, as in the black races, the length of the lever of the heel is increased, and thus a provision to make up the other deficiency. It was by particularly noticing this fact of the graceful rising of the heel by the achilles muscles, as if the foot were performing a circular motion, that an ingenious person constructed a valuable substitute for a leg to those who had had the misfortune to lose that very necessary member. Next to the tarsus are five bones, laid parallel, ealled 'metatarsus,' from which proceed the three bones of each toe, except the great toe, which has only two. As the foot comes to the ground the heel touches first, the ball of the toes resting in a beautiful arch. The surfaces of each bone do not touch, as they have a layer of cartilage between each, and are lubricated with an oily fluid; and thus in consequence of the number of joints, and the value of the surfaces, the whole is completely elastic and fitting for the various shocks in walking, running and leaping; for what can we conceive permitting of a more easy, springing carriage than that of an elastic arch? If a small arch was built of wedges, having pieces of indiarubber placed between each, it would resemble the mechanism of the foot.

In walking, we sway a little from one side to the other; but were the leg inelastic, as when a wooden one has to take the place of a natural one, the lower part would have to be advanced in a kind of half-circle. From a slight bend of the knee, and the contraction and lengthening of the muscles, the leg can be moved straight forward, and thus the body more easily and steadily progresses.

Even this cursory and popular glance at the mechanical arrangement of the framework of the human being must strike all with gratitude that we are so "fearfully and wonderfully made." Still, there are a few points worthy of attention which have not yet been noticed.

A teacher in the sixteenth century who was accused of promulgating doctrines contrary to a belief in the existence of a Supreme Ruler, picked up a straw, and repudiated the charge, saying, " If there was nothing else, this straw would be sufficient to teach me the existence of a deity." Let us now put aside many other important particulars, and merely examine the mechanical construction of a straw. If the material composing it were solid, it is palpable to the commonest understanding that it would not have strength enough to support the invaluable head that it does, so gracefully and securely. On this point it has been proved by Tredgold that when the inner half diameter of a hollow cylinder is to the outer as seven to ten, it will possess twice the strength of a solid one of the same weight, arising from the substance being further from the centre and therefore resisting with a longer lever. This, then, is conclusive of the wisdom of the constructive form of a straw; it has at once lightness, economy of material, and elasticity; and besides these circumstances mentioned, its outer surface is hard, comparatively to that of the inside, and in many vegetable stems their forms are ridged, angular and fluted. In describing the straw, we have generally been describing the structure of the bones of the human frame. In one particular it differs—that is, as to rotundity. It possesses a hard outside in many places, most especially the teeth and spine, and the ' os humeri ' has ridges to give strength, and it is a

27

tube, but the whole exemplifies lightness and economy of material, as in the straw. The hollow of the bones is filled with fine membraneous cells that do not communicate, and are filled with oily substance called marrow. In some of the extremities of the bones that are expanded to increase the extent of the surface of the joints, there is a thin, compact substance that looks like a kind of honeycomb, as we see on breaking those of animals. In the oblique part of the thigh these are seen to converge to a point in the shaft, as if supporting the parts projecting from the centre of gravity. Hard as is the surface of a bone, yet it is penetrated by minute vessels that convey to it nourishment to make up for the waste that takes place and to renew its material; for the law of nature is that during our passage from the cradle to the grave every atom of our bodies shall be continuelly changing. These cells, called ' caucelli,' also exist in broad flat bones, the outer surfaces being named plates or tables. The tough, elastic substance named cartilage, that pads and defends the parts against friction, and fills up irregularities, making a smooth, gliding surface, is of a milk-white pearly colour, and is always found where firmness, pliancy and flexibility are needed, that the body or brain does not suffer as if they were absent.

The weight of the upper part of the body compresses the cartilages of the spine during the day, so that a person after lying down at night is taller than when he goes to bed. The joints are tied together by strong unyielding cords called ligaments, that have a tenacity hardly to be found in any other substance. These hold the bones together and restrict each to their appointed office and motion. The cartilaginous surfaces are smeared with oily fluid

before alluded to, which makes them perfectly slip-
pery. This oil is secreted by appropriate glands,
and confined to the parts where it is required by a
very delicate membrane, called the synovial membrane.

The voluntary muscles of the human body are
composed of a number of nearly parallel fleshy
bundles, the diameter of each fibre being about the
400th part of an inch, containing a glutinous fluid
and threads about the 15,000th of an inch in diameter. A muscle, when contracted, is not larger in
size, but broader than when extended. The action
of contraction is effected in some by the fluid being
forced into tubes, which swells out the sides and
shortens the length ; but in the voluntary muscles
the elasticity which they possess is what renders
them of such value in the functions of the human
body. The temporal and masseter muscles, that
move the lower jaws, are short and strong, and as
they act at right angles to the line of the jaw, their
mechanical advantage or lever power is greater than
those in many parts of the body. This is what gives
great strength in biting hard substances, and power
to crack the obstinate shells of nuts with the back
teeth, like in the hinge of a door.

Bundles of minute fibre are joined together and
form a muscle ; their cohesion is maintained by vital
power, and thus a powerful living muscle is weak
and easily torn when dead. The faultless form of
beauty is preserved by the bulky muscles being
connected with slender tendons, that make up for
their want of substance by their dense and tough
nature. According to the intended action of particular joints, so are muscles placed to aid their
mechanical power. The contraction of a muscle is
towards its centre ; hence it is so placed and shaped

as best to contribute to this mechanical purpose. In some instances there is an increase of tendons to a muscle, in others an increase of muscles to a tendon. One of the muscles of the eyeball is a perfect pulley, and moves the eye in a contrary direction to that in which the force is applied.

It is well known that the size of the muscles depend largely upon their exercise—as, for example, the right-arm muscles of a blacksmith.

Animal power is exhausted exactly in proportion to the intensity of the force used; still, there may often be a great saving by doing work quickly, although with a little more exertion for the time being. The quick mover may exert one-twentieth more force to obtain greater velocity, which afterwards continues, while sloth supported his load four times as long. The rapid waste of muscle which arises from continued action is shown by keeping the arm extended horizontally; few can continue the exertion beyond a minute or two. Nevertheless, the fakirs of India will hold it in that position until the muscles become rigid and wasted, and the arm is immovable.

The power of the muscles of man is far beyond that of any animal of his size, and there are instances of incredible powers of capability and endurance, never equalled by quadrupeds. Carr, the blacksmith, lifted an anchor and carried it over the sands of the seashore to his workshop — a weight that would have broken the back of a horse. This same man once laboured at his fatiguing employment upwards of ninety hours without cessation. In consecutive days' journeys, a horse cannot compete with a man, the former becoming exhausted, while the latter seems to add to his power of continuance.

The skeleton consists of 261 bones, weighing

about 14lbs., and moved by 436 muscles, An Englishman's mean weight is 151lbs., and his height 5ft. 8in. The seat of the mind, the brain, exceeds in weight twice that of any other animal. He tears and grinds the food that nourishes his body by 32 teeth covered with a substance nearly as hard as iron. He breaths 18 times a minute, and inhales in that time 18 pints of air, or upwards of 57 hogsheads a day; every 24 hours he consumes $10\frac{1}{2}$ cubic feet of oxygen, and annually gives forth, to feed vegetation, 124lbs. of carbon. In infancy his blood pulsates 120 times a minute, in manhood 80, in age 60; and the weight of the red fluid in his veins is 28lbs. His heart beats 75 times per minute, and drives 12,000lbs. or more than 24 hogsheads through the body in the space of 24 hours. Our breathing apparatus possesses 174,000,000 holes or cells, covering a surface 30 times greater than the body; and about 7,000,000 pores carry off the used-up material, each of which is about $\frac{1}{4}$in. in length, and thus there is a drainage of nearly 28 miles by means of these tubes. The weight of the atmosphere borne by an ordinary sized person is about 13 tons; and the average duration of life in towns is 38, in the country 55.

It is a principle in mechanics that if the size of a machine be increased, its strength must be increased also at the rate of the square of the increase; thus, if it be made four times as large as before, then its strength must be sixteen times greater; in doing so the weight is increased four times and the strength 64 times. And by progressing in this manner, the machine would at length actually crush itself by its weight. The same principle extends to man, and is the reason why very big men are often a burden to themselves, and exhibit weakness in the legs.

THE MUSCLES AND THEIR NAMES.

A Musculus Palmaris
B The Os Jugale
C Attollens Labij Superioris
D Masseter
E Mastoideus
F Sternothyroideus
H Coracohyoideus
I Deltoides
K Pectoralis
L Extensor Humeri
M Biceps
N Brachiæus
O Flexor Externus Carpi
P Flexor Internus Carpi
Q Flexor Digitorum
R Flexor Pollicis
S Extensor Carpi Externus
T Alter Flexor Digitorum
a Olecranum
b Palmaris
c Serrati Antici Majores
d Latissimus Dorsi
e Obliqui Descendentes
f Recti Abdominis
g Parts of the Glutæi Muscles
h Fascialis
i Rectus
k One of the Flexores, Femuris
l Vastus Externus
m Vastus Internus
n Triceps
r Patella of the Knee
s Tibialis Anticus
t Extensor Digitorum
u Per næus Posticus
xz Gastrocnemius and Soleus
y Extensor Tertij Internodij Pollicis

FIG. 1, PLATE 5.

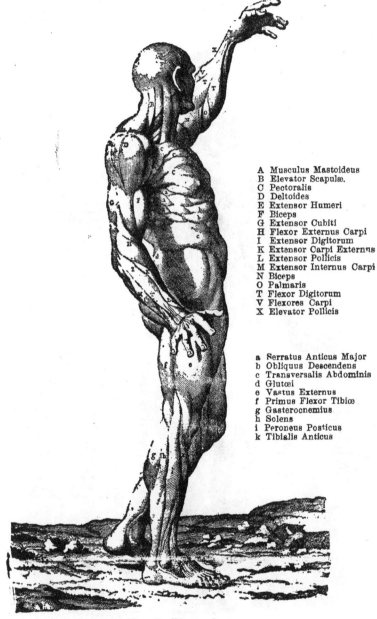

A Musculus Mastoideus
B Elevator Scapulæ.
C Pectoralis
D Deltoides
E Extensor Humeri
F Biceps
G Extensor Cubiti
H Flexor Externus Carpi
I Extensor Digitorum
K Extensor Carpi Externus
L Extensor Pollicis
M Extensor Internus Carpi
N Biceps
O Palmaris
T Flexor Digitorum
V Flexores Carpi
X Elevator Pollicis

a Serratus Anticus Major
b Obliquus Descendens
c Transversalis Abdominis
d Glutœi
e Vastus Externus
f Primus Flexor Tibiœ
g Gasterocnemius
h Solens
i Peroneus Posticus
k Tibialis Anticus

FIG. 2, PLATE 6.

THE MUSCLES AND THEIR NAMES.

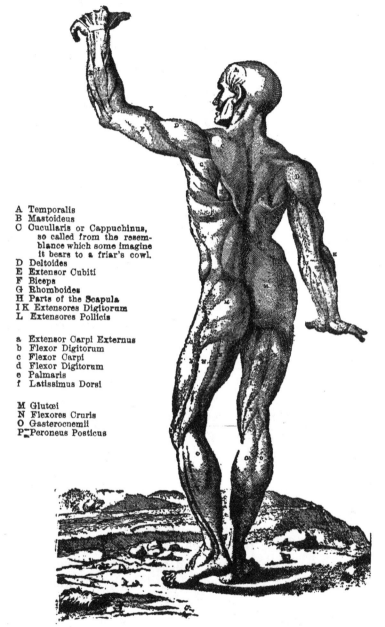

A Temporalis
B Mastoideus
O Cucullaris or Cappuchinus,
   so called from the resem-
   blance which some imagine
   it bears to a friar's cowl.
D Deltoides
E Extensor Cubiti
F Biceps
G Rhomboides
H Parts of the Scapula
I K Extensores Digitorum
L Extensores Pollicis

a Extensor Carpi Externus
b Flexor Digitorum
c Flexor Carpi
d Flexor Digitorum
e Palmaris
f Latissimus Dorsi

M Glutœi
N Flexores Cruris
O Gasterocnemii
P Peroneus Posticus

FIG. 3, PLATE 7.

THE PRINCIPLES OF PLANE GEOMETRY.

This branch being of some importance, as much of it is given as is necessary for the least educated to understand the subject in its elementary aspects. It is all the more necessary that this should be done because authorities differ in their definitions, even on such a subject as positive science, and also make mistakes in consequence of not being able to thoroughly grasp themselves what they presume to explain. To go no further, we have before us a class book, used in schools and colleges, which defines a point as that which has no parts or magnitude, thns making a mistake at the very outset of the work. Correctly speaking, a point is a position which has no extension, as

Fig. 6.

And even the second definition is just as bad which states that a line is length without breadth. A line is length, and there is no necessity or sense in adding, 'without breadth.' Again, the third definition is also bad which states that a straight line is that which lies evenly between two points. The correct definition is that a straight line is the shortest cut between two points, as the solid line of

Fig. 7.

The dotted line is a broken line, or points or positions, and the waved line not the shortest cut between two points.

A superfice is that which has plane length and plane breadth in the horizontal, and height and width or length in the perpendicular; length and width being interchangeable terms in the latter connection.

The extremities of surfaces are called lines; but, correctly speaking, they are boundaries having no magnitude, but composing part of the surfaces.

A superfices is that in which any two points being taken, the straight line between them lies wholly in the superfices, as

Fig. 9.

A plane angle is the inclination of two lines to one another, in a plane, which meet together, but

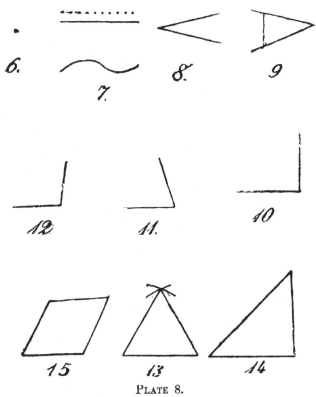

PLATE 8.

are not in the same direction as

Fig. 8.

A right angle is when a straight line, standing on another, makes the adjacent angles equal to one another, or of 90 degrees, as

Fig. 10.

An acute angle is that which is less than a right

angle, or less than 90 degrees, as
Fig. 11.

An obtuse angle is that which is greater than a right angle, or greater than 90 degrees, as
Fig. 12.

A plane circle is a figure containing an equal radius from its centre to its boundary in every direction.

A radius is a straight line from the centre to the boundary line of circumference.

A diameter is a double radius, or a straight line through the centre, terminated both ways by the boundary.

A semicircle is half a plane circle, bounded on the one side by the straight line of the circle's diameter.

A segment of a circle is a figure bounded by a straight line, and that portion of a circle which it cuts off.

Rectilineal figures are those which are contained by straight lines.

Trilateral figures, or triangles by three straight lines.

Quadrilateral by four straight lines.

Multilateral figures or polygons by more than four straight lines.

An equilateral triangle is that which has three sides equal, as
Fig. 13.

An isoceles is a triangle which has two sides equal.

A scalene is a triangle whibh has three unequal sides.

A right-angled triangle is that which has a right angle, or hypotenuse, as shown by the longest line of
Fig. 14.

An obtuse-angled triangle is that which has an. obtuse angle.

An acute-angled triangle is that which has three acute angles.

A square is that which has four equal sides, and all its angles right angles.

An oblong is that which has all its angles right angled, but not all its sides equal; or two equal boundary lines of length, and two equal boundary lines of breadth.

A rhombus is that which has all its sides equal, but its angles are not right angles, as

Fig. 15.

A rhomboid is that which has its opposite sides equal to one another, but all its sides are not equal.

The terms oblong and rhomboid are not often used. Practically, the following definitions are used: Any four-sided figure is called a quadrilateral; a line joining two opposite angles is called a diagonal; a quadrilateral, which has its opposite sides parallel, is called a parallelogram; the words square and rhombus are used in the sense defined by Euclid; and the word rectangle is used instead of the word oblong.

THE PLANE GEOMETRY OF THE HUMAN FIGURE.

The most studious and learned of men (may they rest in peace!) have arrived at conclusions and data given below regarding the natural arrangement and proportions of the human species. Names need not be mentioned, although nearly a hundred could be given, from Vitruvius and Polycletus downwards. Suffice it to say that we are almost entirely indebted to the Ancients, who, by means of writing, established the wise and useful practice of handing down to posterity their sentiments on different subjects, so that not only those might not be lost, but by their

works continually increasing a gradual advancement
might be made to the highest point of learning.
Our obligations to them, therefore, are great and
many, from their not having sullenly kept their
knowledge to themselves, but on the contrary have
recorded their opinions on every subject. Had they
omitted to do this, we should not have known what
happened in Troy, nor the sentiments of Thales,
Democritus, Anaxagoras, Xenophanes, and other
physiologists, respecting the nature of things; nor
the system of ethics laid down by Socrates, Plato,
Aristotle, Zeno, Epicures, and other philosophers.

The ancients, whose ideas of the human edifice,
calculations and measurements, were based upon
the very primitive foundation of the width of the
palm or hand, still prevalent among horse dealers,
divided the human figure into four cubits or twenty-
four palms, six palms being a cubit. Their method
of calculation was as follows: Four fingers make a
palm, four palms make a foot, six palms make a
cubit, four cubits make a man.

From the top of the head to the top of forehead
was considered to be one-fortieth; from the top of
forehead to the top of nose one-thirtieth; the nose,
one-thirtieth; the ear, one-thirtieth; and from the
nose to the bottom of the chin also the one-thirtieth
part of man. From the chin to the roots of the hair,
one-tenth; from the top of breast (second line on
plate 9) to top of head, one-sixth; from the nipple
to the top of head, one-fourth or cubit; from the
nipple to the horizontal line A, which marks the
middle or centre of the figure, one-fourth or cubit;
from the line A to below the patella or knee, one-
fourth or cubit; and from below the patella to the
sole of the foot, the remaining fourth or cubit. The
greatest width of the shoulders was considered to

contain in itself the one-fourth part of man, or the
one shoulder one-eighth ; from the elbow to shoulder, one-eighth ; from the elbow to the tip of the
middle finger, cubitus or forearm, the fourth part of

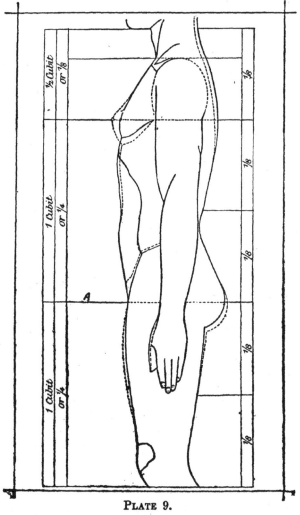

PLATE 9.

proportionate man; the length of the hand one-tenth;
the length of the foot one-seventh, and the width
thereof one-sixteenth ; the depth of the head, one-
eighth. Thus we have accordingly the figure

divided into eight heads, or eighths ; and it was upon this data, handed down to us by our forefathers'
that Wampen based his theories.

But although the ancients arrived at what they
considered to be correct data as regards a proportionate man, so far as indicated, they did not finally

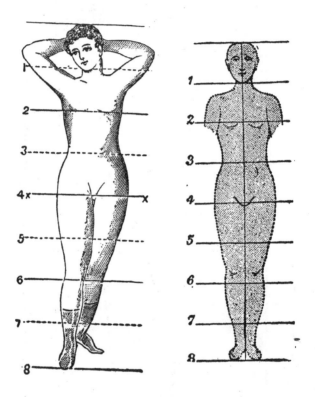

PLATE 9A.

establish or set at rest other points of importance,
such, for example, as the question, What are the
other measurements of constituent parts of a proportionate figure? much less arrive at any decision
as regards the laws that govern human development.
For we find them quite at a loss to understand

which of the measurements or plane diameters of the statues Venus de Medicis, the Venus of the Capitol, Appollino of Florence, or the Achilles of the Louvre, produced the most proportionate or harmonious result. All they were really able to conclude was that eight heads make a man or constitute the human edifice, and that seven of these go to make the height from the chin or head to the ground. Some modernist, however, has arrived at the conclusion that 144 square inches go to make a man. And a more reliable French academician, after forty years' study, has come to the conclusion that the eighth head terminates at the end of the extended foot, and not at the ground, as heretofore supposed; in which case the width from finger-tip to finger-tip of the extended figure agrees entirely with the length from crown to end of foot, and also relatively with the length of the fully-extended reach of the figure.

The heights of the statues mentioned are said to be: Apollo Sauroktonos, seven heads nine minutes if he stood upright, and thus he wants three parts three minutes to complete eight heads; the Venus de Medicis, seven heads, three parts, ten minutes, thus wanting two minutes to complete eight heads; the Achilles of the Louvre, seven heads, one part and eleven minutes, thus wanting two parts one minute to complete eight heads.

An inspection of plate 10, which contains a portion of a figure taken from the drawings of the ancients, will convince those open to reason that the perfect human figure has no space or division between the top of the thighs, as foolishly stated by latter-day tailoric theorists. No modernist who is really an authority, however, ever made such a statement. We need not go any further than the classical work of Charles Rochet to prove this, whose work is not only perfect as far as perfection can be attained on this head, but in all other respects also.

Charles Rochet to some extent traverses the

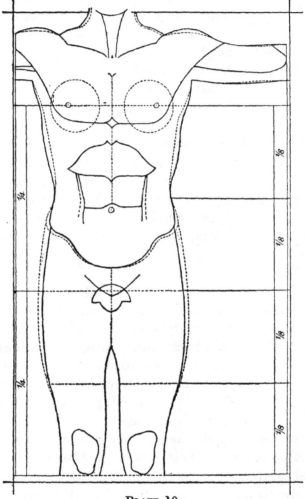

PLATE 10.

opinions and conclusions of the ancient authorities, as before stated, notably regarding the matter of height, which he shows to be 2½in. in the male and 2in. in the female greater than arrived at by the ancients ; and as his views are undoubtedly worthy of attention, they cannot be ignored.

Of man it may be truly said that in unity there is diversity, and in diversity there is unity.

Charles Rochet states that the head, which is the starting point of all measures, is itself divided into ten parts, counting from the median line ; and that the person laid out at full length on a plane (floor) with the arms extended over the head, is also ten parts from the tips of the fingers to the end of the toes. One of these is from the finger-ends to the wrist, another from the wrists to the elbows, which are level with the top of the head, another from the top of the head to the neck, the next to the nipple, then to the navel or waist, then to the pubial point, the lower part of the thighs, top of the calves, small of the legs, and great toe joints. The head is certainly divisible by two and four, and it has ten parts ; further than this, however, it is hardly possible for any scientist to go with any degree of certainty, although the ancients may have come to conclusions not specified, or others may have followed and still may follow in their path. Yet the natural divisions will remain the same, well marked and defined as they are, and furnishing within themselves the most positive and plain evidence that they are reliable and cannot err.

The first great division of the human figure is the median line, which takes its rise in the brain, which it divides into two lobes, as anatomists well know, separated by a physical band of union and demarcation called the median or longitudinal fissure, and passes downwards afterwards through the face and body to the centre between the feet, in its course dividing the face, shoulders, breast, waist, seat, thighs and legs, into two equal halves or parts, each

having two appendixes of five members—the hand
and foot, together equalling in number one forehead,
one nose, one mouth, one chin, two cheeks, two eyes
and two ears. This line then divides the body into
right and left, and all measures of proportion proceed from this line.

The second great division is that which passes
from side to side through the navel, thus dividing

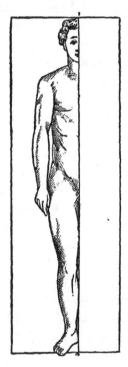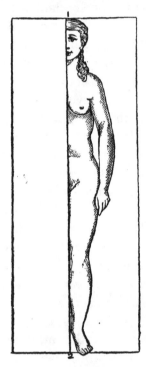

PLATE 10A.

the figure into two equal halves of length when the
hands are extended over the head, five parts being
above and five below, either equalling the five parts
of half the head or together the ten parts of the
whole head.

Following these comes the line marked A on the
plate 9, which here divides the figure into halves
of length when the figure is extended on a plane

with the hands and arms by the side. When the figure is so extended, with the arms straight out from the shoulders, in the form of a cross, this line intersects the median line at the centre of the crutch, and it and the median line also form a cross; and if the figure, so extended, were placed in a maximum square, it (the figure) or the space it occupied would then be divided into four equal minor squares, thus bringing the figure into the cubicle character assigned to it by the ancients. And it can now be seen that any smaller or sub-minor divisions must be the result of dividing the minor squares into sub-minor divisions, as, for example, a cubit divided into two is found to equal one-eighth of the square of height of figure which is found to readily lend itself to divisions by half cubits or eighths. And that this figure is cubical in form may be readily tested by placing it in the form of a St. Andrews' Cross,.

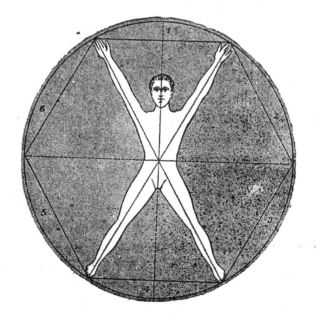

PLATE 10B.

when the fingers will touch two corners, and the toes the other two corners of the cubic—of six sides—and the navel be the centre; and the horizontal line passing through it touch the other two corners of the cubic figure, and equal the entire height of the extended figure with the arms above the head. And as a figure of six equal sides will stand within and touch the boundary line of a circle at each of its six points, it will be observed that it is as nearly spherical or perfect as it is possible to be, and may therefore be justly pronounced proportionate, and accepted as the standard of proportion by the tailor.

It is therefore evident, although he did not see it, that Rochet's conclusions agree entirely with those formulated by the ancients. Rochet's conclusions were that—

The head is the principle of unity, the base of all measurements.

The trunk, three head heights, with distinct centres.

The thighs (including knees), two head heights.

The legs (including feet), two head heights.

The arms (including hand), three head heights.

The upright man (the heels elevated and without arms), eight heads.

Man in a square, eight heads, lengthwise and breadthwise.

Man lying down, arms over head, ten head lengths.

Man kneeling, six head lengths.

Man on horseback, four head lengths.

One very curious point about Rochet's work, and which marks his learning, if possible, more than any other, is the fact that he arrived at the conclusion that the average length of a man's head is 9in., and not 8in., as laid down by some modern expounders.

This, then, is his canon of proportion for the perfect male figure, and $8\frac{1}{2}$in. for a head is his canon of proportion for a perfect female figure, while to both the same laws apply perfectly, the other sections merely differing in the same ratio as the head in size, while the laws of proportion are strictly the same in both sexes, and not different, as some

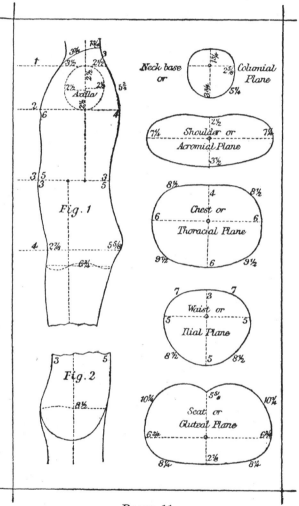

PLATE 11.

imagine. But perfection and imperfection are two different things, both as regards the male and the female ; and if it were not for these imperfections tailors would find it easy to fit everyone, and perfect

systems of cutting would be wholly unnecessary
once one good set of patterns had been produced.

With the object of arriving at a clear conception
of the construction of the human form, the positions

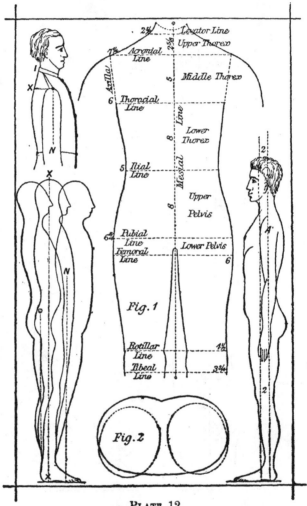

PLATE 12.

denoted by the neck and horizontal lines 1, 2, 3, 4,
on fig. 1 on plates 11 and 12 may be regarded as so
many plane sectors—not sections. The sections lie
between the sectors. The diameters, each way,

taken by means of a large callipers, and their
measurements on plate 11, are termed columnial,
acromial, thoracial, ilial, and gluteal planes. These
measures are merely given as examples ;ﾟ it is not
presumed that they are positively the actual measurements of a proportionate figure. The profile
diameters are also indicated on fig. 1, plate 11, and
the lateral diameters on fig. 1, plate 12; while the
perpendicular lines of fig. 1, plate 11, indicate the
positions of the planes above each other in the figu re,
and fig. 2, plate 12, the position of the thighs under
the lower pelvis, and fig. 2, plate 11, the generally
accepted notion of the form of the seat or pelvis of a
human figure internally. The classical names of
the sectors are also given on the side marked fig. 1
of plate 12, with the exception of the axilla, which
is shown on fig. 1, plate 11. The lines and the planes
are one and indivisible; and the names of the sections are given on the other side of fig. 1, plate 12.
The line marked mesial is the same as named also
median line — which is the truer term of the two.
While all the other sectors in the body are horizontal ones, the calumnial is an inclined plane sector.
The height or depth divisions are given down the
centre of fig. 1, plate 12.

It will be apprehended that in no other position
than perfectly erect would these lines cut the figure
in the places denoted. In standing at ease a man
loses the one-fortieth part of his height, and the leg
and haunch which bears the weight become enlarged.

The difference between the construction of the
male and female figure of the same size is shown by
the dotted lines, for the latter, on the figures on
plates 9 and 10.

The formation of the different plane sectors and
heir diameters, as already pointed out, are shown

on plate 11 ; their circumferences are also added on
the outside, around the plane figures, while the
position of the scye sector is seen on fig. 1 of the
same plate.

Although the diameters of a model figure may be
useful to the sculptor, they are useless to the tailor,
for the very simple and all-sufficient reason that
they are only applicable to the formation and construction of solid figures and not of their surface
coverings.

ART.

WHILE Science is a collection of principles
and their inferences, the combined result
of which may be understood by their careful invertigation, Art is a complement of rules,
which, skilfully carried into execution, will result in
the perfecting of some work. Fine art was for-
merly divided into four classes — poetry, music,
painting, and sculpture.

Both science and art are combinations of certain
fundamental truths; one is simply for knowledge,
the other for work; what is called in the former a
principle, is in the latter denominated a rule, and
the latter is founded in the former, while the foundation of the former is constituted by the unchange-
ableness of nature's laws.

That tailoring and cutting is not only an art, but
one of the fine arts, cannot be doubted; as all art is
founded in science, and all science is capable of use
as the foundation of some useful art.

The poet is an artist in words, the musician in
sounds, the painter in light and shade, or colour in
relation to form, or a designer, modeller or artist on
canvas; the sculptor deals with form, and is a
designer, modeller, and artist in stone. The tailor,

besides having to deal with form and colour in their relationship to each other, and being a designer, modeller and artist in cloth, has also to deal with the mind, and the eternal fitness of things in their relation to matter, or man himself, who is the fountain-head or foundation of all science and art.

The branches or divisions of art and science primarily concerned in draping the human form, are æsthetics, drawing, designing and anatomy ; geometry, trigonometry, gravitation and arithmetic — in short, mathematics generally ; while tailoring and cutting is more or less connected with and allied to all other branches of art and science, because of the very simple fact of having its origin and foundation in the selfsame source as all other sciences and arts. But for the sake of brevity, the tailoric science and art may be divided or subdivided into or classified under the following six grand or leading divisions or heads :—

1st, a knowledge of the human form.

2nd, of æsthetics, designing and drawing,

3rd, of geometry, trigonometry, gravitation, arithmetic and mathematics generally,

4th, of taking out cuts and fulling-on, and their application, uses and effects,

5th, of stretching and shrinking, and their application, uses and effects,

6th, of the use and application of the needle and heated iron scientifically,

And the influence of each and every one of these upon or in the production of form to cover form.

A knowledge of the human form implies a knowledge of anthroposophy, human proportions and disproportions. A knowledge of æsthetics, designing and drawing implies the power of recognising and the ability of constructing the beautiful ; of geometry, of man-measurement, for the very origin

of geometry as applied to ancient science meant
man-measurement, or the mensuration of lines, surfaces and solids in their relationship to the human
form, and there is good grounds for believing that
the standard of measurement designed for Creation
was the person of man; of trigonometry, the power
of determining the sides of angles; of gravitation,
the power of recognising and determining balance;
of arithmetic, the power of calculation; or of mathematics generally, the power of measuring and num-
bering, or determining the size and magnitude of
anything that can be measured or numbered, and of
transferring the same to a flat surface; of taking out
cuts, fulling-on, stretching, shrinking, sewing, &c.
—a knowledge of providing suitable form to cover
form artistically.

SUGGESTIONS RE ÆSTHETICS, DESIGNING AND DRAWING.

Good taste and ingenuity is the offspring of the
mind. But there is no reason why the inborn or
intuitive, nor yet the most mediocre qualifications
may not be improved, enlarged and extended, by
the aid of judicious cultivation or proper training.
Those who wish for a thorough insight into the subjects of æsthetics, designing and drawing, cannot do
better than consult such works as are published on
these branches, or if preferred, place themselves
under proper and duly qualified tuition in some
school of design and art, such as that established at
South Kensington; it not being within the proper
scope of this work to enlarge upon these subjects.
Yet it may not be outside our province to give a few
hints or suggestions on the art of using the crayon.

A good draughtsman generally makes a good
cutter. But those not accustomed to drawing can
very easily learn the art of using the chalk by care-

fully observing the following rules :

1st, Always hold the crayon between the thumb and forefinger, perfectly upright.

2nd, Always mark with the heel of the crayon, without pressing too heavily upon it, and accustom yourself to work with a light, easy hand

3rd, Always stand behind the work, not in front of it ; with the left leg extended foremost—in short, in such a position as will enable you to command a good long sweep.

SUGGESTIONS RE GEOMETRY, TRIGONOMETRY, ARITHMETIC AND MATHEMATICS GENERALLY.

For a full and adequate knowledge of these branches, students cannot do better than study the standard class books used in the schools, colleges, and universities. Such knowledge is highly essential to all who aspire to become adepts in their profession, or to rise to anything like a position in the trade. A thorough knowledge of arithmetic especially is most desirable in order to be able to make calculations, keep books, make-up accounts, &c.

SUGGESTIONS ON TAKING OUT CUTS, STRETCHING AND SHRINKING, FULLING-ON, DRAWING-IN, ETC.

It is only necessary to study the effects producible by each and everyone of these in order to arrive at a thorough and detailed knowledge of their uses, and the reason of their application. Many tailors who are able to make a fine stitch or a good button hole are apt to fancy themselves very practical. But however well a man may be able to sew, he never can be really and truly practical until he has learned to understand the art of putting together properly; and this is what no one can do until he has gained a thorough insight into and knowledge of the reasons and uses of the application of cuts, stretching, shrinking, fulling-on, etc., and to recognise their

bearing, utility and influence, in the infusion of form
to cover form.

THE PRACTICAL APPLICATION of the SCIENTIFIC AND OTHER DATA ADDUCED AND LAID DOWN IN THE PRECEDING PaGES.

After due and adequate observance, and intellec-
tual investigation of the foregoing data, it will be
readily apprehended that there cannot be very much
difficulty experienced in reducing, condensing and
applying these selfsame principles to the operations
of the cutting room, and engrafting them upon the
same.

It will be observed that the line of form depths
are considerably greater than the line of height
depths. The mesial line (see fig. 1, plate 12) is an
imaginary, artificial, and perpendicular plane line,
struck down through the centre of the figure. On
this line are given the perpendicular or line of height
depths of a figure 64in. high. But by referring to
the back line of form, fig. 1, plate 11, it will be found
that the 2⅜ in the upper, and 5 in the lower thorax,
are increased to 3 and 5¼ respectively. Add to 3
and 5¾ or 8¾ the collarseam makes 9, and we have a
total scye depth of 9in. for a porportionate figure of
about 36 breast measure.

Among the other lessons to be learned from the
anthroposophical, geometrical and other data, are
the following: Starting at the upper sector the
tailor has to deal with, we find that the linear or
line of form depth, from the nape or back of the
columnial plane, to the acrimonial line (see fig. 1,
plate 12, also fig. 1, plate 11) to be about ⅜in. more
than the perpendicular or line of height depth,
or ⅝in. more than the differenre between one-sixth
and one-eighth of total height ; the scye depth from

nape of neck to the thoracial line to be 1in. more
than one-eighth of total height ; the waist length to
be about 2in, more than two-eighths of total height ;
and the length from nape to seat or gluteal line to
be as near as possible 2¾in. more than three-eighths
of total height, and a seam.

And thus we are driven to the conclusion that the
back shoulder depth or neck height is about the
one-twenty-fourth part of the line of form height, or
one-sixth of the waist length ; that the scye depth,
middle thorax, or scye section depth is as nearly as
possible the one-twelfth part of the line of form
height, or one-third of waist length ; that the entire
scye depth from nape to the thoracial line is about
one-eighth part of line of form height, or one-half
of waist length ; and to the knowledge that, if all
these facts are reduced, condensed or massed together as in the following tables, it will be an easy
matter to turn them to practical account as the
foundation of reliable systems by which to work
or carry on the operations of the cutting room, in a
truly scientific and satisfactory manner.

Table 1.

The waist length is the	2/8th part of the total height and 2in	Or one-half of half the height and 2in	Or quarter the whole height and 2in
The shoulder level depth is the	1/24th part of the total height and ⅜in	Or 1/12th of half the height and ⅜in	Or 1/6th of the waist length
The scye depth maure is the	1/8th part of the total height and 1in	Or 1/4th of half the height and 1in.	Or half the waist length
Or the scye sectn or mdle thorax dpth is	1/12th of the total height and ⅜in	Or 1/6th of half the height and ⅜in	Or 1/3rd of the waist length
The length to seat is the	3/8th part of total height and 3in.	Or 3/4ths of the half height and 3in.	Or the waist length & 1/8 height & 1in.

Table 2.

The length from waist to garter is the	3/8th part of total height and 3in.	Pants length 4/8 or half totl height and 4in	To trrs lngth 1/16 totl hght and 1in. extra
The leg length is	To the garter 2/8 totl height and 1in.	To pnts lngth 3/8 the total height and 2in	To trsrs lngth 1/16 of height and 1in. extra

Table 3.

The sleeve length from the centre of back is the	4-8th of total height and 4in less 1-10th the height (lngth of hand).	Or half the hght and 4in, less 1-10th the height.	Or 2-4th the whole height and 4in, less the hand.
The under-arm or fore-arm is the	2-8th of the total height, and 1-30th part of the height.	Or 4-8th the hght, less half latrl diamtr of acromial plne & 1-10th hght	Or half of the height, less 1-3rd breast and 1½in. and 1-10th height.

System, to be really worth anything, must be founded on some such sound, correct and scientific data as is here given, otherwise it cannot be a true system, or indeed anything better than the merest guesswork of the imagination.

THE APPLICATION OF SCIENCE AND ART.

Having reduced our scientific data to within something like practicable working limits, simplicity and usefulness, we can proceed to apply it to the end in view, the work we have to do —the art and science of cutting all kinds of clothing for all kinds of persons, for all kinds of figures, by system.

AN EXAMPLE SHOWING HOW TO FIX THE DEPTH POINTS FOR BODY COATS.

See fig. I, plate II.

From nape to shoulder level (line I on figure) one-sixth waist length. Depth of scye (from shoulder line I to line 2 on figure) one-third of waist length, or half the waist length from nape. Waist length one-fourth the height and 2in.

How to Take the Measures for Body Coats.

In order to carry out all kinds of work successfully there should be order, arrangement and method, even to the smallest detail, so as to avoid muddling and mistakes; therefore measures should be taken consecutively according to some set rule, and not mixed up either in the taking of them, nor in the entering them in the order book.

Rule.

1 The length from nape to waist, and full length
2 The width of back from arm to arm, and from X, fig. plate 12, to X, fig. plate 13.
3 The widths of sleeve
4 The width of shoulder from neck to X (see small fig. plate 13), thence on to elbow O, and hand W
5 The width of breast from arm to arm
6 The circumference of the breast
7 The circumference of the waist

These are all the measures it is necessary to take to enable artists to apply the rudiments educed, though the other measures may be taken which are mentioned further on.

The widths across back, shoulder and chest especially should be taken very correctly. Two pieces of elastic, made with a loop on the one end and button on the other, for the purpose of putting round the socket of the arms when measuring, are very useful in case of uncertainty, as in measuring the inch tape can be applied from that round the one scye to that round the other.

During the operation of taking the measures, observations should be taken of the person's form, to see if it departs in any particulars, as far as the eye can tell, from preconceived notions of proportions or normality; and if so, notes should be made under the measures of those departures for guidance when cutting out

We should never stand in front of a person while measuring, nor behind him only, when taking stock of his figure, but view him carefully from the side also.

When about to apply the measures and do the cutting, the first thing that should be done is to compare the measures and notes regarding the form with the data laid down in Table 1. For example, if it was observed that the figure's body or legs was longer or shorter than half the height, naturally it would affect the lengths or depths of the coat; and it may be taken for granted that if the waist length appeared to be long in comparison with proportion, the notes in the order book should say that the body is long in comparison with the height, or there is a mistake somewhere. Or if it was observed that the neck was longer or shorter than normal, this again would affect the depth of itself, and the scye too, as the axilla cannot go downwards or upwards without the scye depth being affected.

HOW TO APPLY THE ELEMENTS, MEASURES AND SCIENTIFIC DATA EDUCED BY RULE OR SYSTEM.

EITHER of the following methods may be pursued, as it makes no difference to the working of the system which plan is fallowed :—

1 The back may be cut separately

2 Then the sidebody separately, by the back

3 Or sidebody and forepart together after the back

4 Or the forepart separately, by the back and sidebody

5 Or the forepart and skirt, under one, after back and sidebody

Just according to convenience.

59

Drafting the Back.

Dia. 1, Plate 13.

The commencement is made by drawing line X2.
From X to J is one-sixth of waist length and a seam;
X to E half waist length and a seam ; X to W the
natural or fancy waist length ; X to 2 the actual
waist length and a seam, or one-fourth the total
height and 2in. The lines X8, J H K, E1 F, and the
waist are drawn at right angles to the backseam.
The bottom of the sideseam of back is drawn ¼in.
below the square line, and line 2 Y 10 is drawn from
1 through this ¼in. drop at Q. X to 8 is half the
breast, and JK and LF the same. XV is one-eighth
breast and ⅜in, rising ⅜in. The shoulder line is drawn
from V to K. The width of back is half full back width,
from arm to arm, or a third of breast and 1½in. 8 R S
gives the curve of back scye. VH, the fashion slope
of shoulder, being governed by fashion, the drop
from R to H is variable accordingly. Depth of back
scye is also governed by fashion or taste, and the
run of sideseam too. As a guide, WM may be made
one eighth breast for the 36 size, and ⅜in. for every
two sizes sizes larger, and E I double the width of
W M. It is customary to hollow the backseam
slightly between E and 2.

The Back Skirt

Is got by going out from 2 to 1 about ¾in. to an inch
according to the style being produced, whether
bound edges, plain, or full dress; and drawing a
straight line from X through 1 to 7; drawing lines
2 3 and Q 5 parallel with it, adding as much inturn
as necessary.

The Sidebody.—Dia. 2, Plate 13.

SS is swept from pivot I. The waist is suppressed
by taking out 1½ at M and a trifle at top of sideseam for

ordinary figures; for figures flat in the region of the
blade, less; for figures prominent in the blade, more
is taken out, in accordance with the changes in formation. The line from 1 through Q to 10 is square

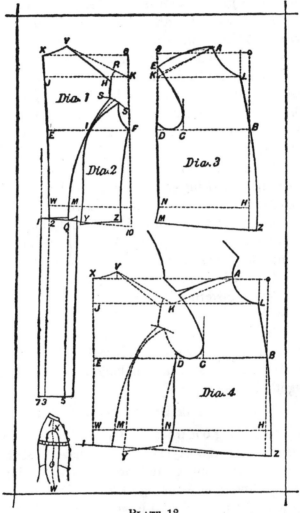

PLATE 13.

with line X 7. The length of sidebody is made to
correspond with back sideseam; the curve of scye
part to start at about ½in. above line EF to S; and its
width is governed by taste or fashion; it may

therefore reach point F or not, but if not, whatever
is taken off inside line K 10 at F must be added to
the forepart outside point D. A wide, gouty sidebody does not look artistic. Point Z is ¾in. to 1in.
above line Q 10.

THE FOREPART.—Dia. 3, Plate 13.

After squaring the lines O 8 and O H, the depths
O L, O B, and O H are made the same X J, X E and
X W of the back ; lines L K, B D, and H N square
with O H ; O 8, L K, and B D each half the breast
and 2in., thus finding line 8 N. K to A is one third
breast and ½in. The end of shoulderseam is risen
as much above K as the back shoulder H is dropped
below R, and its length made to correspond with
that of the back. D C is made 3in. for all sizes, or
B C half the across breast measure and two seams.
In drawing the scye, it is made to touch a line drawn
up from C, at about 2in. above C, and finished off
above D as much as the sideseam of sidebody is
above F. As much is taken out at N as will make
the amount taken out at waist of undearmseam 1¼in.
for ordinary figures, or if the figure is hollow or full
there, more or less. M is as much below N as Z of
sidebody is below line W M, and Z below H as much
as Y is below M. The top of sideseam is one fourth
square and not pointed. When the one side of a
seam is to be stretched, the amount of stretching is
to be cut off, and when to be fulled on allowed on,
or else the opposite seam lengthened or shortened.
The waist measure is applied across the back at
W M, across sidebody, and continued from N through
H, taking in nothing but the widths of the parts.
2in. is (same as at breast) the allowance for seams,
and if more is allowed at the breast, owing to the
substance of material or for any special purpose

except padding and wadding, the same is to be
allowed at the waist.   But allowances for padding
and wadding in breast have nothing to do with the
waist.   The gorge is drawn high or low according
to the style of front opening and turn or no turn
required.   Of this further on.

As the divisions of the waist length correspond with
the divisions of height (see table of analysis), it is
quite correct to work the system by those divisions
made use of; moreover it is very much more simple
to work by divisions of the waist length than by
divisions of the height.   But at the same time no
one is debarred from using the divisions of height,
if preferred, as when rightly understood the one is
the same as the other.

THE PLANE SECTORS GIVE THE CIRCUMFERENCES.

As regards the widths, the diameters of the plane
sectors of any figure can be taken by means of callipers, the planes reconstructed on the cloth, and
thus their circumferences ascertained.   But this
process being so tedious, for practical purposes it is
better to take them on the figure.

The circumference of the acromial plane is about
1in. more than the breast measure — 37in.   Many
figures are considerably more than this.   The circumference of normal axilla (scye) equals three
times the depth of the middle thorax, less $1\frac{1}{2}$in.;
those of the other planes are given on them.

THE SYSTEM MADE AVAILABLE FOR ALL FORMS.

By introducing a slight change in the mode of
procedure, the system becomes self-varying for all
forms, whether long or short in the neck, high or
low in the shoulder (axilla), stooping or erect, it

being only necessary to include the measure from 1
to X, X to dot at the end of shoulder, and thence to
depth of scye front, in the rule of measuring (see
small fig., plate 12), and apply the same in drafting.
Thus the depth of neck XJ becomes governed by
the measure 1X, the depth position of the axilla by
the downward or upward movement of itself, the
depth and circumference covering of the shoulder
by the width and depth from dot at the end of the
shoulder to depth of scye front. The straightness
becomes governed by the measure X to dot at the
shoulder-end, and the measure from neck to X, fig.
W, plate 13. The front of scye moves forward or
backward with the dot at shoulder-end, because the
axilla cannot move backward or forward without
carrying the dot with it.

When the shoulder-end is thick (lateral diameter
of the axilla large) it causes an increase in the
measure governing the circumference C K, and de-
notes that the shoulder line K A must be risen to
the extent of the excess in the measure over the
normal quantity; for commonsense tells us that extra width (circumference) is not extra depth, and
must not be treated as such, but the extra quantity
required to cover the increase in the circumference
of the shoulder-end allowed where the diameter and
circumference of the figure are both increased.
The shoulder line only can be risen the same amount
at A as at K, or the lines K L and O 8 risen first,
then the straightness measure applied from K's new
position to A's new position.

A normal axilla cannot go upwards or downwards,
backwards or forwards, on the trunk, without its
boundary lines (the shoulder and bottom of scye
lines, and front and back of scye) moving upwards
or downwards, backward or forward with it. But a

shoulder-end (axilla) can increase or decrease in circumference and diameter with or without any upward or downward, backward or forward movement of itself on the trunk.

When a figure stoops, the waist length being increased, it increases the scye depth, and an increase in the neck length or shoulder slope increases it still more, and vice versa when the figure is erect and the shoulder slope less than normal.

Figures of all postures—stooping, erect and normal—have high and large, low and large, high and small, and low and small shoulders (axillas), leading many to believe that mankind is divided up into a far greater number of classes of formation than is actually the case. All formations are ascertained and provided for by this system.

Dia. 4, Plate 13.

This diagram serves to snow the back, sidebody and forepart drawn out together for a normal figure. It also shows how the waist length line, from 1 through Q and 10, continued straight on to Z, finds the length of forepart in front; in other words, the drop of the ½in. below the square line at Q does it, while also serving for a waist line by which to draft the skirt. The amount to go up from this line at the bottom of the underarmseam is governed by fashion, and ranges from nothing or ½in. to 1½in.; about 1in. obtains the most favour. The amount of hollowing, in its turn, influences the form of the waistseam of skirt, whether frock, dress, or morning coat skirt.

DISPROPORTION OF HEIGHT TO WIDTH.

IN cases of disproportion between height and width, the normal or average waist length can be got by what ought to be the height, reckoning in heads of certain depths; or, in lieu of same, estimated by judgment and the measure taken, assisted or not assisted by the width from finger tips to finger tips when the arms are outstretched at right angles to the body; then the slope of shoulder and depth of scye found by one-sixth and one-half of it; the width in JK found by one-third breast and 3in., the front of scye by half breast and 3in., the depth BL (giving the depth and width from C to K) by one-third the breast and ½in., and the front slope by the same means as the back slope XJ — viz., one-sixth waist length. For large waists the suppressions may be filled up according to the figure — say 1in. out at M for flat blades, and so much out at N according to the hollowness or fullness at the side.

A third of the axilla equals one third of the waist length. In working the system without the measures XJ, JK and KC, shortness of the waist length modifies this rule, reducing JE below one third of the axilla. So for short and stout figures the modus operandi may be altered to harmonize with the development, by first making XE half the waist length, then EJ one third of the axilla if taken, or by increasing EJ by the probable amount of the difference between one third the waist length and one third the axilla (scye) measure. Short and stout figures, whether corpulent or not, generally require less upper thorax depth, and not more.

All old systems provided more upper thorax depth for big sizes, whether short or long waisted; and the first system published to operate differently was the Students' Guide System, which system instructed the operator to double the back (waist) length into two, to find the depth of scye line, and then divide the upper half of waist length into three to find the slope of shoulder, the slope of shoulder being one third of it.

STRAIGHTNESS & CROOKEDNESS.

WHEN a coat is on a man and buttoned, its backseam and actual breast lines have travelled, to approach each other, the difference between the breast measure of the coat and the profile diameter of the thoracial plane.

The tops of backseam and actual breast line travel still further towards each other, by the amount of the difference between one-third of the neck and ⅜in. and the profile diameter of the thoracial plane. Thus, if the diameter of the thoracial plane is 10, and the breast measure 18, the backseam and actual breast line travel 8. And if the diameter or a third of neck and ⅜in is 5½, and the thoracial plane 10, the top of backseam and of actual breast line travel 4½. This and 1in. deducted from the thoracial plane gives the straightness.

The profile diameter of the neck is about ½in. more than the profile diameter of the scye.

The approximate profile diameter of any size breast may be guaged by deducting two-eighteenth parts from one third the breast measure. Thus, one third of 48 is 16, and two eighteenths from 16 leaves about 13½.

The straightness may be known by deducting one third of neck from any profile thoracial plane diameter.

The diameter (a circle) of the neck and half the profile diameter of the thorax are equal to each other. Half the diameter of the thorax is therefore a good rule for the straightness.

In the process of the front and back of a coat approaching each other, and therefore sitting in different positions from those held on a flat cutting board, the scye points travel only about one third the diameter of scye. The straightness of the front shoulder may therefore be known and regulated by leaving a space of one third the diameter of axilla between the back and front shoulder of a coat, and fixing the neckpoint of front shoulder the length of the front shoulderseam of the back, forward from this open space between the scye points.

In probably the majority of cases, the diameter of the thorax is less in the profile, and more in the lateral direction than the rule above laid down gives.

For example, great numbers of 36 breasts are 9 or
9½ through from back to front, and consequently
wider than 12 from side to side. A very common
figure is 9½ by 12½.

SCYES.

TO know whether a scye is formed nicely, close the
back to the top of sideseam of sidebody ; stand the
inch tape on its edge, running with the front of scye,
the end at the end of front shoulderseam, and form
it round below K to meet the shoulderseam of back
in the form of the man's axilla. The form then
given should be 1in. more in depth than width. The
depth of a nicely-formed scye is one-third of its
circumference, and its width 1in. less.

SLEEVES.

Diagram 3, Plate 14

THE depth of a sleevehead, including round, is on
third of the drafted scye, less the amount the front
pitch point is above the bottom of scye.

The front pitch point is not where foolishly
imagined by ninety-nine out of every hundred writers
on cutting, but exactly where a straight line drawn
from angle C front of scye to V top of back, dia. 4,
plate 13, strikes the scyeseam. This line divides
the scye into halves in normal cases.

Half the one third of scye and ½in. gives the amount
of round above a line drawn from top of fore to top
of hindarmseams, minus any allowance for the reduction of round caused by fulling-in, or for puffed
sleevehead.

A scye is 1½ larger when a sleeve is put in, so that
a 16½ drafted scye must be reckoned as 18 ; and the
sleeve should be drafted by half 18, with ¾in. added,
which should produce a circumference of sleevehead
of 2½in. more, reduced to 1½in. more (for fullness),
after back and forearm and sleevehead seams have
been taken.

The underside should be hooked-in 1¾ to produce
a 9 underside, or 1¼ to produce a 9½ underside, if to
be eased in a bit.

The amount of round of sleevehead above the line
NV, dia. 3, plate 14, equals one sixth of coat scye
when made up.

The fitting points (constructive) of a sleeve are governed by the scye—the topside by the dimensions of the top part of it, and the underside by the dimensions of the underside of it. To ascertain the scale to draft by, the scye is measured all round, or

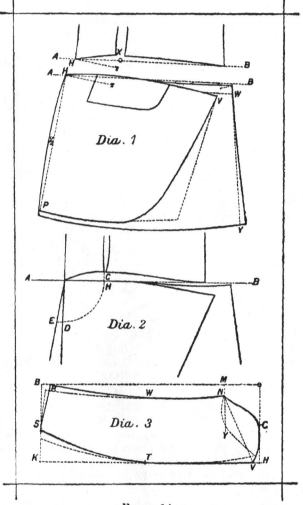

PLATE 14.

from back pitch round to front pitch, a seam from its edge; and this quantity and ¾in. is applied from O to H, after squaring B O H. O to M is half O H, or one third drafted scye less front pitch is above bot-

tom of scye, and O to top of sleevehead the same.
Line M Y is drawn at right angles with O B. H to
V is the amount the back pitch has been dropped
below the level of a point one third of drafted scye
above depth of scye. H to N equal to H O. A
straight line can be drawn from N to W, and the forearm sprung trom W to R, or one from N to B, after
the length has been adjusted by the measure X O W
(see small figure), and the forearm hollowed at W
1in.; then the widths applied from W to T, and R
to S. If the figure is very erect the sleeve should
be drawn more backward at the hand, as indicated
by the dotted lines, and the reverse if the figure
stoops.

SKIRTS.

Diagrams 1 and 2, Plate 14.

THE line A B of the skirt is the same as the waist
line A B of the body part. From this line down to
X is the same distance as X of the sidebody is above
it at O. The spring is got by placing the angle of
square at H with its one arm resting on X, and
drawing line H P by its other arm. All styles are
producible by one and the same system.

If preferred, the line D may be drawn square with
A B, H E swept from bottom of sideseam, and D E
made equal to H C.

The front of the frock skirt should be made to run
square with a point ¼in. down at 2in. in, or with the
bottom of the lapel, which should be first turned
over on the breast as if buttoned over and made to
run with the waistseam of the forepart, which has an
upward tendency in front, as will be seen from the
line running out from the waistseam, dia. 7, plate
15: and the same principle holds good for S.B
frock skirt fronts.

Whenever more drapery is required in frock
shaped skirts of any kind, it should be added above
the line A B, in front, to nothing at the underarmseam of sidebody; because the material thus added
drops into the side of a skirt when it is seamed-to
at the waist.

Whenever less drapery is needed, as in the case
of all kinds of morning coats (remembering that a
gamekeeper's is not a morning coat), it should be
deducted below the line AB, so that when joined to

70

the forepart loose material may be picked up from the side of the skirt. A morning or dress coat skirt may be cut down in front, until its waistseam is as round or rounder than the waistseam of the forepart and sidebody is hollowed. The rounder the skirt in the waist the closer it will fit at the bottom, and vice versa, though extra drapery will not provide for large hips; nothing but extra fullness held on or cuts taken out of the waistseam will do that, more drapery meaning extra spread round the bottom, and giving hardly any extra hip room.

To distribute drapery, the waistseam of skirt should be cut a little hollow between O and B, or C and B.

STYLE.

Diagrams 1 to 7, Plate 15.

DIFFERENCE in style being quite a different matter from fit, the only logical way is to treat it so, in order that it may entail as little trouble and thoughtfulness as possible. The fit of a garment terminates at line LBZ, which is the meeting-edge-to-edge line, or at most allowing for a seam if cut off there; so therefore all added in front of it becomes style of one sort or another, as also does anything cut away from it, as will be seen further on.

The line XX of each of these diagrams is equivalent to the front edge-to-edge line L B Z of the system. The first diagram shows the additions or changes necessary to produce a morning coat button two or three; the second, the style to button three or four; the third, a wide front to button one, or a front to button two with frock lapel; the fourth, the low-rolling style of front; the fifth, the S.B. frock style; the sixth, the same with lapel like D.B. The quantities to allow in front of line X X are: 1in. at breast and a trifle more at lower button for Nos. 1 and 2; the same for No. 3, filled out to second dotted line for full front; and about the same for No. 4. The quantities for S.B. frocks are ¾in. to 1in. for the button-hole breast, and ½in. or more extra for the button stand side. When ½in. is consumed in making up the edges, ½in. extra should be allowed for all styles. For a D.B. frock it is a wise policy to allow 1in. in front of B, and run a line from nothing at Z through this point to neck, before allowing

the overlapping style in the form of a sewn-on lapel.
The reason of this is because such a lapel has the
effect of making a figure appear to be narrow chested,
and so it becomes necessary to obviate it by cutting an artificially wide breast and as narrow a lapel

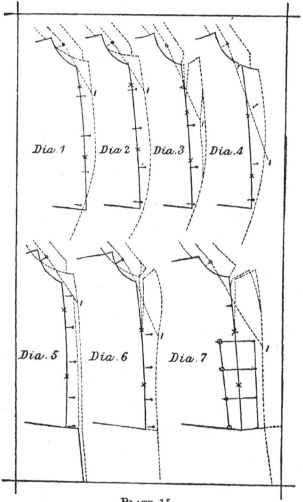

PLATE 15.

as possible consistent with the style. The seventh
diagram shows how the D.B. frock lapel is added
after the amount stated has been added in front of
B. There is a cut showing how the breast has to
be drawn in, and the lapel has to be cut that much

(including seams) shorter, hence the reason it does
not reach to the top of breast of forepart.

DRESS COAT CUTTING.

Plate 16.

O J one third head height and $\frac{1}{4}$in.   J E two thirds
the head height and $\frac{3}{4}$in.   O W to measure or two

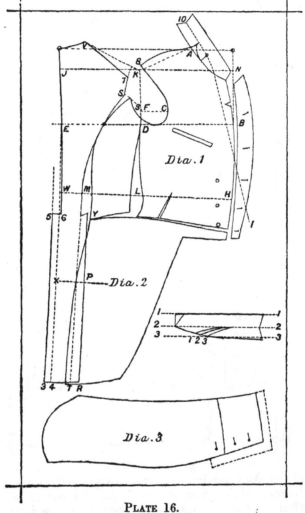

Dia. 1

Dia. 2

Dia. 3

PLATE 16.

head heights and $1\frac{1}{4}$, and O6 to measure or two head
heights and 2in., or fashion.   O V one eighth breast

and $\frac{1}{2}$in. JK one third breast and 3in.; across to 7 or S to measure. ED same as JK. FC one sixth; a third and 3in. and one sixth breast being the same as half breast and 3in. EB the breast measure and 2in. Line BO square with BE, also top and shoulder lines. For the 36 size BO may be made same as OE of back, and the shoulder slope the same as OJ. But for all but slim figures BL (see plate 13) must be made one third breast, or one third breast and $\frac{1}{2}$in., and LO same as OJ KA one third breast and $\frac{1}{2}$in. Shoulderseams according to rule or fashion. $1\frac{1}{2}$ out at M and $1\frac{1}{2}$ out at L. Nothing or only 1in. over net measure to be allowed for width of waist. This cuts the front more backward at H than a frock.

The waistseam of skirt can be made to run with waistseam of body, the spring to run through a point half the breast down from 6 or Y, and the width of the back waist from X, or by the width of the back plait backward from P. If the front of sidebody is to be stretched, it must be cut shorter in front as shown; or if sideseam of sidebody is to be stretched down, or have the back fulled-on, shorter at Y than the sideseam of back. The length of the strap of skirt is one third its waist width; and the run-off of front part and width of bottom to fashion. Dress coat lapels should be cut narrow and tasty, belled inside and straight outside it whole edge, sleeve cuffs as dressy as possible, and collars cut according to the height of the gorge, rounder or straighter, as may be necessary according to circumstances.

COURT DRESS COAT.
Plate 17.

The back and sidebody of this coat is cut as per dias, 1 and 2, plate 13; the forepart as per dia. 3, plate 13 only an inch is taken off at L and $2\frac{1}{2}$ off at Z, as shown by the dotted line behind A to C, the coat not meeting or fastening at the neck, nor at breast, and being well cut away at waist. The skirt is cut in the same way as the dress coat skirt on plate 16.

The other style of Court dress coat is cut similar to the illustration fig. 1, plate 18, only more fish-bellied—i.e , more cut-away. The foreparts of this style are sometimes held in place by links at breast.

FIRST-CLASS MINISTER'S FULL DRESS COAT.

This coat is cut as per dias. 1, 2 and 3, plate 13,

with the addition of sufficient for button-holes on the
left breast, and for button-stand on the right breast,
all the way down from neck to waist, it being worn
fastened from neck to waist, having a military stand

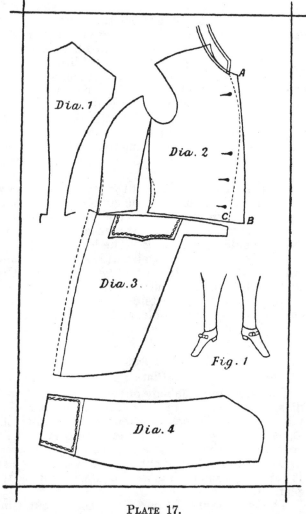

PLATE 17.

collar on the neck, and skirts cut as per dia. 3 plate
17, without the strap part   The waist length is
generally cut as short as if a belt were worn round
the waist outside of coat, a la militaire.

Peer's Dress Coat.

The cut and decoration of this coat is similar to the first-class minister's full dress coat.

Consul's Half Dress Coat.

The cut of this coat is the same as the first-class minister's; but it is decorated on cuffs and collar only, instead of being covered almost all over the breast with gold lace; and is worn with trousers, not breeches.

Lord-Lieutenant's and Deputy-Lord-Lieutenant's Dress Coat.

These are cut in the same way, only are D.B., and button up to the throat with military stand collar. D.B. lapels have therefore to be cut and sewn on, as to the front of dia. 3, plate 13.

Clerical Dress Coats.

Plate 18.

These are cut as per figs. 1 and 2, dias. 1, 2 and 3, plate 18—viz., similar to Court dress coats. The dotted lines show how both styles are got by altering from the forepart dia. 3, plate 13. Not quite so much is taken off at neck 2 3 or 4 5, as in the case of ordinary Court dress, as clerics are supposed to be more staid and not given to such extremes as regular votaries of fashion. However, this matter is regulatable by taste and current fashion.

D.B. Frock for Wearing Unbuttoned.

Plate 19.

The diagrams on this plate are of a D.B. frock coat for wearing open, or only buttoned occasionally. The rule of drafting is as follows: X J one third head height and one seam, X V one sixth neck and two seams, J E two thirds head height and $\frac{3}{4}$in. Waist lengths to measure, or two head heights and $1\frac{1}{4}$ and 2in. All horizontal lines square with the backseam. J K one third breast and 3in., V K back shoulder line, V 8 fashion. Width back to measure. Back scye depth to fashion. Width W M to fashion. E to sideseam double W M.

K A one third breast and $\frac{1}{2}$in., and front shoulder line, A 7 fashion shoulder line. F C one sixth always. E B breast measure and 2in.; W H waist measure and

5in., reduced to 2in. by taking 1½ out at M and N.
Gorge, lapel and collar as shown. Skirt as per the
system plate 14, or the spring can be got as for
dress coat plate 16, The seat measure, with due
allowance, can be used for frock skirts as indicated

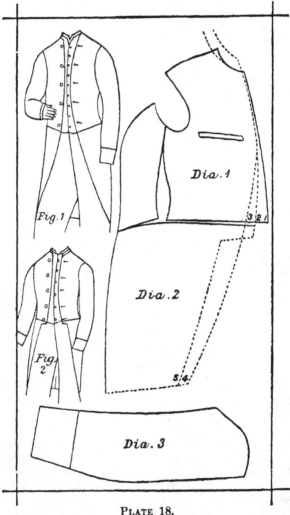

PLATE 18.

by line PRQ. The side should be a trifle longer
than back or front.

When an easier-cut garment is wanted, J K may
be made ½in. more. This will have the effect of

forwarding point A the same amount, and the
straighter shoulder will admit of $\frac{1}{2}$in. being allowed
in front of B.

A straight line drawn at right angles to top square
line through point V, continued when V 8 is placed

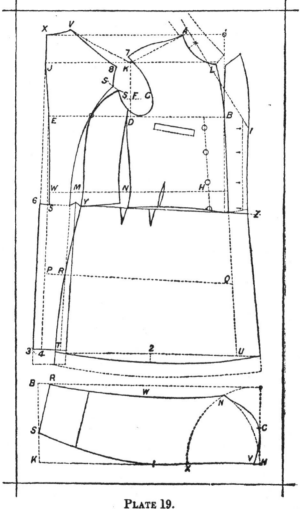

PLATE 19.

to A7, will find the front of the gorge as at L, one-
third the neck from A, which, hollowed 1in., will
give the gorge; and thus the neck will be a trifle
over three thirds of neck measure. When the back

is so laid, the line J K will run from K to a point
equal to J X from A. And a line drawn from the
point one third neck from A as at L to K will give
the front shoulder slope; thus showing the double
quantities in the closed position, with neck and all
in their true relationship.

SLEEVE SYSTEM.

Halve the scye from forearm pitch, also the made-
up scye size. Square OB and OH. Make OH half
the made-up scye and $\frac{3}{4}$in. Square H I K. Sweep
OX from pivot H, and HN from pivot X Drop from
H to V the amount the back pitch point is below
the level of a point one-third of drafted scye above
bottom of scye.

CLERICAL FROCKS.

Plate 20.

These garments being the same as other frocks,
excepting in the neck and style of front, unless they
are wanted a little easier in the waist, the system
is applicable in the same way as for other coats—
i.e., the size up to the actual breast line LBZ is first
to be got (see dia. 3, plate 13), then the style quantities added on in front of it — $\frac{3}{4}$in. on the left and
$1\frac{1}{2}$in. on the right breast. To get the neck, the
operator may mark forward from A one sixth the
neck, and square down from that point one sixth of
neck, then sweep from the angle so formed from A
to L. Multiply one sixth neck by two, and its pro-
duct by three, which divide by four, to find the
approximate length of the curve A L. This added
to the width of back top gives the answer, Fully
half the size of neck. So as to be certain, however,
that the neck is the right height in front, the practitioner may take an opening measure while taking
the size of neck, thus : Place the tape at the back of
the neck, and measure to B or Z, and back to L.
The best way is to take no notice of the measure to
B or Z, but hold the tape there, let it go from the
back of neck, and run it through the fingers backwards up to L, and whatever that quantity says,
enter it in the order book. For example, it may be
7in. In drafting, apply the tape in the same way—
from the back of neck to B or Z, or anywhere on the
breast line BZ ; then wherever 7 falls on breast line

B L, as at L, gives the height of gorge required, ·certain.

POLICE FROCKS.

In producing these the system is applicable in the :same way as for clerical frocks, only the style width

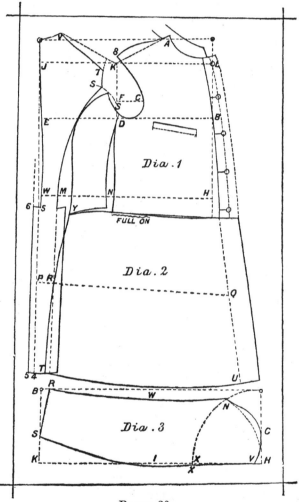

PLATE 20.

·of the back at the waist is broader, the waist length shorter, and cut sufficiently close to allow a belt to be worn over it without causing creases.

80

ALL OTHER FROCKS.

The system is applicable in the same way in producing all other styles of frock coats, the size up to the actual breast line first being got, then the style made as required.

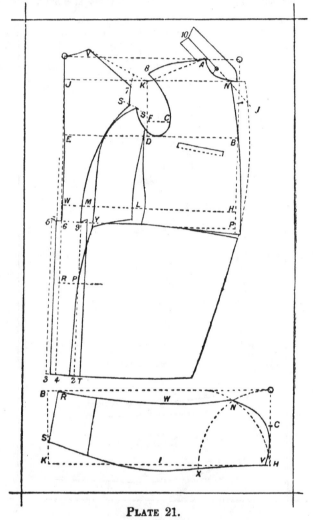

PLATE 21.

Increase of skirt width round the bottom (drapery) may be got by splitting the pattern up where wanted and letting a wedge or wedges in at the bottom to nothing at the waistseam. This plan is the same and much more easily understood than altering the style width of skirt by system.

MORNING COATS BUTTON ONE.—Plate 21.

The principal differences between morning coats and frocks amounting merely to a difference in style of front and skirt, the system is equally applicable to the one as the other, without changing the rule of finding the points and drafting. After getting the size up to the actual breast line, the style is added in front of it as per dotted line. Both the front and skirt can be cut more or less off, and the latter round or angular, according as required. The waistseam of skirt can be made to run with the waistseam of the body part, after the sidebody is stretched down or the back fulled on, or slightly rounder to allow for the reduction in round caused by fulling it on, or otherwise.

MORNING COATS BUTTON TWO, THREE OR FOUR.—Plate. 22.

These diagrams, with the preceding ones, will be sufficient to illustrate the working of the system in full detail in drafting all styles of morning coats. Cut away from the third button or higher the fronts could be made to roll lower and button two ; also to button three by cutting from below the third hole and changing the positions of the buttons. The actual style shown is to button four. In order to get these coats to button in the centre 1in. is allowed in front of the actual breast line on the left side, and $1\frac{1}{2}$ on the right side. If to button four, a little more than these amounts is required at the lower button and hole, graduated off to the amounts stated at the top hole and button.

DOUBLE-BREASTED MORNING COATS.—Plate 23.

These coats being exactly the same as single-breasted morning coats up to the actual breast line, are drafted in the same manner as to size ; then the amount added necessary to produce the style wanted. The dotted lines show three different shapes of cut-away D.B.'s to button one, and the solid lines the style to button two, which also may be cut more or less off and round, angular or corners of skirts blunted. In finding the set of the top button, $\frac{1}{2}$in.,

1in., or as the case may be, must be deducted from the width from the actual breast line to the front edge, and the button set the remainder back from the breast line. The run of the dotted line shows how the positions of the other buttons are found.

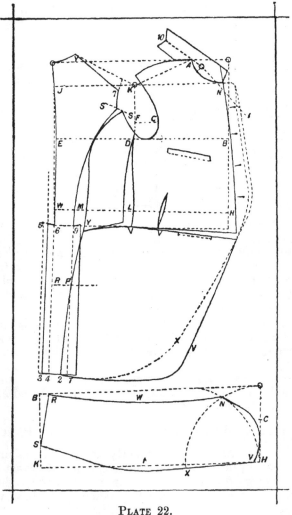

PLATE 22.

SLEEVES FOR MORNING COATS

May be produced by the system shown on the frock and morning coat plates, or the system on plate 14.

PALETOTS, SELBYS, PADDOCKS, AND FROCK OVERCOATS. — Plate 24

For all kinds of overcoats, the breast, waist and seat measures are taken on the undercoat. The

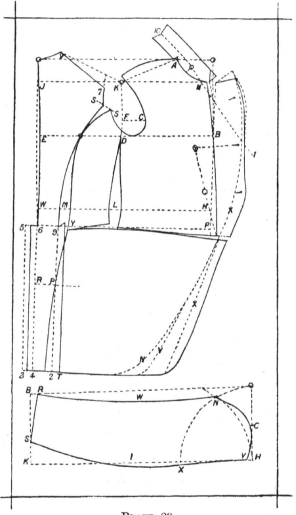

PLATE 23.

approximate waist length of all waistseam overcoats is two head-heights and from $2\frac{1}{2}$ to 3in. In measuring. the waist length need not be taken longer than usual, as the necessary additions to scye depth and waist length can be made afterwards, or by the approximate rule.

In drafting by the waist length, O to J is one sixth and JE one third of waist length and $\frac{1}{2}$in., and

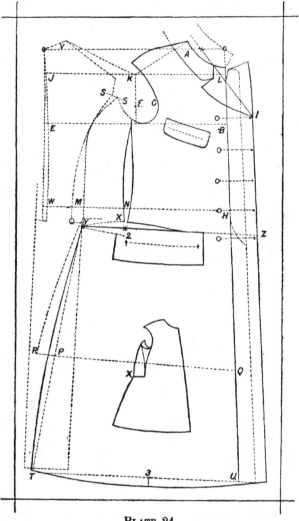

PLATE 24.

the full length to fashion. Lines O, J, E and W are drawn at right angles to the back centre line; Y Z as fashion dictates. OV is one eighth and half inch, point V risen $\frac{3}{4}$in., J K one third and 3in., width of back to measure. W M to fashion. C is 3in. in

front of line K F. A is one third and 1in. from K,
and 1in. above top line. Front shoulder-end the
same above K as back shoulder-end is below it.
About 1in. comes out at M, and fully half-inch at N.
* to X is ¾in. to 1in. 2 is the same below * as X is
above it, and the plait is found by placing one arm
of the square on 2 Y, letting the other arm find line
Y P. If a fuller skirt is required, the pattern can
be split up to points a little in front and behind 2,
and wedges let in at the bottom to nothing at the
waistseam.

B is the breast measure and 2½in. from E. H is
the waist and 4in. or 4½in. from W; this allows for
the suppressions to be taken out. More can be
added if a looser waist is wanted. QP should be as
much more than measure as the waist is more than
measure, at least.

The small sketch on skirt shows one way of getting
the spring, also the style of the old paletot.

GAMEKEEPERS' COATS. — Plate 25.

OJ one sixth the waist length, JE one third waist
length, OW waist length. Lines O, J and E square
with backline OW. Width of back top one-eighth
breast and ½in., neckpoint ¾in. above top line. J to K
one third breast and 3in. E D the same. K to A one
third breast and ¼in. F to C 3in. E to B the breast
measure and 2½in. Back width to measure, position
of shoulderseam to taste, width W M about 2½in.
The front line is square with top line. Point A can
be got at a fourth back from O for all proportionate
figures. 8 is as much above as 7 is below shoulder
line. In making, point A should be well stretched
up. 1½ comes out of waist at M and above L, and
spring allowed at the bottom of seams. The front
of waist is found at the waist measure and from 5½
to 6½ inches from W, which allows for 3in. of suppression and 2½ to 3½ for seams and ease   Ease in
the waist should not be allowed at L and M, as the
hare-pockets full of game drag the coat outwards
from the figure, spring at L being chiefly necessary
to render it easy to put on sufficient skirt width
round the hips. The spring of skirt is ½in. over the
perpendicular line drawn from 9 to 2, at P, variable
according to prominence of posterior. The skirt
shown is the style modern gamekeepers like best.
More width round the bottom can be got by splitting

up the pattern at various places and letting in wedges to nothing at waistseam, or by rising front of waistseam to nothing at L. About 13 or 14 inches is usually the length of skirt. The amount of overlap

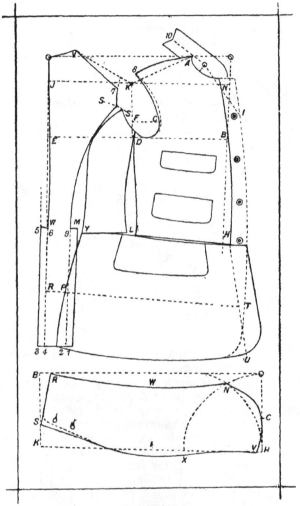

PLATE 25.

allowed is $1\frac{1}{2}$, including the amount consumed in making-up the edge; and the skirts are cut to overlap at U, hence they must be run well forward, as indicated by the line drawn down to U.

The sleeve is drawn out in the usual way.

SHOOTING COATS.

These are cut the same shape as gamekeepers'
coats, except that the front of skirt is run off as per
dotted line through R.   There are old shooters and
new shooters.   New shooters are merely run off
more in front, or more morning coat shape.

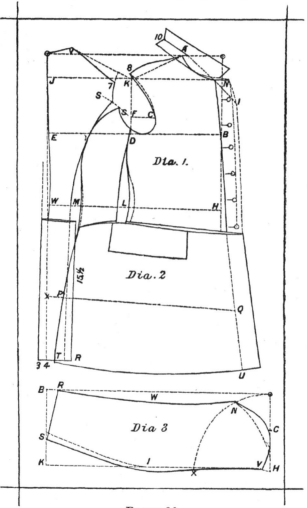

PLATE 26.

COACHMEN'S LIVERY FROCKS.

Dias. 1, 2 and 3, Plate 26.

These garments are usually cut to button high,

with a small morning coat turn, ends of collar cut
as diagram, or morning coat style. In some cases
the waist length is made a little longer than the
waist length of a morning coat, but it does not tend
to smartness of appearance.

The waist length of a livery frock is two head-
heights and 2in. or 2½in.

O to J is one sixth and JE one third waist length,
or O E half waist length and E J two thirds of O E.
O V one eighth breast and ½in., and neckpoint risen
¾in. J K one third breast and 3in., and E D the
same. F C 3in. K A one third breast and 1in. 8 as
much above shoulder line as 7 is below it. The scye
can be cleared out as dotted line, or more for coachmen. E B the breast measure and 2½in., W H the
waist measure and 5½in. 2in. or more can be taken
out at M, and 1in. at L   The allowance in front of
the size line B H is 1¼in. the left and 1¾in. the right
breast, which allows for half-inch being consumed
in making-up the edges.

The spring of skirt is found at half-inch over the
perpendicular dotted line M1 at P. The waistseam
is hollowed a little across the bottom of forepart,
and the front well sprung forward as the line Q U
indicates.   If a fuller skirt is wanted, it can be got
by splitting the pattern up and letting-in wedges
where the extra fullness is wanted, or by rising the
front to nothing at middle of sidebody.

Coachmen's sleeves should be run well forward at
the hand.

Grooms' Frocks.

Grooms' frocks are cut short and close-fitting in
the waist, so as to allow the belt to be worn over
the waist without creasing it, and rest on the back
buttons without rising, which it would do if the
waist were cut too long. The skirt is 2in. shorter
than a coachman's. The waist is reduced at the
underarmseam as indicated by the dotted line. The
same sleeve will do for groom's as for coachman's
frock.

Livery Overcoats or Box Coats.—Plate 27.

The measures are taken on the undercoat. Waist
length two head-heights and 3in. O J is one sixth
and J E one third the waist length ; or O E half and

E J one third the waist length. O V is one eighth breast and ⅛in., and up ¾in. J K is one third breast and 3in., and E D the same. S C is 3in., K A one third the breast and ¾in. to 1in. E B is the breast

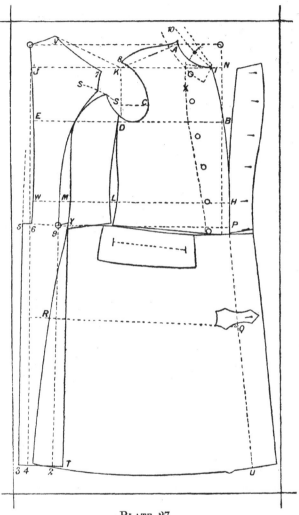

PLATE 27.

measure and 2½in., and W H the waist measure and 5in. to 5½in. W M is 3 to 3½. About 1in. comes out at M and ¾in. at L. The neck is reduced to size at 1; the collar and lapels are shaped as shown. The spring of skirt passes ¾in. over the perpendicular

line drawn down from 9, or 1¾ behind P. Coachmen
have flaps, footmen have not. Skirts are sprung
well forward as per line Q U. When fuller skirts
are wanted, they are wedged at the bottom to noth-

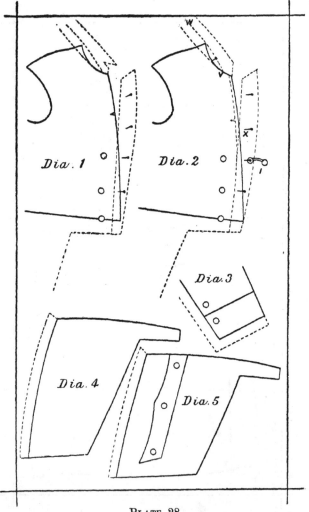

PLATE 28.

ing at the waist. A good figure requires ¾in. on
above A to nothing at 8. The diagram represents
thy common coachman's figure. The measure O J,
J K, and K to depth of scye front, reveals the truth
about figure.

BUTLER'S DRESS COAT.—Dias. 1 and 4, Plate 28.

A butler's dress coat is just an ordinary plain dress coat, cut shoit and neat-looking. The collar may have notched ends or be cut plain. To produce a butler's dress coat all the change that has to be made from the net size draft, dias. 1, 2 and 3, plate 13, is to take 1in off at the front of waist to nothing at the breast, as shown by the position in which the dotted lapel is laid, and to cut the skirt after the form shown by dia. 4.

FOOTMAN'S COATEE.—Dias. 2 and 5, Plate 28.

A coatee is simply a short, neat dress coat with sword flap and side edges to match. It is usually held together in front by means of two buttons and a loop, as indicated on dia. 2. To produce this syle $1\frac{1}{2}$ is cut off at the waist behind the meeting edge-to-edge size line at the waist, and $\frac{1}{2}$in. off at breast, as shown by the dotted line. The length of the skirt, flaps and side edges are regulated by family custom. When no such family regulations exist, the proper thing is to cut as indicated by the diagrams—the skirt shorter than the butler's, and wider at the bottom, with sword flaps three-fourths the length of the skirt, and side edges about after the proportion of 1 1in. to the $13\frac{1}{2}$ length of skirt. Dia. 3 indicates how the cuffs of sleeves are arranged—whether of the plain, round description, or with slits.

COACHMANS FULL DRESS COAT.—Plate 29.

The diagrams show the extent and character of the changes from the net size draft of a coat in order to turn it into a coachman's full dress coat—viz , 1in. taken off the breast at the front of gorge, and $1\frac{1}{4}$ off the front of waist to nothing at the breast, as shown by the dotted line; then a stand collar, waist flaps, side edges, and skirts added. The sleevehands are made up in the various styles shown according to family regulations. The breasts and collar-ends are decorated with notched holes, or cords. When flaps are put on in the ordinary way, they are of the form shown on dia, 2, plate 30. The bottom edge of the flap shown requires stretching straight or else cutting straight. Stretching is best if the coat is close-fitting, straight cutting if loose-fitting. When a cuff is decorated with notched holes, it is a round one.

FOOTMAN'S FULL DRESS COAT.
Dias. 1 to 6, Plate 30.

THE cut of this garment is similar to the coachman's, the difference being that the footman's is the smarter

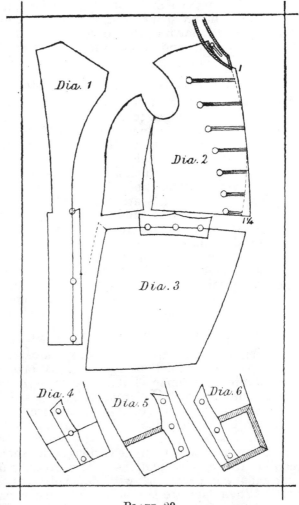

PLATE 29.

coat.   To produce it, the front is cut away more at the waist, and the skirts made longer and narrower at the bottom, as per diagrams. The hip flap is not inverted, and the sleevehands and other decorations are made to match the coachman's, according to the

regulations of the family. The diagrams indicate all
this, also how the notched-holes or other decorations
are usually arranged. There is usually a hook and
eye at the prominence of breast.

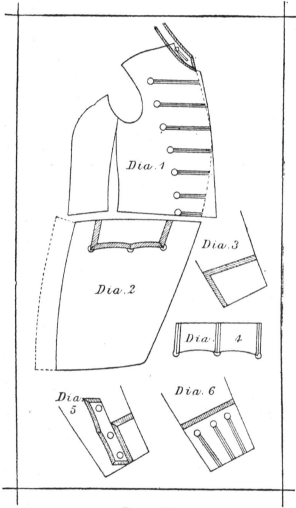

PLATE 30.

LACING AND SIDE EDGES.—Dias. 1 to 9, Plate 31.

These diagrams show how side edges are cut and
put on, also the common shape of the livery flap.
Dias. 2, 4, 5 and 9 show how the coachman's frock is
sometimes laced, In the case of plain or piped edges

the buttons are set both ways shown. The collar of a laced frock is generally cut as indicated.

Dias. 1 to 12, Plate 32.

Dia. 1 shows how short laced holes are formed; dia. 2 a laced flap with notched hole; dia. 3 laced or

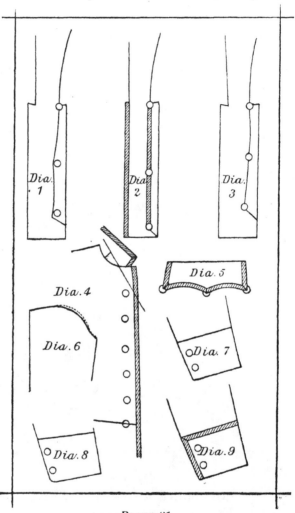

PLATE 31.

notched skirt trimming, with skirt side edge; dia. 4 laced cuff decoration; dia. 5 laced, braided or notched breast decorations, with crown diadem collar-end; dia. 6 revers skirt facing; dia. 7 front skirt ditto;

dia. 8 laced sleeve trimming; dia. 9 laced skirt trimming, with swallowtail revers and laced back tack; dias. 10 and 11 how some liveries of both the higher and lower orders have been made-up. Flap

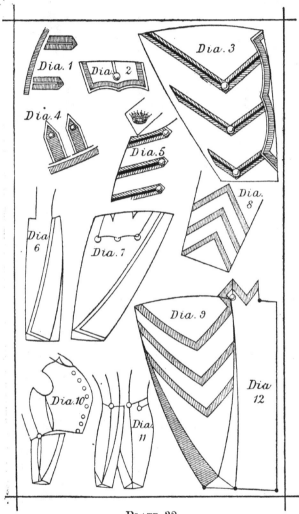

PLATE 32.

5, block 2, plate 20, is the form in which a framed flap is cut. These are seldom used except on coachmen's frocks. In old times skirts were often cut more forward.

Figures 1 to 6, Plate 33.

The revers and skirt side edge on fig. 1 shows
how the the white ones used on Lord-Lieutenant's
and Deputy-Lieutenant's skirts are formed, which

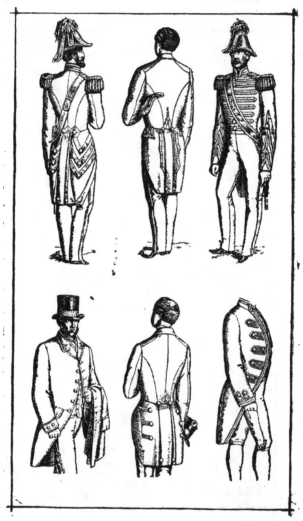

PLATE 33.

skirts are similar in form to the skirt dia. 10, plate 32.
Epaulettes and shoulder sword strap are seen on this
figure; a different kind of back-waist lacing and
skirt side edges on fig. 2; breasts as per fig. 10.

plate 32; or fig. 3 with long uncommon sleeve lacings, such as have been used on some of the higher orders of liveries. Fig. 4 shows a very uncommon style of livery dress, still in vogue on the Continent;

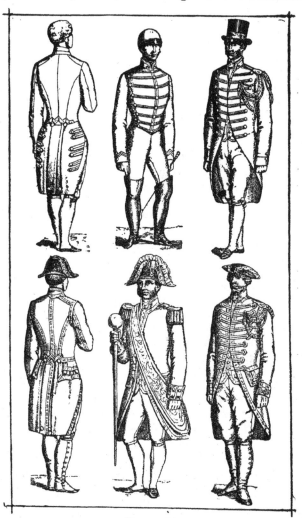

PLATE 34.

fig. 5 slashed skirt with notched holes; fig. 6 laced breast, holes, sleeves and edges.

Figures 1 to 6, Plate 34.

Fig. 1 shows double notching and lacing; fig. 3

shoulder cords and notched holes ; fig. 4 laced seams and an extraordinary style and size of framed flap ; fig. 6 a front view of this stye of decoration, with shoulder cords, laced edges, notched holes, livery vest, gaiters, &c. Fig. 5 shows another very uncommon style, in so far as England is concerned. It will be seen that framed flaps can be worn on this kind of livery coat without appearing out of character with the run of the front of skirt, especially when the skirt fronts are cut still more forward ; part of such a flap is seen on this livery. Some of the French fulldress servants' liveries have been cut much more forward in the skirts than with us, and some of their livery frock fronts to run backwards from the top button to the bottom almost to the extent shown by fig. 5.

Many of the German liveries are very ancient and singular in form and detail to what we are accustomed to, and our liveries have changed considerably during the last century. One instance of this is that large decker capes have given way to close-fitting fur shoulder capes, and gaiters largely to top boots; and indoor liveries have become slightly less imposing and ornate, yet still in high families pretty much the old style is kept up.

The long side-edges of a coachman's frock are sometimes represented by buttons only ; and frequently imitation side-edges are stitched on overcoats and grooms' frocks.

Sometimes livery garments are piped or the edges edged with cloth of a different colour. Edging should be cut in strips on the crossway of the wool, and stoated together, then pressed double. After second press, edges of garment are felled on to the edging, then facings and linings. The facings and linings should be kept a shade over the first sewing.

The shanks of all livery buttons which are for ornament only should be bodkined through, and the holes thus made closed round the shanks, a strong thread cast several times round the neck of the shank, the eye filled with a roll of cotton, the shanks knocked down a little, and the ends of the cotton rolls sewn to the canvas.

In making liveries, strength and durability should be attended to, and their distinguishing peculiarities displayed.

99

Postilion's Spencer.—Dia. 1, Plate 35.

This diagram shows how these round jackets or spencers are cut—viz., close-fitting in the waist, and not to extend below the waist. Fig. 2, plate 34,

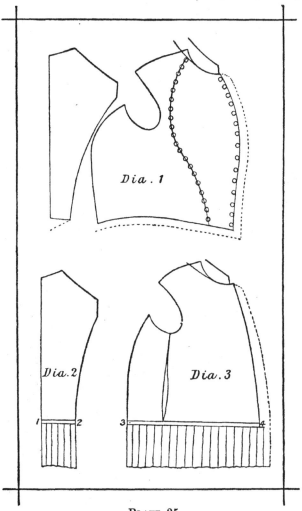

Plate 35.

gives a clear view of the style of this garment. It has a stand collar, fastens with hooks and eyes, and is sometimes decorated one way and sometimes another way, as intimated by the diagram and figure. In old times they were cut without an underarmseam ; but this is not imperative.

The actual cut is as per the original groundwork, dia. 4, plate 13—short-waisted, with sidebody closed to the forepart, a little round placed on the prominence of the breast, neck to size, the sideseam hooked in a little, and a little off the front of the waist to make it close-fitting, the side of the waist being stretched a little in making if the length extends the least below the smallest part and the figure is good.

PAGES' JACKET.

A page's jacket is only a postilion's spencer with underarmseam, cut with less fullness over the blade, longer waisted, and pointed behind as well as in front. See shell jacket for shape.

Referring to the original diagrams of the system plate 13, nothing is taken out at the top, and only 1in. or less at the waist of sideseam, or a trifle at top and less at waist ; besides which the back is cut shorter at the top, all youngsters being flat (undeveloped or immature in form) in the back.

RACING JACKETS.—Dias. 2 and 3, Plate 35.

These are formed after the manner shown by the diagrams, the back being cut long, and wide at the waist, very little suppression being taken out, a covered drawing-string inserted round the waist, and skirt parts for going into the breeches, added as indicated. Being a sort of silk shirt waist, anyone can cut and make them without difficulty from dia. 4, plate 13, leaving out the waist suppressions, barring half-inches or so, placing the seams as shown by the present diagrams, making the waist length very long to measure, inserting the drawing string 1, 2, 3, 4, and adding the skirt part.

INNOVATION UNIFORMS.

Since feudalism was abolished, and the general public discarded uniforms as liveries, numbers of innovations have occurred. Sir Robert Peel's police, and the Irish Constabulary, for instance, have been dressed in uniforms or liveries ; and nowadays it is a common thing to see hall porters, doorsmen, &c., in some sort of hybrid livery or another.

IRISH CONSTABULARY UNIFORM.
Diagram 1, Plate 36.

This diagram shows the style in which the uniform or livery of the Irish Constabulary is cut — viz, the same as an ordinary coat up to the actual breast

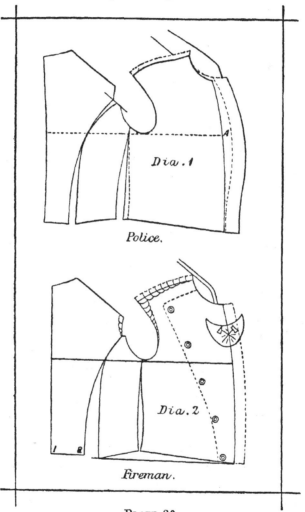

Police.

Dia. 2

Fireman.

PLATE 36.

line, excepting that less is taken out at the sideseam and more at the underarmseam of waist, and the breast has extra round added on at A, and more shoulder length is allowed, see dotted line alterations

The skirt is cut after the manner of a frock skirt or gamekeeper's or tunic skirt, and as short as the latter. As will be seen, the changes are similar to those described for police frocks. In fact, these

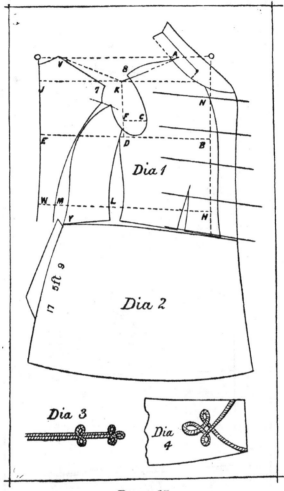

PLATE 37.

changes do very well for the body part of an ordinary police frock, well wadded out in the chest.

The Irish Constabulary tunic is a semi-military garment.

Such decorations as Austrian knots are shown on the military diagrams.

FIREMAN'S TUNIC.—Dia. 2, Plate 36.

These are cut and made very similar to a policeman's tunics, only some are cut single and some double breasted. When double breasted, the lapel is usually similar to a Lancer's, as indicated in dots and buttons on the diagram. The back is cut wide at the waist from 1 to 2. The metal scales and breastplates frequently used on firemen's tunics are indicated on the diagram, and will convey a pretty clear idea as to how and where they are put on to any who may need such information.

MILITARY STAFF OFFICER'S FROCK.

Diagrams 1 to 4, Plate 37.

Military garments being cut shorter in the waist than civilian, 1in. is dropped in the waist length; but the depths OJ and OE or JE are calculated as usual. See rules in Table 1.

OJ is one twelfth the half height and ⅜in., JE one sixth of the half height and ⅜in, or OE one fourth the half height and 1in. O to top of backseam is from ⅝in. to ¾in., O to V one eighth breast and ¼in., JK one third breast and 3in., ED the same, FC 3in., KA one third breast and 1in., and EB the breast measure and 2½in. 1½in is taken out at M, 2in. at L, and a cut as shown out of the bottom of forepart to throw breast. The waist is made up to measure, and a good ½in. of round allowed outside B.

As regards variation of position of shoulderseam, that may be done at will. But for good style for shoulderseam under shoulder strap or other decoration, O V can be made one-fifth neck measure and ½in., and the shoulderseam placed on line V K and A K, especially when the position of K has been found by direct measures from back top to J and on to K.

OTHER MILITARY FROCKS.

All other S.B. military frocks are cut after the style and form of clerical frocks, with the exception of the position of the shoulderseam; and as changes in military clothing are brought about so frequently, it would serve no useful purpose to show such past or present styles as 1st and 2nd Lifeguards' S.B. frocks, Grenadiers' S.B. frock, chaplain's frock, &c.

MILITARY TUNIC.—Dias. 1 and 2, Plate 38.

The system is worked the same way for these as for officers' frocks — viz., O 9 is two eighths of the height and 1in., O 3 one twelfth the half height and $\frac{3}{8}$in., O E one fourth the half height and 1in., O

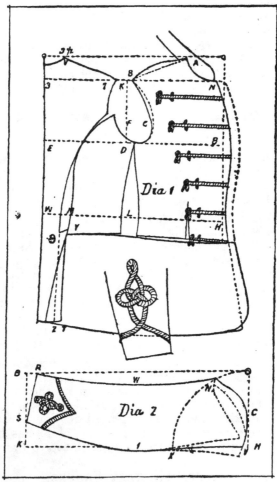

PLATE 38.

to top of backseam $\frac{3}{4}$in., O V $3\frac{1}{2}$ for the 36 size, or one fifth neck and $\frac{1}{2}$in. For flat backs only 1in. or $1\frac{1}{4}$in. is taken out at M, and fully 2 or $2\frac{1}{2}$ out at L, the waist drawn-in to close measure at H, and a good $\frac{3}{8}$in. allowed for wadding, &c., outside B. The sideseams of these garments should be brought up to about where the backseam of a sleeve is usually pitched. If this is done, no change in the sleeve is needed ; if not, as much must be added to the topside as the sideseam is below this point, as per dots behind V, dia. 2.

Sufficient has to be allowed for button-holes, &c., on the one breast, and for stand on the other breast.

The skirt can be cut from any frock or gamekeeper's skirt pattern, or by system as shown, about 9in. long. An Austrian knot is sketched on the sleevehand lying on skirt.

NAVAL UNIFORMS.

These consist of (1) dress coat cut D.B., button all up front, stand collar ; (2) the same, with ordinary frock lapels and collar ; (3) D.B. frock coat ; (4) D.B. reefer ; (5) Eton or round jacket ; (6) the S.B. spencer with stand collar, for midshipmen. These are all, in so far as the cutting is concerned. The decorations used on the made-up garments and the way they are worn constitute the distinctions.

An admiral of the fleet's or an admiral's full dress coat is cut as No. 1 ; his or a commodore's or lieutenant's frock as No 3 ; a captain's full dress as No. 1, and his undress as No. 4, and so on. When the cut for a high and a lower grade officer is the same, the decorations make the distinction. The regulation trimmings for military and naval articles can be got from any military trimming house.

NAVAL OFFICER'S MESS JACKETS. Dia. 3, Plate 39.

These are sometimes cut as shown, and sometimes with rolling collar ; also with narrow D.B. lapel, button up to the neck, the back and sidebody as per the shell jacket.

SHIP STEWARD'S JACKETS are cut the same as dia. 3 in front, and back and sidebody the same as shell jacket. SHIP CARPENTER'S JACKETS are cut the same as ship steward's jackets. OTHER PETTY OFFICER'S JACKETS are cut the same, or as dia. 4. MIDSHIPMAN'S ROUND JACKETS are cut same as military mess jackets, and held together only at neck.

LANCER'S TUNIC.—Dia. 2, Plate 39.

These are the same in cut as other tunics, except the fronts, which are cut off at the meeting edge-to-edge line, and a lapel added of form shown, the front seaming edges being pressed back to the dotted line.

HIGHLAND TUNIC OR DOUBLET.

These are cut the same as an ordinary tunic, except the tashes, which are about 7in. or 8in. long, and which can be cut by the skirt system, taking out 1½in. at the waist to nothing at the bottom between them, to produce spring over the side of hip.

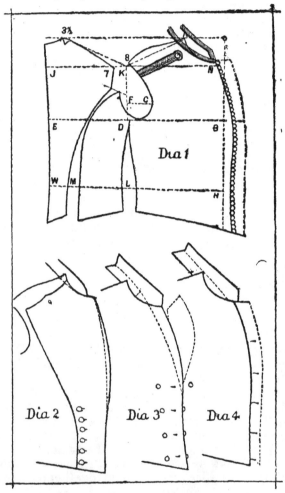

PLATE 39.

SHELL, MESS, STABLE JACKETS.—Dia 1, Plate 39.

A shell jacket is only a sort of glorified page's jacket, and has usually been cut for officers as shown by the diagram. For the men the shoulderseam is

on the top. The working of the system is the same
for these as for tunics, excepting the full length,
which may be made 3in. more than two head heights
or to taste.

OFFICER'S MESS JACKETS

Are cut in the same form as shell jackets without
catch, and are just held together at the neck. Mess
vests are no-collar dress vest in form or S.B. clerical
stand collar form. See vest diagrams.

STABLE JACKETS

Are cut after the shell pattern, only loose and care-
less-fitting, the back being wider and heavier looking—more in the form of a pantry jacket back. As
this is not an important garment a diagram is not
given.

MILITARY PATROL JACKET.
Dias. 1 and 2, Plate 40.

O to W is two head heights and 1in.; O E one
head height and 1in.; O J one-third of O E; O to
top of back ¾in.; O to V one-fifth neck and ½in.;
J K one-third breast and 3in.; E D the same; F C
one-sixth; K A one-third and 1in.; E B the breast
measure and 2½; width of back one-third and 1½in.
After shaping the back, 1in. to 1½in. comes out at
sideseam, and 1½in. to 2in. at underarmseam, which
seam is sprung for seat room as shown. The waist
is made to measure and seams, and the front is
shaped as shown, cut off at solid meeting edge-to-
edge line, and a hook catch sewn on, the eyes coming out through the seam. The same conditions
govern the cutting of the sleeve as the tunic sleeve.

MILITARY FATIGUE JACKETS.

Are cut both with patrol and ordinary three-seamer
backs, without underarmseam, the loose stuff being
gathered in by means of a belt, or plaited.

Military men seem to have peuliar ideas and ways
at times, for the fatigue jacket has at times been
called a frock, especially in India, the only difference
being that no belt was worn round it, or plaits made
in it. It should be borne in mind that the shoulderseams of officers' military garments are often placed
the same as in civilian garments, and it is only the
rank and file that must have the shoulderseams on
the top of the shoulder. Officers' outfits are frequently made by private tailors, and the army tailors
have little or nothing to do with them. This is the

reason of the existence of so many private tailors who call themselves military tailors.

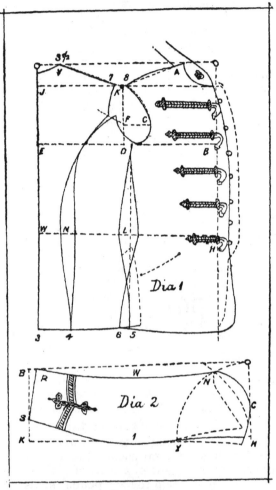

PLATE 40.

THREE-SEAMERS.—Dias. 1 and 2, Plate 41.

To ascertain a man's height, multiply his natural waist length by 4.

To ascertain a man's head height, divide the total height into eight equal parts—as 8 times 9 are 72 for 6ft. Two 9in. head heights and 2in. gives the proportionate waist length for this height, and any variation from it is disproportion, consisting of

elongation or the reverse of the form length below
or above the thoracial line, or of both sections;
proportion meaning each depth section in proportion
to each other, or to the head height. I here is no
such a thing as proportion in height to the breast
measure. The St. Andrews' cross, or full reach of
the arms from finger tip to finger tip in a straight
line explains what proportion of height to width
really means.

The operation of the system is precisely the same
for three-seamers as for body coats, save and except
that the waist line is placed ½in. higher than two
head heights and 2in. gives.

THE BACK.—Dia. 1, Plate 41.

O to J is one-third the head height and ⅜in.; O E
one head height and 1in., and O to W two head
heights and 1½in. Or the points may be got thus:
O E one head height and 1in., O J one-third of O E,
and O W two head heights and 1½in. O S three
head heights and 3in. O V one eighth and ⅓in.; J K
one third breast and 3in.; and EF and O Γ the same.
The width of back to measure. V K the shoulder
line; V 7 the fashion line. Back centre seamed or
whole. If to be close-fitting, shaped in as solid line.
Sideseam placed so as to give fashionable style
width of back. After fixing the width 3 to 5 or 4, a
straight line is drawn from scye to 4, and the sideseam hollowed in from it ¾in. or 1in. as per solid line.

THE BACK AND FOREPART.—Dia. 2, Plate 41.

The cut-cut back is laid down and the horizontal
lines continued; or the front depths O N B H and P
are found by the back depths, lines squared backwards and the back placed down at the breast
measure and 2in. from B; or else the draft is made
all in one.

K A is one third and 1in.; F C one sixth breast.
The shoulder, neck and scye are produced in the
same manner as for body coats. 1¼ to 1½ is taken
out at M: too much causes excess of spring in close-
fitters, and bagginess at back of waist in whole-
backs. The waist measure is applied across the
back and continued across the forepart to find the
solid front line at 1½; and the seat measure is applied across the back, S to T, and continued from H
to G to find the spring over the seat. Loose-fitting

means halt the quantity out at M, none out at back
centre, little or none out under arm, and the spring
increased to the same extent as the hollow is filled
up at M.   When the spring has been found at G,

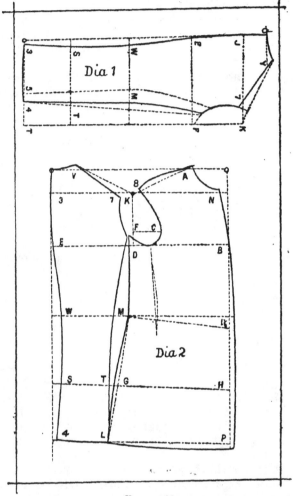

PLATE 41.

the square is put on as at $1\frac{1}{2}$ M G L, and the seam
shaped from M to L as shown.

ı N B H P is the net size line or actual breast line
down the front, and whatever is added in front of it
is style of overlap or lapel and revers (turn back), if
not buttoned to the throat.

VARIOUS STYLES.—Dias. 1 to 6, Plate 42.

All the different styles of front are produced by
adding on in front of, or cutting off behind the actual
breast line, after the manner shown by the dotted
lines of diagrams 1 to 3. The dotted line 1 of dia. 1

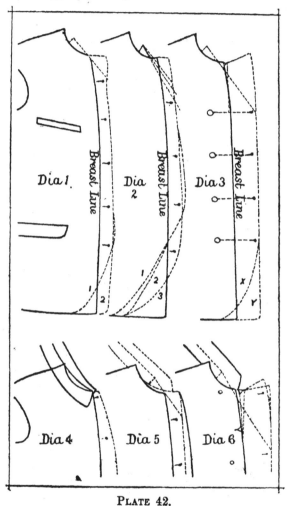

PLATE 42.

is a cutaway, and dotted line 2 the S.B. reefer style.
Lines 1, 2, and 3, dia. 2, indicate various forms of
lounges; and lines X and Y, dia. 3, the cutaway and
and ordinary D.B. reefer. Dia. 4 shows the button-
to-throat Prussian collar style, dia. 5 the addition

for a fly front, dia. 6 the form of D.B. lapel to button to the throat, and the occasional button to throat style.

DRESSING GOWNS.—Dia. 1, Plate 43.

1 HE system is worked in the same way for these as for other three-seamers, the style and length only

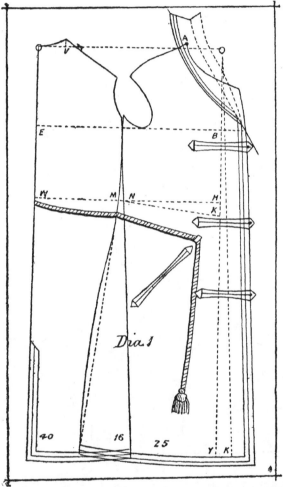

Dia. 1

PLATE 43.

being different. If the operator prefers, however, he can use only the chalk lines shown, going back from O to A a fourth, and finding the front of scye at half the breast and 3in. from E, or 1in less than

half the breast from B, after making E B the breast
measure and 2in or 2½in.

A fair length for a dressing gown is 40in; the
back 16 and the forepart 25 wide at the bottom. The
sideseam of back may be straight, or slightly hollowed, also the sideseam of forepart. If desired
shaped a bit, the square can be placed as K M, and
the spring line run to meet the width 25 at the bottom. As these garments are long, 2in. or more
spring should be allowed from Y to K.

The way to draft the collar for a lower gorge is
shown. The same method is available for any
height of gorge, and is the best ever published.

CHESTERFIELDS.—Diagram 1, Plate 44.

For overcoats the measures are taken over the
undercoat; or if on the vest 3in. added to the breast
and waist measures on the vest, thus making a 36
on the vest 39 on the coat. Very thin or thick coats
modify this difference but little.

The system is used in the same way for chesterfields as for three-seamer under coats, with this
difference—¾in. is added to the depth 3 E, E W, and
W 9. F C is one sixth, and K A one third and 1in.,
point A being risen ½in., and the same additional
amount put on at 8.

When a vent is wanted, it is added from 9 to Q,
and a straight line drawn from O through Q to P.
The suppression at L for a close-fitting chesterfield
is from 1in to 1½in, or ½in, none, or half-inch overlap
for a sack. The application of the waist measure
finds the run of front outside line O T. Whatever
is allowed more than the waist measure, must be
allowed over the seat measure, with at least an
additional inch added to it. Example: If the waist
size is 17½ on the vest, and 19 on the coat, and 2in
or 3in is added to that, the addition to the seat
measure must be 3in or 4in at least. After applying
the measure 9 R, continued from S back to U, and
thus finding the spring, the square is placed as 2 L 5,
and the spring rounded a little. The front of a
long garment, to counteract the effect of weight,
should always be sprung forward a little, whether
the waist measure produces this effect or not, unless
the edges are drawn-in a fair amount, when the
shape should be in harmony with the working-up.

The solid front line is the meeting edge-to-edge or size line; the overlap, whether S.B. or D.B., is to be added in front of it—2in or 2½in for an S.B., and 3in or 3½in for a D.B., or more or less according to taste or fashion.

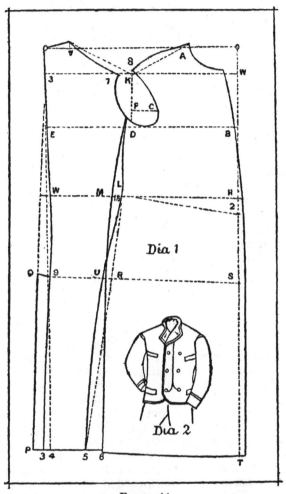

PLATE 44.

THE UNDER JUMPER.—Dia. 2, Plate 44.

This little jacket is specially designed for wearing under chesterfields. It may be S.B. or D.B., both of which are shadowed on the diagram.

FULL SACS AND ULSTERS.—Plate 45.

These are cut after the form shown by this diagram. About 1½ is allowed from 3 to 4, and the back made 11 or 12 inches wide at 52 long, the sideseam being a straight line or hollowed a trifle. The fore-

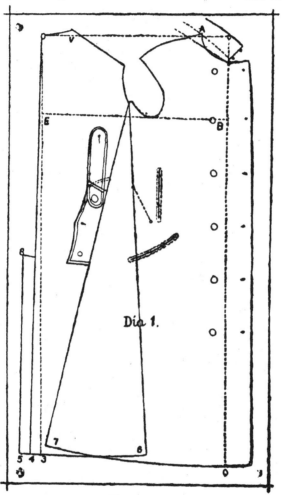

PLATE 45.

part may spring over to the back line O3 at the full length. All other details and points are found and adjusted as for chesterfields.

MILITARY GREATCOATS

Are cut in the same way as ulsters, as indicated by

the diagram, the width of the skirt part being governed by class of service and whether officer or linesman. If an S.B., it is cut in front like an S.B. chester, but usually to button to the throat. If a D.B., as per the diagram. If no V is to be taken out at the top of the breast line (gorge), point A must be brought nearer to O, so as to prevent the neck being too large.

SERVICE CAVALRY GREATCOATS.

These are cut in the same way as ulsters, with a triangular piece let into the back centre of about 24in. wide at its base, and 21in. in height.

Horse Guards' Overcoats.

These are merely ulsters cut very wide in the skirts — sufficiently so to spread out and cover the horse to the tail as well as the man—say 85in. wide round the bottom, and balanced so that the bulk of the extra width will spread out behind when on horseback.

Waterproof Riding Capes

Can be cut in the same form as Horse Guards' overcoats, with or without the addition of the old style of coachman's shoulder capes,

Naval Greatcoats.—Dias. 1 and 2, Plate 46.

At one time the frock overcoat was the officers' regulation greatcoat of the royal navy, from admiral downwards; at another time the S.B. waterproof chesterfield-sac form, also the waterproof shoulder cape; at another time, the form shown by these diagrams, which is still the regulation officers' overcoat, only cut D.B. The primary distinguishing feature lies in the large inverted box plait at the centre of back. The collar is of the deep stand-and-fall form; and a back waist belt is added similar to that shown on the military overcoat diagram. These greatcoats are not cut so wide in the skirts as the military descriptions, nor so long. See diagrams.

The Caped Waterproof.

These consist merely of the back and forepart of an ulster, with the scye scooped out all round, and a shoulder cape added instead of sleeves, of the form which has been called Scarboro, button up to the neck, with stand-and-fall collar.

Some foreign nations use plaits in the sideseams of their naval and military greatcoats. If these

were made three-corner in form, the material falling
and folding itself inwards when walking, the back
of the coat would spread on horseback, or in any
other position requiring it, in a similar manner to a
Horse Guards' greatcoat ; and it is a moot question
if the style would not be better, with less encum-

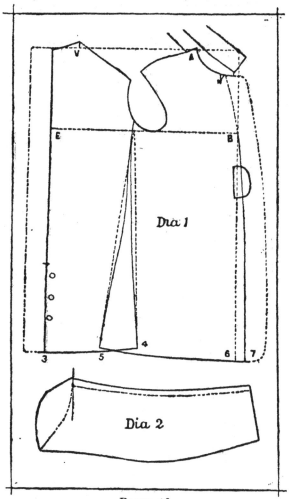

PLATE 46.

brance. This hint is merely thrown out, en passant,
for what it is worth. It may be much, it may be
little ; yet still it is an idea, to those who, like the
military and navy, are always busying themselves
with changes in their dress regulations.

NORFOLKS. — Dias. 1 and 2, Plate 47.

The way to cut these is from a three-seamer pattern of the breast measure of the customer, allowing as much extra looseness round the waist, &c., as wanted, to be gathered up by the belt. But a Nor-

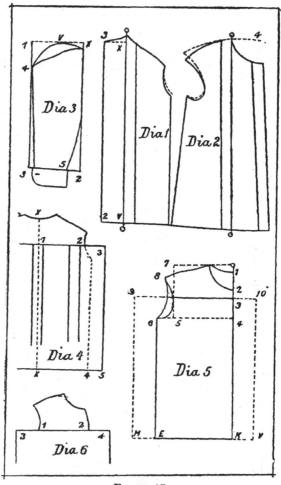

PLATE 47.

folk may be cut by the system in the same way as an ordinary three-seamer, only making the following alterations in the working: First, after laying the plaits, let the lines O O be the starting lines, and mark back from X and V to 3 and 2 one-eighth the breast and $\frac{1}{2}$in., and forward to find the actual breast line a fourth the breast. After drawing the back and front lines, the operator can then proceed as usual, excepting in the case of corpulency, when two-thirds of the disproportion may be marked back from the front line at the waist, and a line to square by be drawn from that point to 4 at a fourth from O. The dotted lines indicate how the Norfolk should vary from a three-seamer in the shoulder and scye.

THE BLOUSE.—Dias. 3 to 6, Plate 47.

Blouses may be constructed by the elementary system hereunder explained. OK is the construction line. It is also the centre of both back and front. O to 1 is 1in. for the back top, and to 2 an eighth and 1in. for depth of front of gorge. O to 4 is 4½in. added to one-fourth breast for depth of scye. O 7 and O 5 are each half the breast. 7 to 8 is 1in., and 5 to 6 2½ to 3in. The construction line of the sleeve is XZ. X to 1 is the same as O4 of dia. 5, and XV half of it. From 1 to 4 is also half X 1. Z to 5 is for boxplaiting into cuff. For boxplaiting of back or forepart, allow from 3 to 10, and from 6 E to 9 H whatever amount is wanted, according to the number and size of the plaits. Dia. 4 shows one style of plaiting, the piece X 1 2 being the back part (yoke) above line 10 to 9, dia. 5. The piece of forepart above line 10 to 9 looks something like 1 2, dia. 6, when cut off, and the part below that line like that below line 3 4 before boxpleated into front part of yoke. Some call these blouses Norfolk shirts. It is a very free-and-easy garment, and with pockets like a Norfolk makes a very fine shooting garment. For any kind of overlapping down the front, whether plain or in the form of boxplait, due allowance must be made, not only in the piece below the yoke, but on the front of the yoke also.

HIGHLAND OR SCOTCH JACKETS.

These form a separate class of garment, allied to no class unless it is the patrol; and in addition they are of a fancy type.

THE KILT JACKET.—Diagram 1, Plate 48.

The system is worked in the same manner for this jacket as for the patrol, the whole differece consisting of small variations in the mere details of the matter of style; so therefore it will not be necessary to re-describe the system of drafting. When this jacket is cut for corpulent men or boys there is a belly on it, as seen in the diagram. The run of bottom, flaps, cuffs, and ornamentations explain themselves.

THE DOUBLET JACKET.—Dia. 2, Plate 48.

As this jacket is drawn out by the same system,

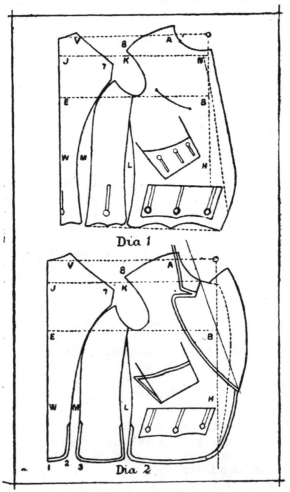

PLATE 48.

and the details of style explain themselves, it is not necessary to repeat the instructions for drafting the system. The front is sometimes made like that of an S.B. morning coat.

ALTERATIONS BY JUDGMENT FOR DIFFERENT FIGURES.

When not using the check measures shown on the small figures plates 12 and 13, the changes have to agree with the changes in the form of the figure.

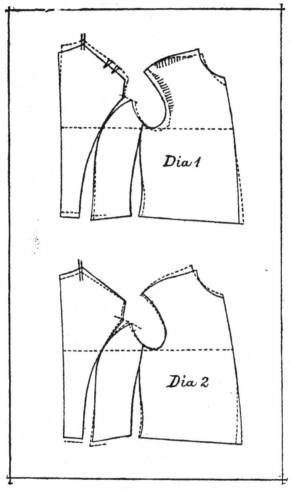

PLATE 49.

STOOPING FIGURES.—Dia. 1, Plate 49.

The changes usually needed for this type of figure are shown by the dotted lines of this diagram, the extent in each case depending up the extent of the change in the figure. As a rule. people are more

inclined to over than under estimate the changes in
a figure.

ERECT FIGURES. — Dia. 2, Plate 49.

The dotted lines of this diagram show the character of changes that are needed for this type. The
stooping figure needs a tightened back scye, a
rounded back, a forward and deeper scye, a longer
back and shorter front balance, and the waist more
suppressed. Fulling-on the back shoulder tightens
the back scye, while rounding the back and making
it sit close to the figure, whether the blade is prominent or not, or the waist hollow or not. The erect
figure, on the other hand, needs the reverse of the
changes made for the stooping figure — viz., a narrower back, shorter back balance and longer front
balance, crookeder instead of straighter shoulder,
and a less-suppressed instead of more-suppressed
waist. The back shoulder should not be fulled-on.

HIGH AND LOW SHOULDERS, LONG AND SHORT
NECKS.—Dia. 1, Plate 50.

The simple alterations for these figures, as explained in the working of the system, amount to the
scye going upwards and downwards to 1 1 and A
for high, and to 3 3 and X for low shoulders.

COMPLEX AXILLA AND SHOULDER CHANGES.

A figure may have low while normal, small or
large shoulders; or high while normal, small or
large shoulders. As a rule, the change is not so
much in the width 1 to X, fig. 4, as in the width of
the arm, 3 to 4, fig. 5, which figure illustrates a high
and small, and a low and large shoulder. The extra
width 3 to 4, fig. 5, often occurs without any increase
—or it may be with a decrease in the breast or the
shoulder horizontal widths. Thus the width in 1 to
2 fig. 1 may be less, and the depth 3 to 4 more, owing
to 3 to 4, fig. 5, being wider, and vice versa. On the
other hand, increase of depth and width of axilla
may occur as in fig. 2. In this case the figure
broadens out in every direction from breast sector
to shoulder sector, until 1 to 2 and back width become quite broad, and the man is said to have fine
shoulders. A man can, however, have fine shoulders
and yet small axillas, just the same as the man of
narrow shoulders may have big axillas. In each
figure the axilla may be large, normal or small; and

it is suchlike complexities that form the difficulties of cutting to fit well.

The best way to view a figure is from the side, as it can then be seen whether the width and depth of the axilla fig. 3 is large or small, also whether large

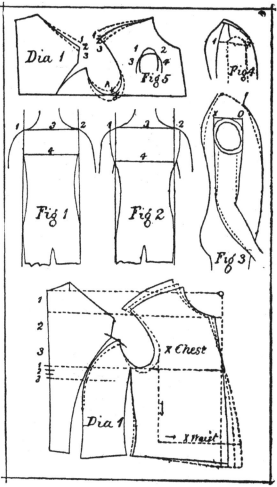

PLATE 50.

or small as compared with the size of the figure. The small axilla may be as per inner oblong and dotted arm to the solid line figure; or the large axilla as per the outer oblong and solid line arm to the dotted breast and back line figure. The cutter's art lies in viewing intelligently and correctly estimating when cutting by divisional proportions or judgment alone.

SHORT AND STOUT OR CORPULENT FIGURES.
Lower Diagram 1, Plate 50.

In cutting by judgment for short and stout or corpulent figures, the operator can mark down half the length of back first, as 1 to 1, then half the breast as 1 to 3, then divide the difference into three parts, and sink the scye and clear it out one part, making the front shoulder one part crookeder and longer. To get the shoulder line, 1 to 1 may be divided into three parts, as 1, 2, 3, the upper part finding the shoulder level line. In cases of difficulty about distribution of material round the waist, a measure can be taken from a point perpendicular with scye front across to front of waist, or as indicated by the arrows.

THREE-SEAMERS FOR CORPULENT FIGURES.
Dia. 1, Plate 51.

In cutting these, the plan is often adopted which is shown by the dotted lines of this diagram, any excess of spring being taken off after the forepart is drawn back by the process

BALANCE. — Dias. 2, 3, 4, and 6, Plate 51.

This matter has been frequently misunderstood. According to the ancients, it meant the length of front shoulder in relation to the suppression of the waist and straightness. Old Thirds men made a point at one-third of the breast or some other quantity in from the back of the waist, as at 1, 2, or 3, dia. 2, and swept forward for the length of front shoulder (balance) from X to 1, 2 or 3. Diagram 3 shows a similar idea. Dia. 4 shows the Reliable balance, with variations for stooping and erect types, 2 5 being the normal, 1 6 the stooping, and 3 4 the balance for the erect figure. Dia. 6 shows the star-axis system of balancing, while the straight line from 1¼ to the bottom of forepart shows the real front of breast line after the breast of a coat, minus lapel, has been pressed back.

OPENNESS AND CLOSENESS. — Dias. 1, 2, Plate 52.

More open is when the distance from 3 to 2, dia. 1, is greater, either through more being let in at X to

nothing at waist, or more in at the top of sideseam.
It must not be caused by 3 being more forward as
dots, as that is a straighter shoulder. Closer is the
reverse of opener cut, just the same as crookeder

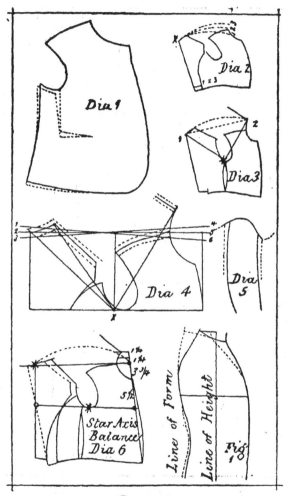

PLATE 51.

dotted shoulder, dis. 2, is the reverse of straighter
dotted shoulder dia. 1.

The measures X2, dias. 1 and 2, are unreliable for
several reasons. That of dia. 1 is influenced by the
amount let in or taken out of top of side or underarmseam, causing the back balance to be too short

or too long. That of dia. 2 is influenced in the same
way, with the addition of errors in waist length
brought about by error in the back balance. And
besides this, there is the unknown quantity of the

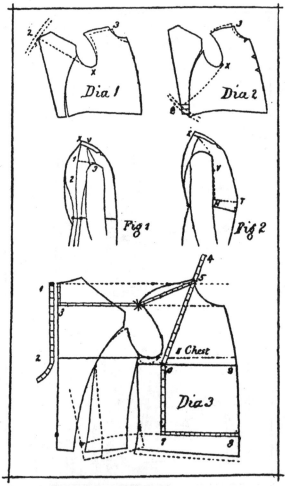

PLATE 52.

underarm waist suppression, which must first ¦be
correctly ascertained and taken out before measure
1 to 2, dia. 2, can become reliable.

FORM AND ATTITUDE.—Fig 1, Plate 51.

Attitude is form, and form attitude, the one being
produced by the other, if we except the result of

some local weakness in the physique. An habitual attitude will affect the form in time, just as the extent of a local growth affects both form and attitude. Example : The dotted lines show that an erect or flat-back figure is shorter in the line of form or back balance in relation to the line of height. In the case of the stooping figure, naturally the reverse is the case. And in like manner, the front balance lengthens in the first case, and becomes shorter for the stooping type. Line of height means shortest distance between top of head and bottom of feet ; line of form the measurement following the surface of the body.

The balance of a sleeve is not altered by changing the location of the seams, as per dia. 5, plate 51.

THE SYSTEM CHANGED INTO A DIRECT MEASURE SYSTEM.—Figs. 1 and 2, Dia. 3, Plate 52.

Point 3, fig. 1, is the same as point * of dia. 3. The direct measure system of measuring may be as follows : From X to 1, and on to the depth of scye point 2, and full length ; the sleeve measures ; from 1 to 3, and up from 3 to V, fig. 1 ; the front shoulder length XV. on from V to N, continued from N to T, fig. 2 ; width across chest, continued under arm to centre of back for breast size; and the waist measure over the coat. If the operator prefers, the acrosschest and front of scye can be taken separately.

HOW TO DRAFT BY THE DIRECT MEASURES.

Apply the length measures from 1 to 3, and on to 2 and full length, dia. 3. Square the horizontal lines from these points. Make the width of back to measure, and the design as wanted. Lay the cutout back down, continue the horizontal lines right across. Then apply the measures 1, 3, V, taken on fig. 1, from 3 to *, and on to 5, dia. 3. Apply the breast measure backwards from 2 to 9, chalking off the width across chest for front of scye while doing so. This gives the front of scye both ways — viz., from backseam and front of breast. Now place the width of back top from 5 to 4, and apply the front shoulder measure from 4 through 5 to 6, and if this places 6 below the line squared from 2, draw a parallel line across the forepart from 9 through 6, and sink the scye, of forepart only, the same amount. If the front shoulder length should place 6 above the

line squared from 2, the scye of the forepart must
be risen. The first necesitates lengthening as per
dotted line at the bottom of forepart, while the latter
necessitates shortening the same. Apply the
measures V N T taken on fig. 2, from 6 to 7 and on
to 8, to find the front of forepart at waist, and draw
the actual breast line through 8 and 9. The waist
measure will now show how much it is too large
from 8 to dot at back of waist, and consequently
how much has to come out as suppressions, which
total amount can be divided into halves for the normal, and the greater or less portion taken out at the
sideseam for full and flat blades or backs.

JUVENILE GARMENTS.

The system is applicable in the same way for boys
as for men. But as boys are specimens of disproportion in minutæ, it is simplest to take the natural
waist length by measure, and add $\frac{1}{2}$in. to 1in. to it,
to find the depth points by, using half of it for the
depth of scye, one third of depth of scye for depth
to shoulder line, and the waist length and the addition and half of the same for depth to seat line, &c.
This same method can be applied to drafting for
short and stout-waisted men, varying the addition
made to the natural waist length from $\frac{1}{2}$in. to 1in.,
in accordance with the flatness or roundness in the
back. Boys being undeveloped are usually very
" bladeboneless " and flat in the back.

THE ETON JACKET. — Dia 1, Plate 53.

Top of back to J a sixth of scale of depth, or one
third depth of scye ; to E half scale, to W natural
waist length. Fashion length 3in., or more or less,
longer than natural waist length.
Width of back top one-eighth breast and $\frac{1}{2}$in.
Width back to measure. J K one third breast and
3in. Front of scye one-sixth breast in front of line
squared down from K. K A one third and $\frac{1}{2}$in.
Point A $\frac{1}{2}$in. to $\frac{3}{4}$in. above top line. A to 8 same
width as 6 7. Point 8 as much above K as 7 is be-
low it. EB the breast measure and 2in. Line O H
square with top line. Point A may be found by one
fourth breast back from O. 1in. out at M, and $\frac{3}{4}$in.
out at L, varied according to the figure. Waist
measure made up at H ; and the lapel, front, bottom,
&c., formed as shown.

THE ROUND SCHOOL JACKET.—Dia. 2, Plate 53.

This jacket is formed in the same way as the Eton, excepting in front and at bottom of forepart.

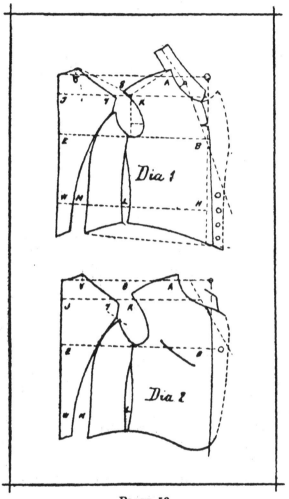

PLATE 53.

And as the diagram plainly shows this change in style, this is all that need be said about it.

THE KILT DRESS.—Dias. 1 to 3, Plate 54.

The jacket dia. 1 is formed in the same way as an Eton or school jacket, excepting that its waist length only reaches a little below the natural waist, and its back is cut a little heavier-looking. Its neck must be filled up the depth of collar stand. The tashes and cuffs are cut as shown, and the kilt formed as shown by dias. 2 and 3. A little above the knee is

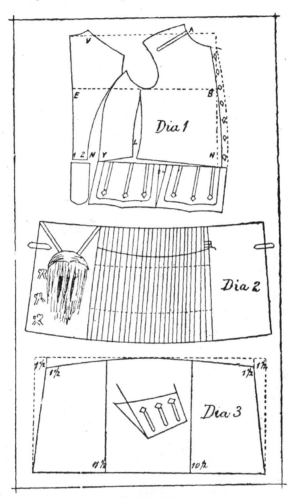

PLATE 54.

the proper length of a kilt. Three times the width of the part to be kilted must be allowed for that part. The outer front part is plain, excepting the sporran decoration, &c., and so is the underlap of same.

BOYS' THREE-SEAMERS. — Dia. 1, Plate 55.

See the method of getting the scale of depth for juveniles, and the manner of getting the points for the Eton jacket. The system is the same for three-seamers, the difference being only in the style. The

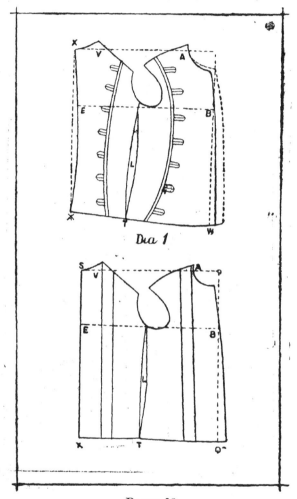

Dia 1

PLATE 55.

top line and E B are square with the back line, and BW with EB, in front of which line the size of waist generally projects, the waist being nearly or quite as large as breast. Boys' three-seamers require very little shaping — i.e., no great suppressions or curves, but gentle depressions and ovals, excepting in the matter of style of front edges. As a rule, it is well to take as little as possible out at L. The waist measure is then applied across at L to find the

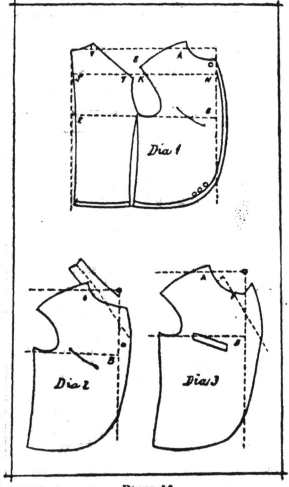

PLATE 56.

actual size line down the front, and finally the seat measure at half the waist length below the waist.

The diagram shows an S.B. reefer. If to be made without collar, the neck requires filling-in the depth of the collar stand.

BOYS' NORFOLKS.—Dia. Plate 55

The system is the same for these, the style alone varying, and the difference being mainly produced by plaits, for which kiltings may be substituted if desired.

BOYS' CUT-AWAY JACKET.—Dias. 1 to 3, Plate 56.

The system is the same for these as pages' and reefers. I he short round jacket dia 1, not reaching the seat, does not require spring to cover it. Being collarless, the neck needs filling-up the depth of the collar stand. The same or similar style jacket is made-up with coat collar, as per diagram 2. In this case there is no filling-up of neck. The style can also be varied as per diagram 3, or otherwise; and varied, or not, in length.

BOYS' REEFERS AND LOUNGES.

Dias. 1 to 4, Plate 57.

Dia. 1 illustrates how the style is added in front of the actual size line, and any amount of cut-away desired made from this to make a lounge. Dia. 2 shows how the overlap and revers, usually called lapel, is added in front of the size line for a D.B. reefer; dia. 3 the more or less blunted-corner lounge; and dia. 4 the bevelled-corner jacket or lounge with Prussian collar.

I hese suffice to show what endless changes can be made in style, which is a separate matter from system and fitting. The latter is a matter of science and art; style a matter of cultivated taste or personality. Frequently a tailor's individuality can be seen or traced in his work; but this has nothing to do with system, as often falsely assumed.

FANCY JACKETS. — Dia. 1, Plate 58.

This diagram is given to show that any boys' three-seamer forepart can he easily changed into a fancy style, such as the appearance of jacket and vest, or whatever other style may be wanted.

BOYS' S.B. FANCY BLOUSE.—Dia. 2, Plate 58.

This diagram shows how an S.B. boys' blouse can be cut if to button to throat and have Prussian or Shakespeare collar. Many modifications can be made to this design A system for blouses is embodied in diagram 3.

BOYS' D.B. FANCY BLOUSE.—Dia. 3, Plate 58.

A general idea of the form and outline of a boy's fancy sailor blouse can be obtained from diagram 3, whether SB or DB. There is no need to apply an elaborate system of cutting to the production of

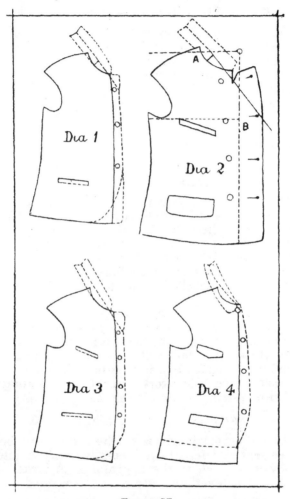

PLATE 57.

these garments. The length of waist, sleeve, and breast and waist are all the measures that need be taken for garments to be cut to measure. The cutter can draft in the following simple manner:—
Square lines O V and O B; make O B half breast.

Square B E, making it the breast measure and 3in
or 4in or more, according to the amount of looseness
wanted. Square up and down from E. Make the
back length, including half waistband, as much
longer than measure as will give the amount of

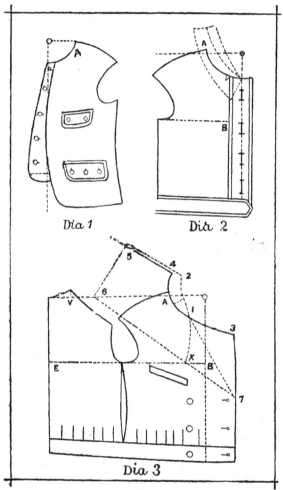

Dia 1   Dia 2

Dia 3

PLATE 58.

droop over belt required. Make the width from B
to front of scye half the breast, or more, according
to the amount of looseness wanted on breast. Make
O A one sixth breast and ½in, and the width of back
1in or more wider than measure. Make the slopes
of back and front shoulder equal to twice one third

the depth of O B, and the length in front 1in longer at the waist than behind, or to style wanted. Make the width of waist the amount above measure of the fullness required, cutting the band to measure, with a button-stand on one end and the amount of overlap to take the hole on the other end. The gorge and collar can be cut to either form shown, and stand or turn-in allowed as dots 1 to 2 If a stand is used, OA should be made one fourth breast, and collar stand well stretched. The back balance is about right without collar stand; it may be lowered for collar stand and the difference added at the bottom; but it is of little or no consequence in this class of garment.

THE SAILOR BLOUSE.—Dia. 1, Plate 59.

Any style can be cut by this system, the variations being only a matter of detail.

Square O2 and OK; make OB half breast; square BD; make BC half breast, CD 3in. Square up from C; make O A one sixth breast. Let shoulder-end project about 1in over line C, and 2 to 3 be the same quantity, or less. Square down from D to 3, and shape back and front scye as shown. In cutting a pattern, O B is the front of breast line; and in the case of half a pattern, the front edge is also the back centre; or if the dotted part is folded in under, it is the front and back crease edge. The forepart is cut down in this crease say half the breast and 3in or 4in, and the material turned back to the neckpoints A; then the remainder of the collar is cut to meet the turn-backs as shown. The length must be long enough to be tucked into the trousers. French people do not follow this practice, but allow them to hang loose, and they cut them rather closer-fitting.

In drafting the sleeve, make 1 to 2 half the breast, and 2 to 3 one-eighth breast. Shape the back of sleevetop as 1 X 3, and the front as per dots. Cut a piece away as from K to 3 for the front half, so as to make the cuff button right. 1 to 6 is the crease, and 6 to 5 is plaited into cuff. If a plait is wanted on the top of shoulder, it must be allowed behind 1 6, and thus leave the crease say 1in behind line 1 6.

FANCY SAILOR BLOUSE.—Dia. 3, Plate 59.

This diagram shows how the closed-to-the-throat style is formed. It must have a laid-on box plait like a shirt-front; or a piece laid under, and the edges of opening held together by cord and tassels at neck. if only a short one to admit the head. The collar is cut by the neck, and as shown in form,

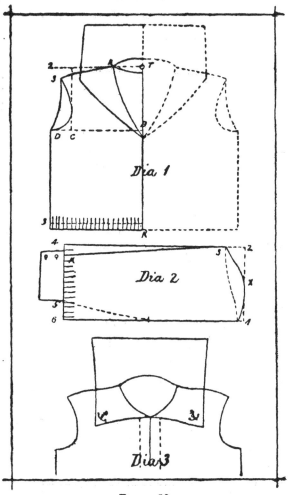

PLATE 59.

THE REAL SAILOR BLOUSE.

Diagrams 2, 3, 4, and 5, Plate 60.

To cut, take material three-quarters the whole breast measure in width, of double the length of blouse, fold it double as shown by dia. 2, to form the back and front, leaving it whole at crease line A X

Find the centre line X*; make X to 1 and X to 2
one-sixth breast, and X to 3 half the breast and 4in.
Slit the crease from 1 to 2, and the front from X to
3; lower the front neck to 5 and 6 ½in. or nothing,
and turn back the pieces 3, 6, 2, and 3, 5, 1, to form

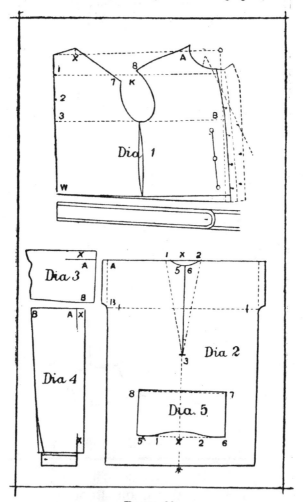

PLATE 60.

the opening. Make AB about one-fourth breast and
4½in., and cut about an inch off, on the double, at
each sideseam, from armhole down, as shown.

The collar is formed as per dia. 5, hollowing at X
about ½in. As in making 2 6 and 1 5 of the collar

join to the turn-backs 2 6 and 1 6 of the gorge, and
X to X of back neck, it will be seen that X to 2, X
to 1, X to 5, and X to 6 of the collar must correspond
in width. The collar can be cut on the double,
making X 2 and 2 6 agree, and the depth 6 7 6in., or
to regulation or taste.

The sleeve is formed as per dia. 4, straight from
A to B; its length being adjusted by the length of
fore or underarm, and its widths at top and bottom
by the armhole and cuff. A B sews to A B, as indicated by dia. 3; and if boxplaits are to be laid, they
must be allowed for as from A to X, and outside the
centre of cuff. The projections outside of A B can
be cut off, and the other blouse sleeve used for this
blouse. Real sailors use straight seams as a rule.

THE COAT-FRONTED BLOUSE.—Dia. 1, Plate 60.

This style being similar to the fancy blouse, excepting in front, can be drafted in the same way,
and made closer-fitting or not. It can also be drafted
in the manner laid down for the Eton jacket; or by
squaring OX and OB, making OA one-fourth breast
and OB half breast, B to front of scye $\frac{1}{2}$in. less than
half breast, B3 the breast and 2in. to 3in., the waist
length to measure; finding the shoulder line two-
thirds of the scye depth above 3, the shoulder points
an equal amount above as below K, the front of the
waist the waist measure and 3in. or 4in. from W,
making the length in front more than behind, and
adding on and shaping SB or DB front overlaps as
indicated by the dotted lines.

Belts are cut the amount of overlaps longer than
waist measure, to allow for hole and button-stand.
Collar like coat collar and sleeve like a coat sleeve.

CHILD'S REEFER.—Dia. 1, Plate 61.

Square OV and OB. Make OA one-fourth breast,
O B half breast. Square B E the breast and 2½in.
Width of back top one-eighth and ½in., width back
to measure. Shoulder line two-thirds of scye depth
and ½in. above E, B to front scye ½in. less than half the
breast, neckpoint ½in. to ¾in. above A, find points 7
and 8 as equidistant above and below K, or to taste.
Shape the back as shown, and for spring allow from
6 to 7 2in. more than the difference between breast
and round the skirt of dress. Coat sleeve. If to be
collarless, A must be advanced towards O the depth

of collar-stand. This reefer does for children wearing skirts, of either sex.

BOYS' SCULPTOR BLOUSE.—Dia. 2, Plate 61.

This garment is drafted in the same way as a reefer, only, being worn over short trousers, the

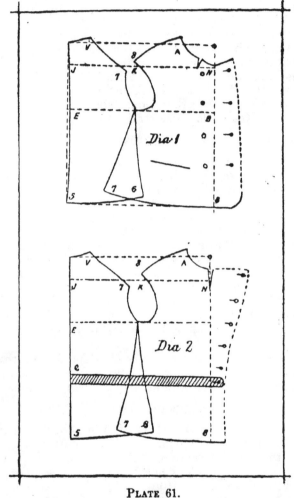

PLATE 61.

width in 6 7 must be reduced accordingly. The length terminates near about the knee, and a loose belt is worn round the waist. O A is the depth of collar-stand less than quarter breast for making-up without collar, for wearing with white linen Eton

collars. The sleeve is coat shape. This blouse can
be cut like an SB fancy sailor's blouse in front, or
like the real sailor's front, and have a deep sailor's
collar on it It looks well, en suite, made of brown
(drab) holland or drill, with blue sailor's collar edged
drab. The waist should not be cut too loose, and the
short trousers should not be wide, but close and short.

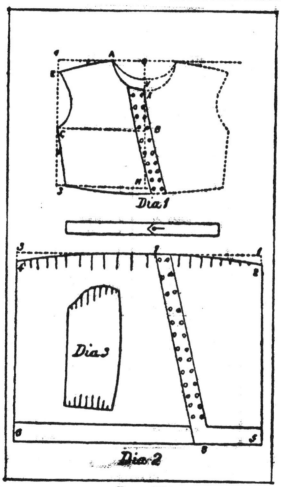

PLATE 62.

GIRLS' PLAIN DRESS SYSTEM.—Dia. 1, Plate 62.

The most modern dress for a little girl, or up to the
age of 13 or 14, is merely a yoke, with straight
material gathered into it, after the manner women's

dresses used to be gathered into a waistband. This dress hangs curtain-lke from the yoke all round, and is handsome in many materials, such as the highest class delicate-coloured velveteens for winter, and fine white materials for summer; although, in a

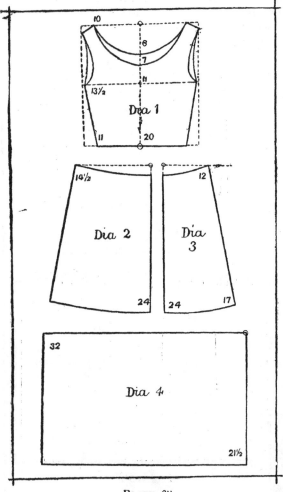

PLATE 63.

manner of speaking, there is no "cut" in it, and it is all a matter of draping. A yoke can be cut by the sailor's blouse system, dia. 1, plate 59, or by the system for girls' plain dress.

Square O H and O 4. Make OA one-sixth breast,.

or as much more as the neck opening is to be cut down. V one-eighth, X one-sixth and ½in. O B. half breast. B C half breast and one or more inches, according to whether to be close or loose-fitting. Make the waist length to measure and ½in. or so, and the width H 3 half the wais; and 1in. or whatever additional ease there is to be. Shape the front of scye as shown, and the back of same a trifle straighter, or not. The sleeve may be cut in the form of dia. 3, wide at the hand and fulled into a cuff. The skirt, dia. 3. Square lines 1 to 3 and 1 to 5. Make 1 to 3 the width of waist and whatever fullness it is desired to plait or gather into waistband, and cut down from 1 to 2 and 3 to 4 about 1in., shaping off to nothing at centre 7. The back and front parts are the same shape, and are seamed together up the sides. Of course there may be other seams, and the front may be made up fanciful, as indicated, instead of plain. This kind of dress has often been used for little boys also.

GIRLS' LOW-NECK FROCK.—Dias. 1 to 4, Plate 63.

Draw the line O O, and take a graduated tape equal to the breast measure, and mark the depth to 7, 11, and 20 by it. Square each way 13½ units from 11, and each way 11 units from 20. O to 10 is 10 units. Shape shoulder and scye as shown ; the eye is near enough for this. The skirt part may be cut as dias. 2 and 3, squaring from the O's to 24, and applying the widths in units shown. 14½ is the front, and 12 and 17 the back crease edges. The front length, also the side and back length, is made to measure. A sash may be worn round the waist, twice 32 units long and 21½ units wide, as indicated by dia. 4, fastened by gold safety pin or brooch, or any other decorations considered desirable, and suitable and fashionable.

CHILDREN'S SLIPS.—Dia. 2, Plate 64.

These are cut as shown, to fasten up the back, seamed or whole down the front of breast, and can be produced by the vest system.

CHILDREN'S DRAWERS.—Dia. 1, Plate 64.

These are made to fasten up behind, and are fulled into waistbands cut to the size of waist. They can be cut by the short trousers or knicker system—

only allowance must be made in the width of waist for fulling into waistband.

SMALL CHILD'S OR BABY'S FROCK.
Dias. 3 and 4, Plate 64.

Square from O each way. Then with a graduated tape the size of the breast measure, make O to 4½,

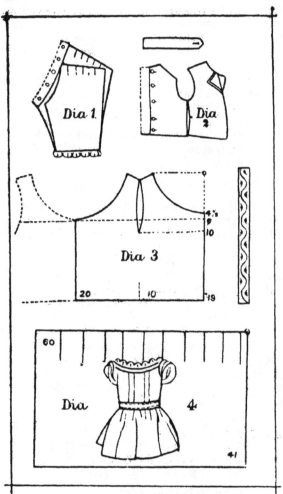

PLATE 64.

6, 10 and 19 those numbers of units, and square cross lines as shown. Along the top line mark 7½, and along the 10 line 10 units, also 10 units along

the bottom. Square up from 10 units at the bottom
to the top. Shape the neck from 4½ to 7½, slope the
shoulder strap about ½in., and clear out about ¾in.
inside the line squared up from 10 for the scye. The
line 4½ to 19 is either the actual front or back line.
To get the other half, fold the material over on the
line squared up from 10, and cut it by the part already shaped and folded over. 20 indicates the full
width of half the garment, either from centre of front
to centre of back, or from sideseam to sideseam if
the seams are placed at the side.

For a looser fit the depth 10 may be increased to
10½, and the width 7½ and 10 increased from 1in. to
2in., and the width 20 twice the amount added to 10.

To produce the skirt part, square from O to 41
and 60, and mark the depth and width by those
numbers of units, or as required for length, etc.

The small sketch on dia. 4 shows how this frock
is made up, the waist going into a band, and the
armholes finished with needlework or lace frillings
in place of sleeves. A sash, fancy or otherwise, can
be worn round the waist.

Having shown how to cut the smallest outdoor
dress that is worn by those who follow European
styles of costume, let us now cap the edifice by
showing how to cut the smallest over-garment.

THE CHILD'S PELLISE.—Dias. 1, 2, 3, Plate 65.

Square from O down the front, and across the
top, dia. 1. Square the depth of scye line at half
the breast down from O. Make the width across
the breast half the breast, and the entire width from
front line to back centre the breast measure and
2½in. if to be plain, or if to have plaits the difference
between 1 and 2 extra. The difference is the amount
the plait or plaits take. Make the length about 60
units, the width of back 40 or less at bottom, the
width of back to pitch and shoulder slope as per the
rules given in the other juvenile systems. Shape
the neck, spring the front well forward, taking a
piece off front of neck as shown, and cut the collar
as indicated. A catch goes on at top of breast as
per dots. The width of forepart at the bottom to be
made a little wider than back, hence 43.

The sleeve, dia. 2, can be drafted by the blouse
sleeve system, or cut like a coat sleeve. From 1 to

2 is half the scye, 2 to 3 an eighth of breast; 1 to 4
the crease, 4 to 6 plaited into cuff, 2 5 square with
1 2, underside of sleeve a little wider than topside
at cuff, hence not cut back so much from 5.

The cape, dia. 3, when wanted, can be cut by laying down the plain back and forepart in the angle

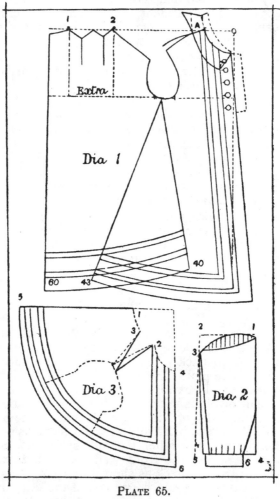

PLATE 65.

of square as shown, which will show how much V
has to come out between 2 and 3. The neck is got
by the neck of the coat, shoulderseam brought forward, and the bottom swept from the angle of the
squared lines.

LADIES' GARMENTS.

THE system does not require "adapting" to ladies' garments, because its principles are correct, and require no changing. The only thing to be remembered is that females are straight and flat in the back, and not round, with projecting bladebones, like men. This flatness renders it unnecessary to add to the line of height to make it equal to the line of form, to shoulder slope, level of scye, and waist. Bearing this in mind, it is as easy to draft females' as males' garments by it, taking the line of height as the scale by which to find the depth points as far down as the waist. Thus, if the height is 5ft. 4in., two-eighths of it is 16 waist length, half of which is 8 scye depth, and a third of 8 a little over $2\frac{1}{2}$ shoulder slope. The height scale is useful in drafting models. But in cutting by measures, it is simplest to use the waist length for the depth points. Half-an-inch should be added to it, or not, according to whether taken net or long. A sixth of it finds the slope of shoulder, and half of it the depth of scye.

The Old Habit or Dress Bodice.
Diagrams 1 to 4, Plate 66.

R D one-sixth waist length, R H half the waist length, to K the waist length. After squaring top and lines D and H, from R to M is made one-eighth breast and $\frac{1}{2}$in., DC and HF one-third breast and $2\frac{1}{2}$ or 3in., HF half breast and $2\frac{1}{2}$ or 3in., DB and HE the breast measure and 2in., and CA one-third breast and $\frac{1}{2}$in. to 1in. Or O A may be made $\frac{1}{2}$in. less than a fourth, and ET 1in. less than half breast. The front length, including the back top, is usually about 6in. longer than back, or to measure taken. A waist line can be drawn from K through 9. From 1in. to $1\frac{1}{4}$in, is taken out at P, and $2\frac{1}{2}$ to 3in. out at N. The breast darts should be about 1in. for flat breasts, $1\frac{1}{4}$ to $1\frac{1}{2}$ for good figures, and $1\frac{3}{4}$ to 2in. for full figures. These amounts are added to what is taken out at P and N and the waist measure, and the whole applied from the back to front to find the front of waist and the run of size line up the front. A line is then drawn from O or B through this point, and the front formed on it as per diagram. In producing models, a point may be marked $1\frac{1}{2}$in. from V towards W, and a line drawn from O through it.

The diagram shows how to shape the bottom, and
the shoulderseam is placed to taste, high or low, the
front neckpoint being risen ¾in. to 1in, above top
line.

Without tail, the draft forms a plain, close-fitting

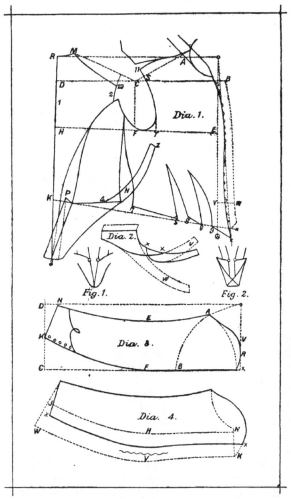

PLATE 66.

bodice. The addition of either form of tail shown
turns it into a habit bodice. Tail W, dia. 2, is the
same as shown running up to Z. Another tail as
per solid lines is in two parts, cut to overlap to X
and X and give spring. Either tail can be curved

more towards V to get more ease round the bottom edge. Figs. 1 and 2 show how habits used to be made-up.

The sleeve system, dia. 3, is operated exactly the same as for a man's garment, only if to be tight it is hollowed out more at E and B, and reduced at K.

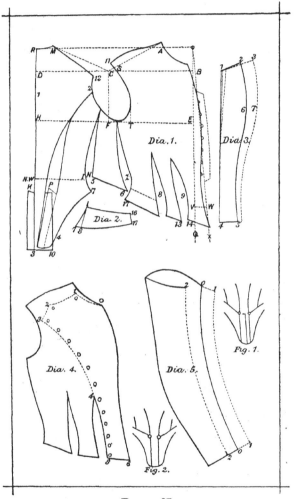

PLATE 67.

Shifting seams, dia. 4, is done in the way shown, by taking from the underside, as per dotted line H, and adding to the topside as per the dotted line V. When a backseam is thus shifted the topside V must

be fulled-on to the underside H, for which allowance
has to be made at the bottom.

MORE MODERN HABIT BODICE.

Diagrams 1 to 5, Plate 67.

The system is the same for these, the differences
being only in the design. Down to the bottom of
scye the design is the same. From there down
another seam is introduced; and the quantity taken
out at N of the older style is divided, and half taken
out at N and the other half at 2, thus producing a
second sidepiece, which is not cut to the full length,
but a short skirt, dia. 2, let in across its bottom to
gain spring over hip. This side skirt can be continued to either of the darts, or even the fronts.

Dia. 4 shows how the Lancer-fronted style is
formed, and dia. 3 shows lapels for ordinary double-
breasted styles.

The old style of habit was made whole-back, as
fig. 2; the more modern ones sometimes as fig. 1.

Forearmseams are shifted by taking off to 2, 2,
and adding on as per dotted line 1, 1.

A more modern habit still is

THE HABIT OR DRESS BODICE.—Dia. 1, Plate 68.

Add ½in. to the waist length taken for scale
of depth points. Make F to 2 one-sixth, F E
half the scale, and the length to measure,
with the ½ in. added. Square the top, shoulder,
bottom of scye, and waist lines. Or the routine
may be as follows : Waist length to measure and
½in.. Depth of scye half of it. Shoulder line two
thirds of the latter above depth of scye line

2 to H one third the breast and 3 in.
E to D the same as 2 to H
Back top one-eighth breast and a seam.
Rise to ½ half an inch.
Draw shoulder line ½ to H.

Make the width of back to measure, and the design
of the back and sidebodies to taste, taking 1 in. out
at 1 and 1½ to 2 out at 3 and 5.
DC 2 in., CN 2 in., and NJ 1 in.
EB half the whole breast and 2 in.
Continue the line DH above H, making it one
third the breast and ½ in., and apply the same quan-

tity from the top of this line forward to the top line
to find A.

Point A can also be got by squaring up from B to
O, and going back one fourth breast.

Make the width of shoulder A to * same as ½ X of
the back. Measure from X up to the shoulder line,
and rise point * from ½ in. to ¾ in. less above the
front shoulder line. Raise A the same amount
above top line as line DH extends above H, which
in this case is about ı in.

Take out cuts at 7 and 9, according to the size of

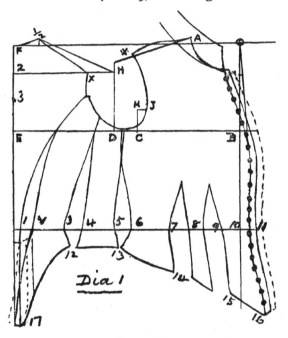

PLATE 68.

the bosom; if large 2ın., if medium 1½in., if flat
ıin. at each cut; unless the breasts are to be enlarged artificially by means of wadding, when inch
cuts will be too little, not giving enough of puff over
the artificial breast.

Form the scye, and measure up waist, making it
about the net measure or ı in. more, and draw a
straight breast line from O through the front of the
waist point so found. Then form the front on or by
the guidance of the straight line referred to.

THE MODERN HABIT.—Plate 69.

The Modern Habit is cut like a ladies' jacket, either with a dress body-like back, or with jacket back, not more than $1\frac{1}{4}$ or $1\frac{1}{2}$in. wide at waist. This diagram shows the form of the first-named style. It is not necessary to show the form of a jacket back, nor to repeat the particulars regarding the modus operandi of drafting, which is the same as for the dress body style. The width around the seat is ad-

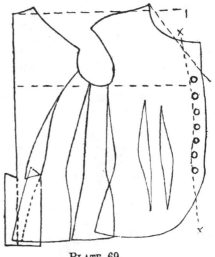

PLATE 69.

justed by the seat measure, as per the method laid down for jackets.

THE NORFOLK HABIT OR JACKET.—Plate 70.

The system is worked in the same way for these

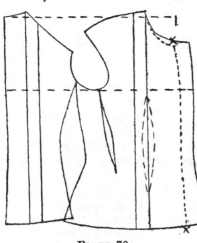

PLATE 70.

as Habits, the form below the arms alone being different. The back is formed in the style, and the waist suppressed in the manner shown. Norfolks as habits are worn by girls; seldom by women, except as jackets.

LADIES' FROCK COATS.--Plate 71.

From the hips upwards these are formed in the same manner as the plain dress or Habit bodices. The back sidebody can be cut first, as in the case of men's coats.

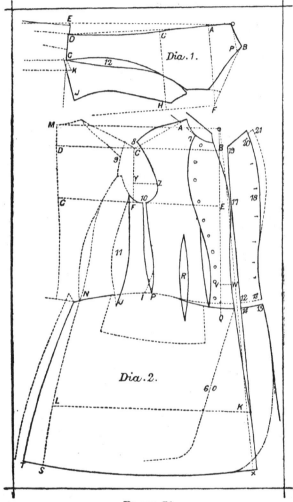

PLATE 71.

The waist seam may be cut to run straight round the hips, or curved upwards at the side, or pointed downwards in front and behind. The spring of skirt is made to follow on in the run of the spring of

the sidebody from waist to N. Or after the run of
the front has been got in accordance with the rule,
it can be adjusted by measure from K to L. Every-

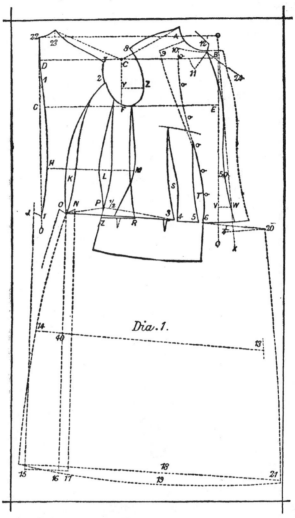

PLATE 72.

thing in front of the dotted line O X is overlap or
lapel.

The Redingote has frequently been turned into a
Morning or Louis XV. coat, by cutting the front of
skirt similarly to dotted line 60. It can be cut
D B to button up as per diagram, with ordinary

frock lapel and turn. Skirt corners can be blunted, more or less as indicated by dot and dash line, or square as men's.

The object of placing the waist seam on the hips is to dispense with taking cuts out of waist seam of skirt, which placing the waist seam at the waist, renders it necessary to do, in consequence of the hips being so much larger

LADIES' NEWMARKETS. — Plate 72.

These are produced in the same way as frock coats. The waist seam may run straight from O to 20, or be curved as per dotted line up to P. Also $\frac{1}{4}$ an inch or more can be taken out between Z and P, and more spring allowed. The run of front of skirt may be got by squaring from $\frac{1}{4}$ below waist seam at 2 or $2\frac{1}{2}$ in from 20. And the width and spring tested by the measure round from 13 to 14. The back skirt is shown. Two styles of D B button-up fronts (lapels) are shown, also the S.B. Various collars are indicated by 11 and 12.

For large hips or seat, extra width can be got by taking a piece out at 10 and waist, or by allowing it from P to 1, or from K backwards, dia. 2, plate 71.

LADIES' FIVE SEAM JACKETS —Plate 73.

THE back and sidebody can be drawn side by side, as shown by diagram 1, to any design, unless it is thought desirable to add spring behind 1 or G. The sideseam can be run into the scye or shoulder seam, and the widths of back and sidebody regulated by fashion. The actual width from A to F, diagram 1 of the Ladies' Frock, as also the measure of the shoulder line A C of this diagram 1, is really governed by the natural width of the figure's back, and half the diameter of the axilla added together. If, for example, the natural width of the back of a figure is $6\frac{3}{4}$, and the diameter of the scye $3\frac{1}{2}$, it would be $8\frac{1}{2}$, to which must be added the seams. The natural width of the back and half the diameter of scye also govern the length of the same line in the case of men's coverings. But a third and 3 inches, or half an inch more for seams is more simple and amounts to the same thing.

The system is the same for the forepart, dia. 2, as for habits, the spring from K to J being regulated by the measure round at that part, after getting the

front line E X. and measuring the width I K, placing
it on 2, and continuing to J to measure and seams
and ease; or K J may be made $\frac{2}{3}$, and 1 2 one third
of the difference between seat and breast measures.

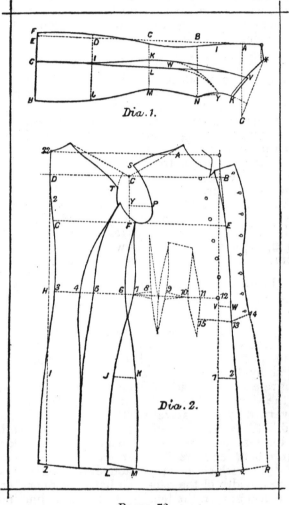

Dia. 1.

Dia. 2.

PLATE 73.

The darts can be taken out as found necessary.
The dotted lines below 7 8 9 10 indicate how to
avoid or get rid of a crease across the side, and the
dotted lines 13 14 15 how to produce the appearance
of a frock in front.

LADIES' SEVEN SEAM JACKETS.—Plate 74.

The back and sidebody can be drawn out in the same manner as the back and sidebody of the five-seamer. Then the forepart and quarterbody, the spring being divided between 2 3 and 4 5, in-

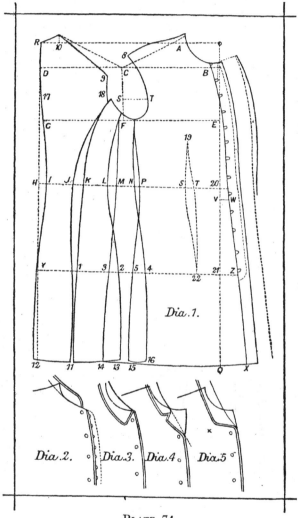

Dia.1.

Dia.2. *Dia.3.* *Dia.4.* *Dia.5.*

PLATE 74.

stead of all of it allowed on the forepart. The seat measure can be applied across back and sidebody, and across the quarterbody, and continued from Z back to 5, after the run of front line has been drawn.

B E W X is the actual front and size line. If to
hook and eye, a catch, as per dotted line, is sewn on
the one breast only, the eyes coming out through
the seam. For a S.B. from $1\frac{1}{4}$ to $1\frac{1}{2}$ is added in front
of the size line, and for a D.B. from $2\frac{1}{2}$ to $3\frac{1}{2}$, all
according to the style wanted.

Diagrams 2 3 4 and 5 are illustrative of the
Military, Prussian, M. C., and roll styles of fronts,
turns and collars.

TIGHT-BACK AND LOOSE-FRONT JACKETS.
S.B.'s Plate 75.

The system is worked in the same way for these,
only part of the one half of the spring allowed is
placed at the sideseam of sidebody. Anyone can

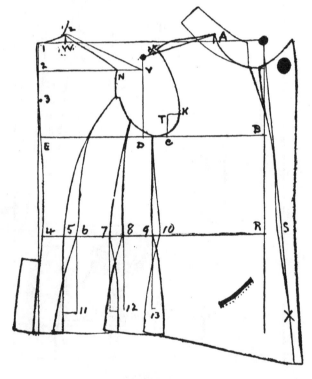

PLATE 75.

make rules for fac-simile reproductions of a good
design by squaring down from 6, 7, 8, 9, and 10, and
going backward and forward the amounts furnished

by a good model. The real thing, however, to
bear in mind and attend to is, to distribute the
spring in accordance with the form it has to cover,
as for instance large hips, or on the other hand a
dress skirt forced out behind by any kind of so-called
dress improver.

The line 2V is one-third of the scye depth from 1,
or two-thirds from E, and O is as much above V as
the neckpoint is above A. It will be seen that the
draft can also be made by the Students' Guide
System. The style is to button one only, and that
at the side of the neck—a very nice style for winter
wear, when made with a deep standing collar or, a
stand-and-fall collar.

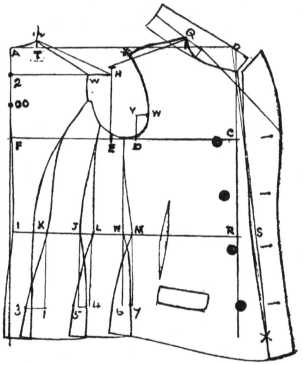

PLATE 76.

TIGHT-BACK AND LOOSE-FRONT D.B.'s.—Plate 76·

The system is worked in the same way also for
these, there being no difference between the S.B.
and D.B. of the same class, excepting in the matter
of such minor details as the way the necks are made

or to be made-up. This diagram shows what is called the frock coat turn and collar. It is not necessary to show all styles of necks and collars, &c., for each style of back and front of jacket that is made, as the variety is almost endless. A short cut

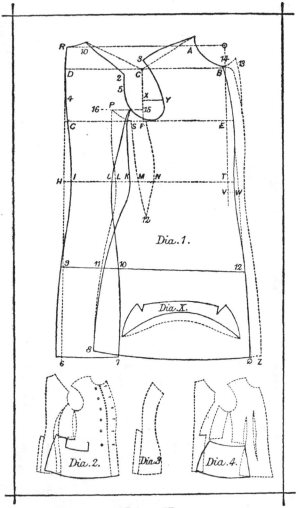

PLATE 77.

is marked to be taken out of the forepart if it is to be made half semi-fitting; it is not taken out of loose fronts.

When a lady orders a jacket, as a general rule she will decide on a back of one style, a forepart of

another style, and collar and neck of another style
—i.e., from three or four different illustrative figures.
It is seldom she can see the force of adhering to or
taking a style as it stands, without suggesting changes and improvements according to her own mind.

LADIES' CLOSE - FITTING THREE - SEAMERS.

Diagram 1, Plate 77.

The system is worked in the same way for these.
The back centre may be hollowed in, or whole and
straight. The less is taken out at back, the more
has to come out at side and cut under arm. If to be
close-fitting at seat, the width of back 9 to 10 must
be placed on 12, and the measure made up at 11. In
order to land ease over the hip, the fish can be taken
out as shown, and what is taken out between F and
S made up at P. V W is about 1½ for long jackets.

LADIES' SACS WITH SIDEBODIES.

In order to produce these, the back centre is left
straight, and 5in. spring allowed as from 7 to 8, and
the forepart made to spring the same amount over
sidebody, at a jacket length of say 33in., and the
front edge made straight.

LADIES' PALETOTS.—Dias. 2, 3, 4, Plate 77.

A ladies' plain Paletot is similar to a gents' Paletot, Selby, or Paddock, and may have the back of
either dia. 2 or 4.

LADIES' FROCK PALETOTS.—Dia. 4, Plate 77.

The frock shape skirt part, designed to give
spring, gives this style its name. This skirt can be
extended to the front dart, or a sidebody of the form
of dia. 2 may be used in place of the short one, making the skirt the amount of its width narrower.

LADIES' SHORT REEFERS.—Dia. 1, Plate 78.

The system is the same for all styles, though the
details relating to purely matters of style may be
various and different. W H J and J S is the short
loose reefer, and the dotted lines at N M and the
hollowed line at P the semi-fitting short reefer.
The positions of the seams can be changed so as to
produce a wider or narrower back or sidebody ; and
the shoulderseam may be varied as a matter of style.

LONG AND POINTED DRESS BODICES.

Diagrams 2, 3, 4, and 5, Plate 78.

A plain, long dress bodice is merely a seven-seamer jacket, the pieces cut narrower and lighter, and as much smaller in size as the difference be-

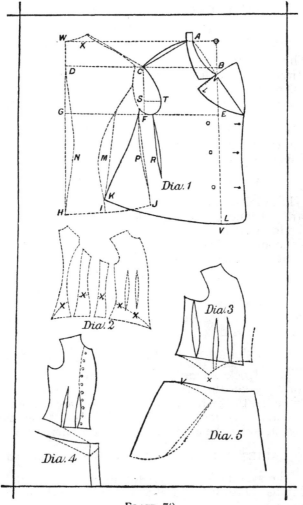

PLATE 78.

tween the waist measure over and under the dress bodice, which may be set down as 1in. The pointed style is produced by cutting pieces off the long bodice pattern, as per the X's.

D.B.'s and S.B.'s with skirts can be produced as per dotted lines of dia. 4, also Newmarket coats or ulsters with waistseams pointing downward in front. S.B. or D.B. cut-aways, with skirts, can be produced as per dotted line down to X of dia. 3, with alterations from frock skirt as per the dotted lines of dia. 5.

LADIES' SACS.—Plate 79.

The system is applied to the production of these the same as all other styles, the variations being in the style only. The measure round at the full length is the best to adjust the width of skirt by, as it in-

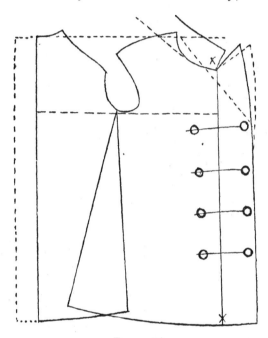

PLATE 79.

dicates the amount of spring necessary, all of which may be allowed at the side, or part at the back and a little in front, and the remainder at the side. The dotted line indicates an addition for a box plait at the centre of back. Plaits can be made to start from yokes back and front, or from a sort of bodice formed by cutting across several inches below the bottom of scye line, straight or in any fancy form, then cutting the part from there down and plaiting it into the upper part, stitching cloth strapping over it or otherwise.   Half-belts or whole ones may be worn round the waist.

When a sac is cut with a fish under the arm, the back style is cut narrower, also when the fish is carried through and a sidepiece thus formed.   Carrying a fish through is in order to allow more width

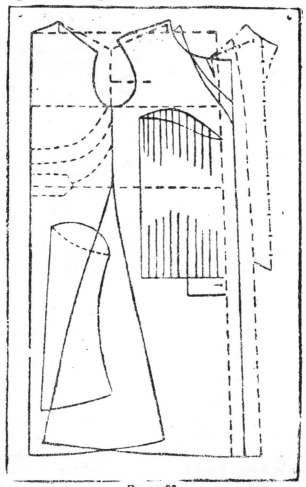

PLATE 80.

(spring) at the side than a fish gives, unless it is made very wide and sharpened, lead-pencil form.

LADIES' SAC ULSTERS.—Plate 80.

These are simply continuations of ladies' sac coats. They may be formed by continuing the length of the sac coat, plate 79, either SB or DB ; or the waist may be cut as per this diagram, or closer-fitting ; this is a matter ot individual taste and fashion. Single and D B fronts of various designs are shown, also the no-collar style. For the latter, the amount ot collar-stand must be added across the back top, or a strip sewn in as per a no-collar vest.

Slated - back jackets or ulsters are formed similar to dotted-line indications on the back, or the same run upwards at centre of back so as to form inverted V's, with curved in place of straight sides, with corresponding slatings on the forepart. A sketchy outline ot a bell sleeve appears on the back, and a bishop sleeve on the forepart. The widths of both are dependent on fashion and taste.

The short belt indicates how sac ulsters, both plaited and unplaited in the back, are sometimes caught up.

Any of the ladies' jackets on the diagram plates of this work can be extended to any length, and thus made into ulsters ; so that it is quite unnecessary to repeat those styles in ulster lengths,

Cape - Stole Victorine Jackets.
Dia. V, Plate 81.

This style is produced by altering from an ordinary style. If from a sac, it is laid down or drawn out by the system ; then the alterations are made as per solid shoulder lines, producing the cape form. This cuts the scye away, except the lower solid line part, giving in its place the bottom edge of a shoulder cape, extending only to the back and front of scye. The remainder of the cape-stole is formed by means of cloth or trimming laid on as per dotted lines. The sleevehead is cut like a blouse sleeve, only wider, or it may be as straight across its head as a sailor's or ancient shirt sleeve. If rounded as much as a plain coat sleeve, its head is sewn to a false scye top made in the lining, from the lower edge of the cape up ; the flat-head style is laid in under the bottom edge of cape, which must be as wide as the amount of scye cut away. In some cases the back of cape is cut off, and plaits laid in the back thence downwards. If only a box plait at centre, the cape can have an inverted V or heart-point over the plait. This diagram shows also how the no-collar front is formed.

SHORT-WAISTED AND ZOUAVE STYLES.
Dia. X, Plate 81.

Short-waisted and Zouave styles of jacket-tops are produced mainly by means of cloth trimmings. Sometimes braidings are used, either in black or to

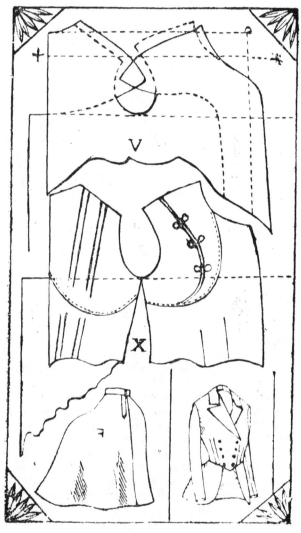

PLATE 81.

match the cloth. The diagram shows two styles; another is shorter and straighter across the back.

Close-fitting jackets that are extensively plaited, kilted or strapped, have these placed so as to produce the appearance of breadth in the shoulders and smallness of waist.

THE NEWMARKET HABIT AND TRAIN.

The sketches on plate 81 show the latest form of Newmarket habit and train.

LADIES' ETONS.—Plate 82.

Ladies' Etons are formed like plain dress bodices

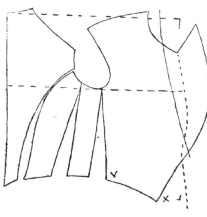

or habits to the waist and across to actual breast line; then an Eton lapel is added, the front run off as shown, and the bottom run similar to the diagram. Something more can be taken out at V, as well as off from 1 to X, if to be worn unbuttoned, and reduced to about the waist size without taking out a cut under the breast.

PLATE 82.

THE BOLERO OR BLOUSE.—Plate 83.

The system is applied in the same way as for other body garments; but the shoulder may be straightened to reduce the size of neck. The solid lines of top diagram show how the short bolero is formed, and the dotted extension lines the blouse, which goes inside the skirt. S B and D B styles of front are shown, with and without collars For rolling and sailor collars of all styles the gorge and opening are formed as for vests and boys' sailor blouses.

THE YOKED BLOUSE. — Plate 83.

The bottom diagram shows how these are cut—viz., the shoulder parts of a plain blouse are used for yoke, and thence downwards is composed of plain material wide enough to allow for being gathered into the yoke parts, and scye width. Both plain and Prussian collars are shown; the stand collar is shaped like the plain collar, only narrower, with the crease line left out ; and the Medici collar similar

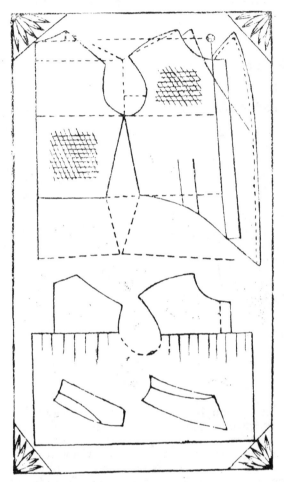

PLATE 83.

to the Prussian collar without crease, its front more or less run off or rounded.

Some blouses are made on tight linings, sleeves and all.

Sleeves for blouses are cut as dias. 3 and 4, plate 60, as bishop sleeves, as sketch plate 80, and as bell sleeves without backseam, and gathered into wristbands or cuffs.

VARIOUS STYLES. — Plates 84 and 85.

Dia. 1 shows how a cut-off lapel for jacket to button to throat is cut, dia. 2 how the roll collar style

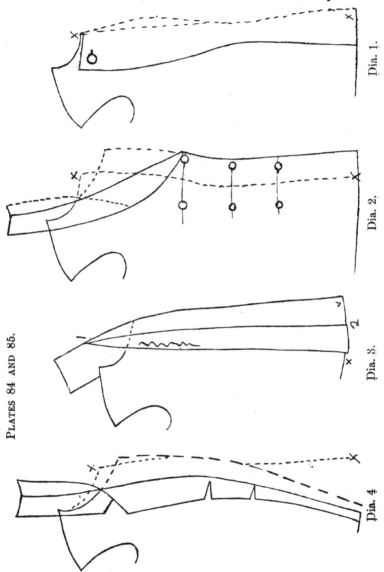

is formed, dia. 3 how the roll-collar roll-back front is formed, and dia. 4 how the roll-back cut-away front with coat collar is designed.

LADIES' COVERT COAT.—Dia. X, Plate 86.

This coat is cut as shown by diagram, 34 breast. The depths from top of back are, to level of shoulder end 2, depth of scye $7\frac{1}{2}$, waist 15, and full length 30. The widths of back are, at top $2\frac{1}{2}$ and up $\frac{3}{4}$in., across

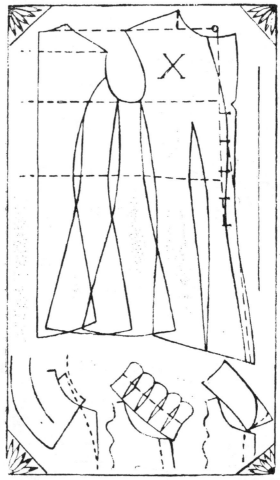

PLATE 86.

to pitch $6\frac{1}{2}$, at waist 3, and at bottom $5\frac{1}{2}$. The other widths on top line are $15\frac{1}{2}$ and $19\frac{1}{2}$, or back 4in from $19\frac{1}{2}$, and up 2in. for neck point of front shoulder. The end of shoulder rests on top line. The other widths on bottom of scye line are, $4\frac{3}{4}$ to sideseam, 8 to next seam, 11 to underarmseam, and $19\frac{1}{2}$ to front square line; on waist line, to sidebody $3\frac{3}{4}$, to front of same 7, to quarterbody near $8\frac{1}{2}$, to under-armseam of same 12, to sideseam of forepart $13\frac{1}{2}$, to breast cut $16\frac{1}{2}$ and $18\frac{1}{2}$, and to form breast line $19\frac{3}{4}$ fully.

At bottom the sidebody springs $5\frac{1}{4}$ over back, and is 10in. wide; the quarterbody 6in. over sidebody and is $11\frac{1}{2}$ wide; the forepart 2in. over quarterbody, is $5\frac{1}{2}$ wide to dart, 4in. from dart to bottom of front line, and another $1\frac{1}{2}$in. to front edge, thus dividing the bottom of forepart into two equal halves. The length of forepart from its neckpoint is $35\frac{1}{2}$, and from front of gorge $32\frac{1}{4}$. From $\frac{1}{2}$in. to $\frac{3}{4}$in. of round is placed on front of breast, to nothing at front line at waist. If a straight line is then drawn from front of breast to size point at front of bottom, and the run of actual breast or front line continued out to it, the shape of the front will be got, corresponding with the result of going down the breast measure from top line and $1\frac{1}{2}$ forward, and drawing a line from the front of breast through this point, then hollowing 1in. at waist to nothing at breast and bottom. The style of turn is got by allowing 2in. in front of the square line to $\frac{3}{4}$in. in front of breast round, and running straight out at top. An inch is allowed for button catch and holes, coming out to $1\frac{1}{2}$ on the slant at bottom. The top button is level with bottom of scye line. The dent shown is only made in the catch side, and is level with the top button. The front may be closed by means of four or five buttons.

Storm, Sectional, and Cape Collars
for Jackets, &c.

The small diagrams at the bottom of plate 86 show how these are formed — viz., the storm collar has a hollow collarseam to make it spring out at its top edge. Springing out from the height of an ordinary stand is also got by taking a lot of darts out, thus making it a collar of sections. This collar can also be cut hollow in its seaming-to edge. A cape collar is merely a flat-lying piece, shaped at the neck the same as the garment, with an allowance for turning-in at neck, and either circular or fanciful in its bottom edge and front. As the diagrams speak louder than words, there will be no necessity for further explanations.

FOUR-SEAMER WHOLE-BACKS.—Plate 87.

This diagram illustrates how the moderately narrow whole-back is formed, with sidebody and forepart. As the lines indicate, there is no change

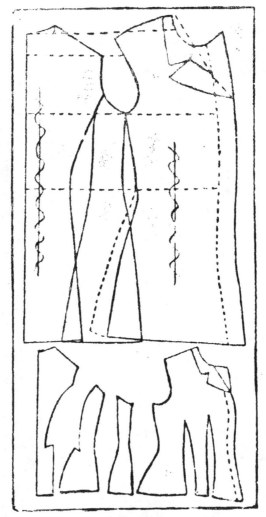

PLATE 87.

in the working of the system, all changes being in design only. In making up, under the breasts and centre of back should be well shrunk. Two styles of lapel turns are shown; and the dotted line indicates where to let out for looser cut or projecting side hips.

HABIT BODY.—Small Diagrams, Plate 87.

This style is cut close fitting all over, with side-seam plaits, and sometimes without them, like a jacket. The pieces are cut narrow and neat looking. Its length of front is sometimes increased, when the spring of front of skirt part must not be skimpy.

FOUR-SEAMER, WIDE BACKS.—Plate 88.

The top diagram illustrates how comparatively wide whole-back with straight front is formed. Its length may be made anything without marring its appearance. The system is used in the same way for this as all other styles, all the changes there are being in design only. As will be seen, a number of styles of turns are given.

BELL SLEEVES.—Dia. *, Plate 88.

Bell sleeves can be cut from jacket sleeves in the form shown by either of the dotted lines — viz., not very wide, or extra wide. All that is necessary is to add to the coat sleeve in the manner shown by the dotted lines. Some of these sleeves are back-seamless, and some not.

PUFFED ABOVE WRIST SLEEVES.—Dia. V, Plate 88

These are formed by cutting up the bottoms of bell sleeves in the form shown by this diagram ; or the point to puff-up may be made longer and fuller if desired.

WING OR CAPE SLEEVES.—Dia. X, Plate 88.

These can be produced from ordinary sleeves in the way illustrated by this diagram, the dotted lines showing the ordinary sleeve, and the solid ones the change into a wing sleeve. The heads of both are the same ; the front of the wing being straight and on the crease instead of hollowed, and the back taking its run from the hinder part of sleevehead. The top of underside is the same as that of ordinary sleeves, hooked-in as per dot and dash line. To economise, a seam may be placed anywhere underneath, so long as it does not come in sight and the front is on the crease.

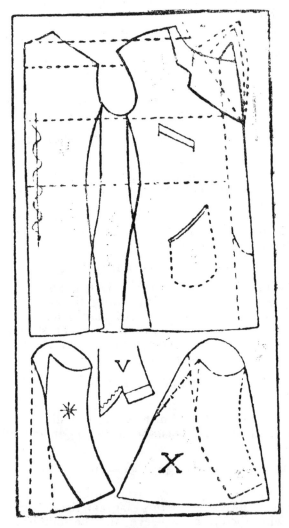

PLATE 88.

SAC-BACK THREE-SEAMERS.—Dia. 1, Plate 89.

These are cut in the manner shown by this diagram, or more or less hollowed in the back and at the sideseam, and of various widths. Some have side pieces, and are thus turned into five-seamers with semi-sac backs. A few have cuts taken out under the arm, and some similarly to dart shown. The

lines of the system are shown on the design, and it
is not necessary to repeat the instructions. Sufficient spring must be allowed to produce the width
round the seat, and the style required. Various

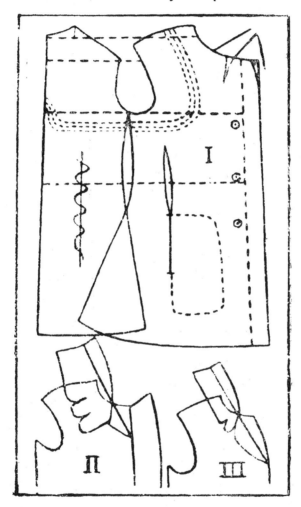

PLATE 89.

styles of turns are shown, also DB and SB fronts,.
also one of the Zouave tops which are used to-
produce a very short waist appearance. A more
circular and longer form of Zouave top is shown on
plate 81.

COLLAR AND TURN DESIGNS.—Dias. 2, 3, Plate 89.

These are given to show how easy it is to produce variety and novelty in a lady's garment by simple means.

YOKES OF ALL STYLES, Dias. 1 to 7, Plate 90,

Are used on almost all styles of bodices and jackets. The way to produce a yoke is from the garment it

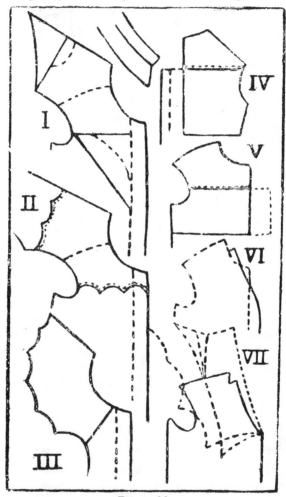

PLATE 90.

is to form part of. The solid lines on the back and forepart of dia. 1 show the horizontal bottom yoke, also the pointed back and front yoke; the dash lines

a curved at back and ditto and pointed one in front
style; the solid and dotted lines on dia. 2 the
series of segments at bottom of yoke, ranging in
number according to taste. The dotted lines of
dias. 4 and 5 exhibit how additional width below
yokes is added for plaiting or fulling in to form
plaited jackets or gathered into yoke blouses; dia. 3
the serial-segmental bottom, shoulder cape; dia.
6 the no-collar style of front, gorge, and neck;
dia. 7 a collar with a segment front, segmental
sides, and pointed cape-like back; also a combination of side edge and sword flap collar, with or
without a pointed back. Enormous variety in
collars is possible. These indicative sketches will
serve to show how wide the field is to designing
genius with the necessary inclination to explore and
exploit the subject.

BODICES WITH BASQUES.—Dias. A and E, Plate 91.

Small sketches are sufficient to indicate the manner in which natural waist length bodices with
basques are produced.

The French no-collar bodice with basque A is
cut both with and without sidepieces, or with one
piece under the arm; also with or without back
skirts, or with basques meeting the back skirts, or
as per A, extending to the centre of the back.
Either description can be plaited at back, in a line
with the position of sideseam, or anywhere. Length
and style in front to fashion.

The plaited bodice with basque E is composed of
back and forepart, after the manner of old-fashioned
bodices, all the waist suppression being taken out
at the undearmseam, the plaits rendering it possible
to take out cuts unseen if necessary, not only out of
waist of bodice, but out of waist of skirt. Styles of
front are almost illimitable. The diagram shows a
novel style of double revers, and fancy panteen collar. Dia. F indicates forms in which lapels are cut
when the fronts are DB.

ORNAMENTAL CUTTING.

Diagrams 2, 3, H and R, Plate 91.

Dias. 2 and 3 indicate how easy it is to cut fancy
saddles or yokes suitable for bodices or jackets of
all styles, whether plain, gathered, box-plaited or

kilted after the manner of all-but-yoke-kilted dresses
Dias. H and R show how easy it is to change the
form of ordinary-shaped turns and collars into fancy

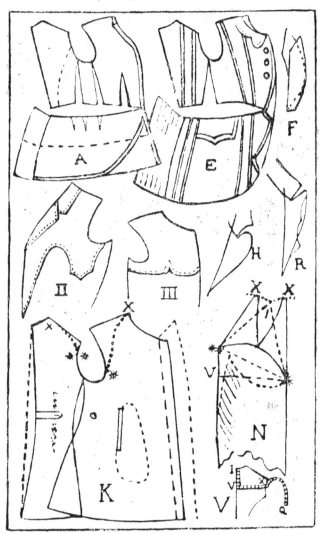

PLATE 91.

revers and collars. It is in such matters as this that
much of the success of a ladies' cutter consists—viz.,
the power to make fresh designs and to please.

Dia. F, plate 92, is a design for lapel and collar.

LADIES' TALMA-RAGLANS.
Diagrams K and N, Plate 91.

Dia, K indicates the form of a hollowed-back three-seamer. A Talma or Raglan sleeve may be put in this or any form of jacket, though it is generally put in the full sac. To produce the style, alter the shoulder as per dotted lines X to * and X to **. To produce the Talma sleevehead, lay down the ordinary sleeve and measure and make * 1, dia. N, the same length as *X of the front shoulder, casting a sweep through 1 by pivot *; then by the measure from ** to X of the back, cast a sweep through 1 by pivot **, dia. N. To produce the Raglan sleeve, sweep outwards from point 1, both from pivot * and **, to X and X ; then take out as much each side of point 1 as necessary—say 3½in. in all. And after allowing seams and running straight lines from X to * and X to **, shape slightly hollow towards the neck, oval in the middle, and slightly hollow again towards the heads of back and forearmseams. The single seam of the old-style Talma sleeve was made to come right at the bottom of scye (armpit).

A SEMI-SACQUE.—Dia. X, Plate 92.

This design has four seams, with or without a breast dart. It may also be cut with a backseam, instead of whole. It has a fancy yoke composed of four pieces, and a slated front, with tab extending over breast. It is straight-fronted.

A WATTEAU-PLAITED BACK.—Dia. XX, Plate 92.

The outline of the diagram is sufficient to show how these are cut, the boxplait being laid on the centre of back between the shoulders, from which it hangs right down to the bottom of dress. Its width is generally pretty broad, say 3in. or 4in., but it may be made any width. It is frequently seen in widows' robes.

DIVIDED SKIRT.—Dia. XXX, Plate 92.

After drawing line O O, O to * is made 13in., O to O the full front length and ½in., * to 7 7in., O to 15 15in., and O to 23 23in. O to X half the seat. The waist is reduced to measure by taking out cuts. If these are made equal, there being a front and a back, a double amount thus comes out at the sideseam by X. The amount from O to 15 goes in

between the legs. The side length by X 23 should
be made to measure, or 1in. longer than front. The
front of waist is lowered ½in., and the back of waist
risen ½in. or more.

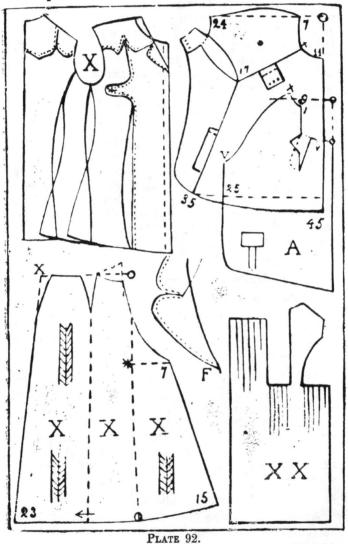

PLATE 92.

SAFETY TRAIN.—Dia. 1, Plate 92.

After squaring O to 24 and O to 45 those numbers
of inches, O to 7 is made 7in. and O to 11 11in.
The waist is then formed as shown, reducing 7 and

11 if too large, and vice versa. 11 to X is made a quarter the waist, and X to 17 the length from front of waist to knee, not the length from side of waist. A sweep is cast through 17, which is 22in. in a straight line from the line O 45. A line is squared from a point 5in. above bottom across to 35 that number of inches, and lines are drawn from X to 17 and from 17 to 35 for the position of the seam. 11½in. is measured out from 17, and a sweep made where the mouth of the big cut comes. This cut starts at 5in. down from 24, and is 5in. across its mouth. It is also 5in. from cut to the lower hole of leg-cuff. Outside line 17 to 35 the width is about 11in., excepting out to the hole-edge of cuff. At its outer edge the cuff is 5in. wide, also 5in. in its side next 24, and the V between it and 24 is 5½in. wide.

O to O of the underside is the same as O to 11, and O to the full length the same as O 45. O to 9 is 9in., and point 1 is 1in. below 9, X being 1½ square up from a point 13in. from O. XV is made the same shape and length as from 7 to 24 of forepart, including the 5in of cuff that joins on to 24. The width of underside at the level of V, and thence all the way to bottom, is 25in.

VARIOUS STYLES OF SLEEVES.—Plates 93 and 94.

All styles of sleeves are cut by the same system, variations being only in the style. Dia. 2 shows the system in full detail, for a close-fitting ladies' sleeve, the width at the elbow being applied forward and the width at the hand backward, thus producing the outline of style.

Full top sleeves are produced by altering from plain sleeves as per dotted lines dia. 4. The amount of extra width and round to add depends upon the extent of fullness wanted. The same sleevetop does for plaited styles, also to be reduced to size by taking out wedges.

Leg-of-mutton sleeves, dia. 5, are produced from plain sleeves, straight from X to 3 and 2 to 6, with 3in. or 4in. added from 1 to 2 and on top. 4 to 5 the quantity for fulling-in.

Puffed-elbow sleeves, diagram 6, illustrated by fig. 1, are cut as dia. 6. 1 to 2 the amount added for puffings.

Variations of the positions of seams are shown by dia. 3. When a topside is made wider behind, it must be fulled on at the elbow; when made wider at the forearm, stretched.

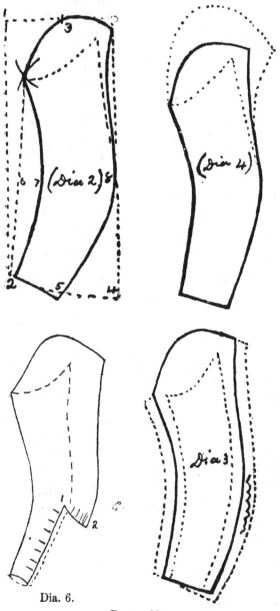

Dia. 6.

PLATE 93.

183

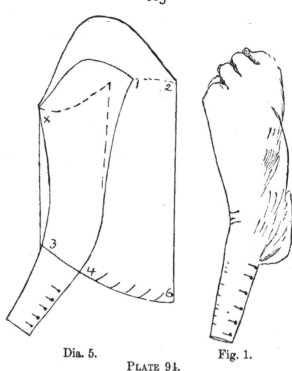

Dia. 5.   Fig. 1.

PLATE 91.

Measure I V, dia. V, plate 91, depth back pitch;
VX width of back; and from X over shoulder to the
front pitch Q, amount of sleevehead minus fullness.

CLOSE-FITTING CAPES. — Plate 95.

An angle is first drawn, as 3 O X. Into this is laid
the back and forepart of a garment corresponding
with the customer's breast measure, as per dotted
lines 1 5 P 6. The back neck is lowered as from 1
to 2 and solid line to 5, which widens the back top,
The finger point is then placed on the forepart at P.
as a pivot, by which it is swung back to the hinder
dotted lines, thus making point 6 fall to 7. The
shoulderseam is then drawn from 5 to Q, which is 1½
in front of P. A sweep is then made from 5 to 7 by
point Q to see that both shoulderseams will be of
the same length. If not, either advance 7 a trifle,
or lower at 5, and draw front shoulderseam, neck
and front by the forepart pattern. Now make a
sweep from 3 forward by pivot O, after having

marked off the length from 2 to 3   This sweep will
come as dotted line.   Add the difference between 6,
and 7, or the amount the gorge has dropped, from

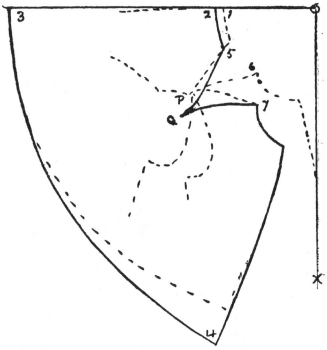

PLATE 95.

the dotted line to 4, and run off the bottom from 4.
to 3 as per solid line.

ANOTHER STYLE. — Plate 96.

All the difference in process and style between this
one and diagram 1 is that two cuts are taken out
at the neck to nothing at the shoulder point, instead
of one.   The cuts 2, 3, and 4, 5, are to be equal to
the one cut 5, 7, of dia 1.   The sweep W Y is
made from pivot O, same as usual, and then what 4
is dropped to 5, as in the case of 6 to 7, dia. 1, must
be added as at X, or the front will be too short.

Both these close-fitting capes have been, and can
still be extended to 52in., or any other length required to make a long cloak.

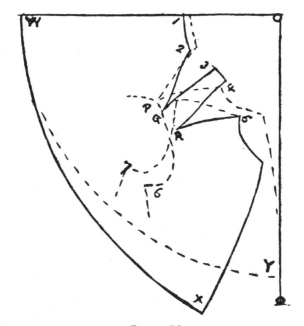

PLATE 96.

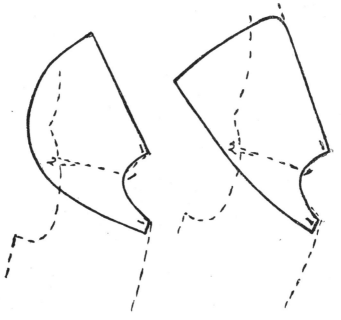

Dia. 1.   Dia. 2.

PLATE 97.

186

HOODS. — Plate 97.

The way to cut these is to place the shoulders of
the garment in a closing position from 1 to 2, and
then mark the neck of the hood to fit the neck of the
garment, as shown, letting the centre of back be
straight with the back of the jacket, and shaping
the remainder to the style required. Diagram 1
shows a gipsy hood, and dia. 2 the monk's cowl
shape, which is by far the most fashionable of any.

THE CORSLET DRESS. — Plate 98.

XX to X is the waist line, half the difference between breast and seat measure, and 8in. longer than
waist measure. XXO front length. After squaring
these lines and bottom lines, O L is made from 3in.
to 5in., according to attitude. LC half entire width
round bottom. If a 2½yd skirt, it would be 45in.
Lines are now drawn from XX to L and X to C, and
the seat measure applied at 8in. below waist line.
If found correct, well and good ; if not, the bottom
width, or both bottom and XX to X, enlarged or
reduced sufficiently to make the seat width correct.
For the bodice part, lines are squared up from X and
XX, and the waist and top reduced to measure by
taking out cuts—the largest one at the side over the
hip, and the others according to the development of
breast and form of back.

The dress can be divided at line V, or anywhere,
after chalked ; or it can be produced in halves, going
from XX towards X and L to V half the full amounts,
and applying half the seat measure at 8in. below
waist line.

THE PRINCESS ROBE. — Plate 99.

The whole of this diagram, including dotted line
parts, represents a princess robe with one cut taken
out under breast ; two breast darts are probably
most usual. This garment is in the form of a long
jacket or tight-fitting ulster trained at back, or
otherwise.

CORSLET DRESS FROM PRINCESS ROBE.

Plate 99.

The solid lines of the princess robe show how a

corslet bodice is cut from it—viz., it is chalked off at the height required, as indicated by the lines X; and thus the robe is turned into a corslet dress by merely cutting off the dotted line parts.

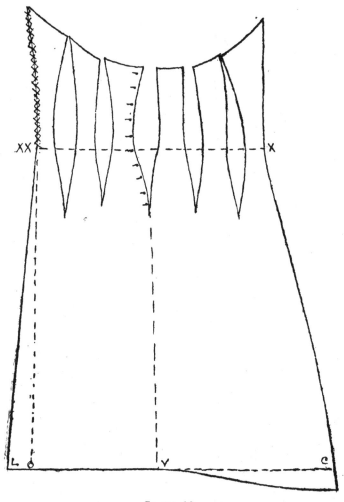

PLATE 98.

When there are two breast darts, the back and two side pieces are made narrower, so that the three parts of the forepart may be equalized with the others in width.

188

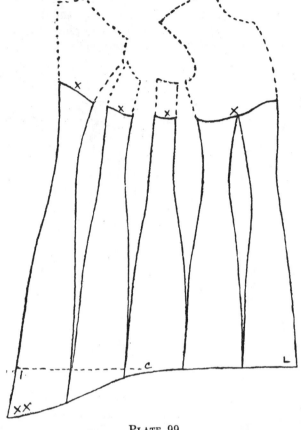

PLATE 99.

PRINCESS ROBES AND PRINCESS HABITS.
Plate 100.
A Princess robe is merely a long jacket, designed
in such a manner as to produce either a plain or else
a trained robe. The right side is lengthened and
broadened for a habit.
Diagrams 1, 2, 3, 4, 5, Plate 100,
Give a fair idea of the general aspect and cut of
the latter, to be made up quite plain. But it may
have boxplaits at centre of back and sideseams.
Dias. 2, 3 and 4 show these added. These diagrams,
with diagram 5, also show how the parts of
FESTOONED DRESSES
Are cut—viz., run down to points sufficiently below

the actual lengths to allow for the plaits forming that end of the festoonings to be made, and leave the length desired at that part right.   Festoonings

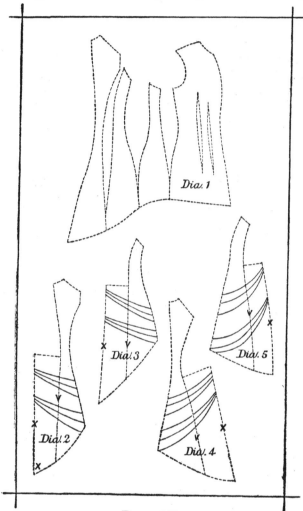

PLATE 100.

can be made at any seam, either on the one side or both sides of it.

Diagrams 1 and 2, Plate 101, Illustrate both ways in which foreparts can be cut and boxplaited or festooned.

The waved lines on the diagrams are intended to

represent festoonings in a sketchy manner.

THE ART AND SCIENCE OF GORING SKIRTS.

Diagrams 3 and 4, Plate 101.

The diagrams show how goring was originally practiced.

Dia. 4 represents a length of material for the

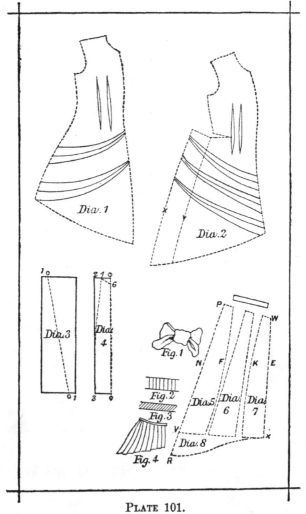

PLATE 101.

front, on the double, O O being the crease line. O to 1 is half the width from O to 2. The piece from

1 to 2 is sloped off, either in a straight line from 1 to 3, or ovalled.

Dia. 3 represents the length of material for the side gores, not folded, the two sides being the selvedges. 1 to O at each end is one-third of its width. A straight line is chalked from O to O, and the material cut through at this line. The thick (wide) end of each piece is for the bottom, and the thin end for the waist part of these two side gores.

The two back gores are the same as the side gores. If the material is 27in. wide, the result will be 49½ round the bottom and 22½ at the waist, or a 2½yd. wide skirt, as dias. 5, 6, 7, to be reduced to size in the waist by taking out cuts and rounding-in at the tops of seams, as if cuts were taken out at the tops of seams. Such a skirt may have two back gores of half width at the top to all the width at the bottom, in place of the same as the side gores.

Two lengths of double-width (54in.) material, cut as dia. 3, into four gores of one-third at the top and two-thirds at the bottom, and back and front on the crease, form a skirt. Or a skirt may be formed of two lengths, the front cut one-fourth the width at the top and half the width at the bottom, using the two pieces cut off from that length for side gores; and the other whole breadth for the back, boxplaited or cut one-third by two-thirds Such skirts, cut from double-width material, come out at about three yards in width.

Skirts from narrow-width goods are gored by half to all of the folded material for the front, one-third to all of the open material for the side gores, and half to all of the open material for the back gores, one-third of the sloping being taken off the front seams and two-thirds off the back seams of the side gores, to give them a backward-flowing form.

The piece dia. 8, below line V X, represents how training is added; and if kilted, it takes the form of fig. 4. Decoration bands of material should be cut on the cross, as per fig. 3, and not on the straight as per fig. 2; and this applies with increased force to flouncings.

LADIES' DOLMANS. — Plate 102.

First of all take a five-seam jacket pattern, and alter the back shoulders and scye as shown by the dotted lines of dia. 1. The pieces added below N show the relation of underside to wings of different forms to scye. To draft a wing, lay down the back and sleeve as dia. 2, and add from 2in. to 3in. from 2 to 3, to make X 3 that much more than the width of back and sleeve together. This is for a plain

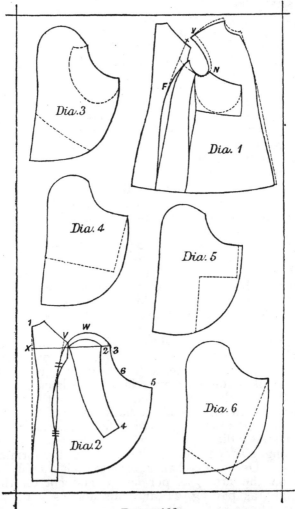

PLATE 102.

dolman. For puffed heads allow another 3in., and add from 4in. to 6in. of round at W. Shape side-seam of wing and front as shown. Other styles of wings are produced in the same way, only made different in form, as indicated by the other diagrams.

LADIES' VESTS. — Plate 103.

These diagrams show how ladies' vests of all styles are formed. No change in the system is necessary in

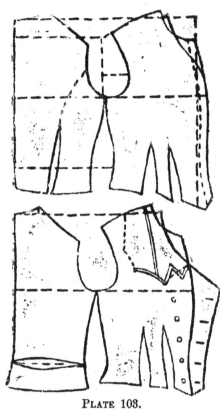

PLATE 103.

producing these, unless it be to deduct an inch from the breast and waist measures taken on the bodice. The main thing is to cut a tight-fitting waist. The back may be cut after the manner of either diagram —suppressed by taking out a fish where the side-seam of a habit or jacket comes, or with a little skirt formed by taking a fish out across the waist.

Indications of various styles of necks and collars for jackets and vests are outlined on these diagrams; the variety possible in this respect is almost endless, and has to do with style or design only — fashion being always on the move and changing.

In reducing the waist under the arm, care should be taken not to reduce the breast also. The D B diagram shows how the breast size may be reduced by an oversight. The no-collar diagram indicates how to avoid reduction to any appreciable extent, by the form in which the suppression or wedge is taken out. Small errors in forming a garment at the seams often make quite another size of it; and then the operator may fancy it is the system, and not himself, that is in error. All garments should

be carefully measured up after drafted, part by part,
or in a closing position at all the seams, so as to
make sure no error has crept in.

Imitation vests, inserted in the fronts of jackets
or bodices, are quite out of fashion for the time being, but may return again into popularity. These
are merely pieces cut to reach as far back as the
front cut taken out under the breast, and may or
may not reach as far back as the scye and shoulderseam, or even to the sideseam of forepart.

LADIES' RIDING SKIRT SYSTEM.—Dia. 1, Plate 104.

Take the measures as follows : The length of left
side from waist to ground, and the waist and seat
measures. In drafting, use them thus : Open the
cloth, draw the line O O down its crease. Deduct
1in. from half the length to find the length to knee.
Make a mark at X, and apply the length to knee
from X to 3. Sweep XV by pivot 3, making it half
the length to knee. Draw a line from 3 through V
to *. V to K one-fourth waist, X to K one-third
knee length, and sweep VK from *, continning from
V to W one-fourth waist. Square 3 2 by line 3 V,
and 3 5 by line O O, making each half the whole
seat measure. Square 2 1 by 3 2, continuing it up
to cut. Draw nearly a straight line from K through
X to cut, making the length from K to cut same as
X 3 or V 3—viz., the length to knee as already found.
Take out 3½in. or more of cut 5in. deep. Make the
width at bottom 4 to 7 same as 3 to 5. 4 to 6 a little
more than 3 to 2, and the length of right side half
the length to knee longer than the left, at the bottom 8, where lifted up by the right knee. This
completes the front.

Cut the back part the same shape as the front,
except 1½in. shorter at 8, and wider and higher at
back of waist to allow for taking a couple or three
1½in. cuts out as shown. When these cuts are sewn,
the back of waist should rise a little higher than the
front of waist. The pocket shade grows-on, and
the pocket goes in as shown.

Diagrams 2 and 3

Show how to put the seams into the back in place
of at side, by allowing a piece outside of sideline OO,
and taking it from the back part so that the side-

seam will go underneath to X; also how cuts are
taken out of fronts to make a receptacle for the knee.

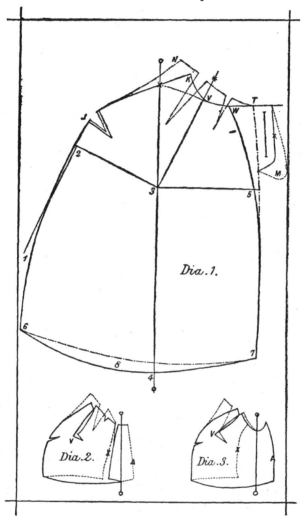

FLATE 104.

LADIES' SKIRT CUTTING. — Dias. A, E, F, H,
Plate 105.

Three times its length of 27in. material cuts a
five-piece skirt 2¾yd. round the bottom, barring the
hem or facing—which latter should be on the cross.
See dias. A A single length is folded down its cen-

tre, and shaped off from half its folded width at top
to all at bottom ; then two lengths, the one placed
on the top of the other, and gored from half at top
to two-thirds at bottom, leaving two gores of the
same dimensions for the two back widths. The top

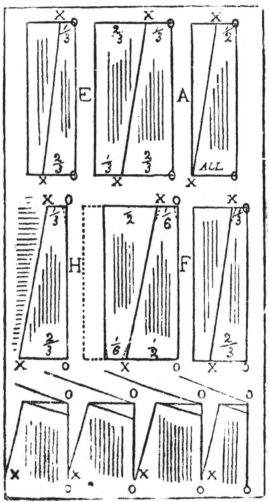

PLATE 105.

widths produced thus are 6¾, 9 and 9, and the bottom
widths 13½, 18 and 18, on the double. The waist can
be reduced by cuts and plaits, or by cuts only.   A
1½ cut and 1in. rounding can be taken from the front,
1in. rounding a side and a 2½in. cut from the side

gores, and 1in. rounding and a 2in. cut from back
gores, and the rest plaited, or no cut and the rest
plaited.

A 2½yds. wide skirt can be got by cutting the
front as per dia. E—viz., one-third at waist and two-
thirds at bottom.

Four times its length and 2½in. of 18in. material
will cut a six or seven piece skirt 2yd. 12in. wide—
viz., one front width 4 at top by 9 at bottom, four
side gores 6 at top by 12 at bottom, and a back width
4½ by 9 on the double. The 2½in. extra allows for
squaring top and bottom by back centre crease. if
there is to be no backseam. The waist can be reduced to size by taking one-third of the excess out
at top of first seam, two-thirds at next seam, and one-
third at third seam ; or by using cuts, or cuts and
plaits also.

Materials narrower than 27in. reduce the width of
five-piece skirts, and those above 18 to 27 increase
the width of six or seven-piece skirts, according to
the before-stated methods of goring.

Three times its length of 27in. material will cut a
seven-piece skirt 2¾yd. wide. See dias. F and H,
plate 105 — viz., one length folded down its centre,
and cut from one-third its folded width at top to
two-thirds at bottom ; two lengths laid one on the
other, reduced to say 18in. wide, and then divided
by one-sixth of 27 at top and half of 27 at bottom.
If an 18in. material, this would be one-fourth at top
and three fourths at bottom. The two back pieces
consist of the slopings left from the front piece.

To get a back centre without seam, another length
2½in. longer than measure, can be creased down its
centre, and the crease used for the back centre.
Skirts gored according to this rule can be reduced
at waist by taking out one-third at first seam, two-
thirds at next, and one-third at next, or otherwise.

Hollowing ½in. in front to nothing at sideseam is
equivalent to squaring from ¼in. down in front to
nothing at side. Doing this gives 3in. of forward
spring at bottom ; squaring by ½in. down to nothing
gives 6in. of forward spring, and so on, adding 3in.
more forward spring for every ¼in. more down.

Raising the waist at the hinderseam of each piece
is the same as hollowing. See top and lower lines of
bottom diagrams O O and X's.

Hollowing the waist is not for the purpose of

making it fit the waist, nor yet to make a good run, but for the purpose of distributing the drapery evenly and preventing dips at seams and their consequence.

Plate 106.

The top diagrams bounded by OX's represent the two side gores and back of a skirt hollowed at waist

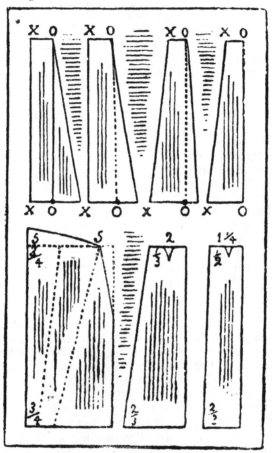

PLATE 106.

in the usual way (equivalent to squaring as bottom diagrams, plate 105) : the front not being hollowed any. It will be seen that all the spring remains at backseam of front piece only. Hardly any of it remains at the hinder seam of first side gore, and still less at the hinder seam of the hinder side gore, while none at all stays at back centre.

If any backward spring is wanted, it must be placed behind back lines that are square with the top of any pieces.

In cutting from double-width materials, half a width does for the front and the other half for back; the material being ready doubled, only one length instead of two is required for side gores. Backseams can be used or avoided. If to be avoided, the length for the back must be $2\frac{1}{2}$in. longer than measure, to allow for squaring and cutting of the right shape.

The bottom diagrams, plate 106, represent the original foundation skirt shown to the tailoring trade by J.F.D.—which is the basis of all more recent cuts. These diagrams show how skirts with a lot of fullness (gatherings or plaits) are cut; also how to provide for fitting over dress-improvers. It will be seen that there are no hollowings taken out at waist.

The skirt cutter must remember that skirt pieces must be laid down as per dias. OX's, plate 106, with the waist of each piece on a perfectly level line, to know how the drapery (spring) has been distributed, unless the waist plane of the customer is tilted either upwards or downwards iu front, when the parts must be laid correspondingly to see how they or the skirt will hang. If not right, it must be altered so that it will balance (hang) right. For a waist plane tilted upwards in front, it amounts to the same thing as lowering behind and letting out at bottom, as raising cannot take place in front if there are no outlets upwards

Lines OO are the crease lines or front edges, and X X the biassed or cut edges, in each case. The exception of the front edges of dias. 3, 2, 1, plate 106, projecting forward of lines OO, is caused by placing mistermed hollowed waists on square top lines. There is no such thing as a hollowed waist. When made, the waist is perfectly straight. The apparent hollowness is caused by letting in the wedges of drapery at bottom, and to cover hips (seat). Strain the waist out on the double, and it is straight; and it is quite level when on a well grown figure.

AN ALL-STYLE SKIRT SYSTEM.—Plate 107.

In skirt cutting, seams can be placed anywhere, any number of them. The diagram shows a seven-piece skirt—viz., a sloped front, four side gores, and

two back widths or gores; the intermediate lines
indicating an equal division of the seven-piece skirt
will turn it into a fifteen-piece skirt, clearly evi-
dencing the fact that a skirt can be composed of any

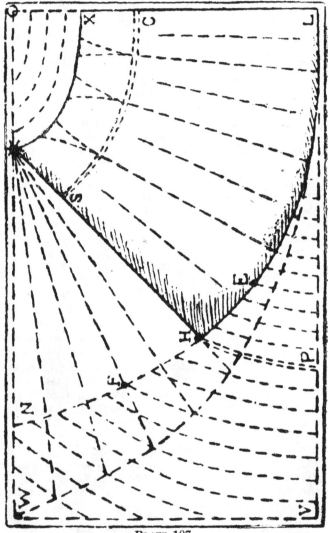

PLATE 107.

number of pieces, from seven to fifteen or upwards.

The narrowest skirt a woman can walk in is three
times the length of her step, exclusive of seams and
the stand-away at back.   This represents a circle

surrounding the length of her step, which is the circle's diameter. This condition is fairly well met by cutting a skirt equal in width to twice its length, or twice the hip width. Whatever the width round bottom may be, the waist must be made wide enough, before reducing it, to allow of the size round the hips and seat being large enough. Thus a straight line drawn for the centre of the back, from the bottom width decided on, must enclose sufficient width from C to S to correspond with the measure at that part or line, no matter what the waist size.

The system of drafting is as follows: After squaring OL, OW; O* is made two thirds and OX one third of CS, to start with, XL the length. LP width of bottom. PH a sweep. Back length applied from * to intersect sweep. From intersection to * a straight line. C to S seat measure and requisite addition. Back centre always runs from H through S after seat width is adjusted. Wherever this line reaches line OW, half the measure from there to O is the depth of CX—which, if not right at the start, can now be corrected, also the length.

As a very wide bottom gives enough width of seat without having to reduce the waist to measure by means of cuts, it follows that the wider the skirt the smaller the cuts, until the no-cuts stage is arrived at.

The front of waist is square with the front line XL for about 3in. in, unless the plane of the figures' waist slants upwards or downwards in front, when corresponding changes are made to the skirt.

Three inches of the back of waist is square with back centre, unless folds of the drapery are to be dropped to and forward of E, or the drapery held well backwards. Lowering at * to nothing at middle cut takes drapery backwards, and raising at * drops it forward. The last may necessitate letting out at H, and the f rmer taking-in at H to nothing at *.

Large and prominent hips need more height at the middle cut than regular figures.

Habit trains can be produced by this method.

The large number of sweeps indicate all widths of skirts round the bottom, and the diagonal straight lines various lengths; while the line from L to W indicates either letting-out at the bottom for any purpose, or training.

VESTS.

TAKING THE MEASURES.—Figs. 1 and 2, Plate 108.

Stand on the right hand side of the customer, and with the left hand place the end of the inch tape at the nape of neck (seventh vertebræ), as at point X, and while holding it there with the left hand, measure with the right hand to the amount of opening required, as from X to V.   Then, still holding the tape at nape of neck with the right hand, measure straight down to bottom of vest point N, or the full length required in front.   Next take the breast and waist measures carefully, not too tight or slack, and also the hip measure if the vest is to be cut long. For an ordinary vest for a 36 breast figure, these measures, when entered in the order book, will stand thus :—

15 25½ 36 32

Such are the measures required to be taken for an ordinary shaped vest.   For vests to button close up to the throat, apply the tape from the nape to any point on the actual breast line, such as from X to V. Then, whilst holding it firmly fixed there, to let go the end of the tape from the nape of the neck, and with it measure backwards, as from V up to the gorge or point of opening required.   By this mode of measurement, a certain number of inches from the end of the tape will fall upon the point of opening ; only these need be entered in the order book, as the tape can be applied in the same way in drafting.

HOW TO DRAFT BY THE VEST SYSTEM.

Diagram 1. Plate 108.

The foundation of the system is the same for vests as for coat cutting, the sectional parts or divisions being obtained in the manner explained in Table I, page 55.   Thus the total height divided by 8 to find the head height, and the head height or waist length used to find depth points.   The waist length can be got by measure, or as explained by the table.

O B and X N may be made either one-sixth waist length and a seam, or one-third the head height and a seam.   O C and X D half the waist length and a seam, or B C and N D two-thirds of the head height and ¾in.   Width of back top one-eighth breast and ½in, or one-sixth neck and two seams.   N H and D Z half breast, and E F 2½in, or to line H Z a third of breast and $2\frac{1}{2}$, and front of scye half breast and $2\frac{1}{2}$, H A one-third and $\frac{1}{2}$in, or O A a fourth of the breast. NB and DC, or vice versa, the breast measure and $1\frac{1}{2}$in. The opening and length to measure; $\frac{3}{4}$in, 1in, or $1\frac{1}{4}$in out at G; and $1\frac{1}{2}$in, less or more, out at K,

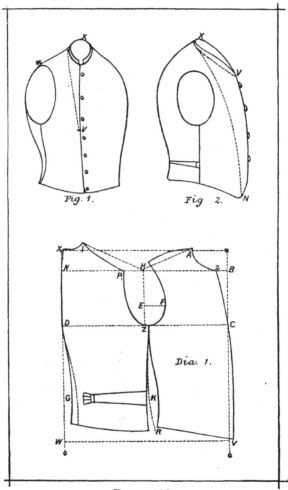

Fig. 1.   Fig 2.

Dia. 1.

PLATE 108.

according to figure. Rise at R $2\frac{1}{2}$, or as required. The waist as well as breast only $1\frac{1}{2}$in instead of 2in more than net measure. C 2 to run with V C. All styles of front, of every description, to be allowed in front of line 2 C V. As will be seen, the scale of depth can be as easily got as the width scale.

FOREPART OR BACK SEPARATELY.

Diagrams 1 and 2, Plate 109.

It is as easy to draft the parts separately as under one; thus A C, B K, and X N half the breast. CW the same line as C N, 1 to 2 2½in. Total width in

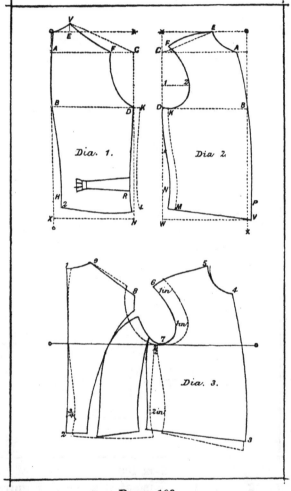

PLATE 109.

B D, D B, the breast measure and 1½. Either part can be reduced, as shown by the dotted line KM, in case of shortage of material, and the difference added to the other part as per line K L.

Vests from Coat Bodies.—Dia. 3, Plate 109.

In cutting vests from coats, the best plan is to draw line OO, and lay the coat body with its bottom of scye line on it, and mark all round it barring the side and underarmseams. Take up the coat, and alter from its outlines by taking 1in out round the scye front, and 1in off at 8 to nothing at bottom of scye; then reduce breast width $\frac{1}{2}$in under arm, taking 2in out at waist if $1\frac{1}{2}$in is the proper quantity to come out, and $\frac{3}{4}$in at the back of waist if that is the amount to come out there, being guided by the figure or the coat suppressions. If the coat is suppressed 3in, the vest will stand the same or $\frac{1}{2}$in less suppression; so that if $1\frac{1}{2}$ comes out at sideseam and $1\frac{1}{2}$ under arm, $\frac{3}{4}$in at back and $1\frac{3}{4}$in under arm can come out of vest; and for 2in and 1in in coat, 1in at back and $1\frac{1}{2}$in under arm of vest. Generally speaking, $\frac{1}{4}$in can come off at 1 and be added at 9. The neckpoint 5 can be advanced $\frac{1}{4}$in, or not.

Back Under Forepart.—Dia 1, Plate 110.

After squaring O E and O X, the depth O C is made one-sixth waist length, or one-third the head height and a seam; O E half the waist length or the whole head height and $\frac{3}{4}$in. O B by one fourth breast; C D, E F, and G N by half the breast and $\frac{3}{4}$in. Z W sufficient to make E F and Z W together half the breast and $2\frac{1}{2}$in. The shoulder line is drawn from B to D, the length applied from B to G, the rise from 5 to 6 to taste. $\frac{3}{4}$in. is taken out at side of waist.

O A is one-eighth and $\frac{1}{2}$in., A 1 $\frac{3}{4}$in., 1 3 same as B4. A $\frac{1}{4}$in. is taken off at O, nothing at E, and $\frac{3}{4}$in to 1in., or to figure, at back of waist. The waist measure would be made up at 9 in drafting the forepart, minus such reductions in the waist suppressions as decided on beforehand.

The operation of the system is, in short, precisely the same in drafting with back under forepart as with back against forepart.

Sleeve Vests.—Dias. 2 and 3, Plate 110.

The system is applied in the same manner for these as for all other vests, except in the case of over-vests, when the widths needed are the same as in a coat. The shoulders and scyes of all sleeve

vests need to be cut like a coat—shoulders as broad
as the figure can carry, and scyes as close up round
the arms as possible, so as to avoid sleeves dragging.
When a sleeve vest is cut long, it must have ample

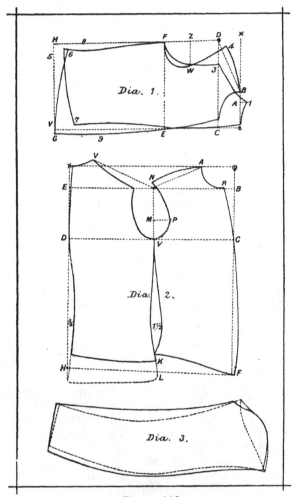

PLATE 110.

spring over the hips, where it should be cut easy to
measure.

All sleeves for vests can be cut by coat sleeves.
The changes in form from the coat sleeve are shown
by the dotted lines of dia. 3 — viz., more height at
top of fore and backarmseams, a less hollowed-out

underside sleevetop, and less width at hand and
higher up. The reduction at elbow should be made
at front seam, and at hand at backseam. The extra
height of forearm is to make it more like a shirt
sleeve, and to prevent discomfort or crampiness in
wearing it under a coat, or in hard labour. In an
over-sleeve vest, the coat sleeve will often answer
admirably, without making any changes in it, unless
it be in the widths at elbow and hand.

THE VARIOUS STYLES OF FRONTS.

Diagrams 1 to 10, Plate III.

After drafting a vest to net size, to seam up the
front, every kind of style is a matter of overlap or
change from the seaming-up net size ; the amount
of opening or height of gorge being another matter,
yet still relating to style. The dotted lines of dias.
1 to 10 represent the front of a vest drawn out to
net size, the XX line being the actual breast or net
size front line. To turn a vest so drawn into an SB
vest of any kind, $\frac{3}{4}$in. is added in front of this line ;
to turn a net size draft into a DB, such a quantity
as 3½ at breast and 2½ at bottom is added, varying
in amount according to the style and form of button-
over required. A cassock vest is only a DB buttoning over almost or quite to the sideseam.

Dia. 1 shows how to change the net size vest into
an SB Prussian collar style, with a gorge of only
3in. or 3½in. in depth, and a neck cut to size. Dia.
2 shows how to change into an S B stand collar
clerical vest, gorge same height and neck to measure,
as in the case of the Prussian collar style. The full
length measure, and the measure back from the full
length to gorge, will find the height of gorge correctly, and the neck measure its size. Dia. 3 shows
how the V-opening clerical vest is formed ; dia. 4
how the jockey vest with stand collar growing-to is
formed ; dia. 5 the step collar style ; dia. 6 another
style of step collar ; dia. 7 the roll collar style ; dia.
8 the low-roll collar, or old-fashioned dress vest ;
dia. 9 the no-collar style ; dia. 10 the DB style with
or without turns and fall collars.

Here it may be well to remark that the turns of
vests are often wrongly called lapels. Possibly it
may be because it is impossible to say rolls or rolling, lest it should carry a wrong meaning. Certainly

most people would understand by 'DB roll collar vest,' simply a front like dia. 8, only DB.

When a vest is not to have a collar, the neck must be filled up to the extent of the depth of a collar-stand.

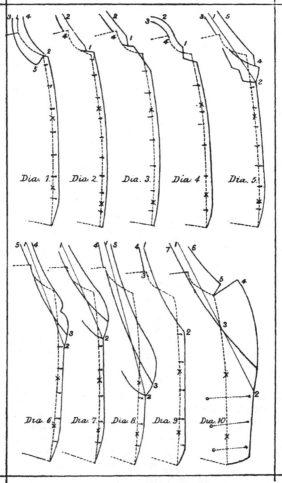

PLATE 111.

Any style of DB can be produced according to the manner indicated by dia. 10, high or low buttoning, or with more or less curved openings, with laid-on, without collars, or with sewn-on collars.

The lines 1 2 in every case represent the top edge of collar, whether it be stand or crease. A Prussian collar is formed more or less curved in its leaf edge, and its stand worked out until it will lie flat on the leaf. Stand collars give less trouble in making up when just the right degree of roundness is given to the sewing-on edge to bring the top edge close to the neck. Roll collars and step collars are best cut fairly straight for high-buttoning vests, and a little more crooked for lower openings.

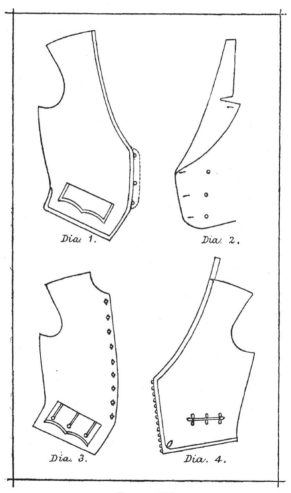

PLATE 112.

FULL-DRESS LIVERY VEST.

Dia. 1, plate 112, shows the form in which a full

dress livery vest is cut, having only a catch sewn to the right front, with eyes coming out through the seam. These are always cut long, after the style worn in the age of Louis XV. ; this arrangement is for the purpose of showing the lace on both the front edges.

Dia. 2 shows how the best of all styles of gents' DB vests look when made up. It is the most suitable for wearing with DB frock.

Dia. 3 illustrates the form in which a vest to wear with a Scotch doublet or Highland kilt suit is cut and finished.

Dia. 4 shows the form in which a military dress vest is usually cut. Sometimes, however, it closes all the way up to the neck, and at others is merely a button-three roll-collar dress vest, worn with a stand-collar Spencer mess jacket, or with a Spencer cut like a roll-collar Eton jacket.

CASSOCK VESTS.—Plate 113.

There are two forms of clerical cassock vests worn by clergymen ; the one style is shown by dia. 1, and the other by dia. 2. The form shown by dia. 1 buttons right over to the sideseam, runs round the front of scye, and buttons by the shoulderseam. It can also be cut as per dotted line 6, to fasten at the side of the neck and down the sideseam.

The style shown by dia. 2 fastens at the side of neck, point 4, and with a fly down through 12 to 3, the right side being cut as per dot-and-dash line. The right side of dia. 1 is formed in the same way.

The easiest way to produce a cassock vest of any description is to take the forepart of an ordinary vest marked out to the net size — i.e., without any overlap or style allowed on it in front of the actual size or breast line X X ; and to mark lines on it indicating the outline, form and position over to which the large forepart is wanted to button, as for example, line 4 12 3, or 4 3 2 1. Then fold a piece of paper on the double. and lay the actual breast line X X of the net size forepart on its crease edge, and mark all round it ; also mark through all by means of a wheel or the thumb-nail, along the line 4 12 3, or 4 3 2 1, so that it will be visible when the net size pattern is taken up, and when the paper is unfolded. If the style being produced is of the form shown by dia. 2, when the paper is opened out an

outline, partly in chalk and partly in thumb-nail
dent, will appear on it as per dia. 2, the lapel portion 6 7, brought out from underneath, being the
part showing the lapel marked by the thumb-nail
right through the lot. As the thumb-nail mark will
also appear at line 4 12 3, it will serve as a very

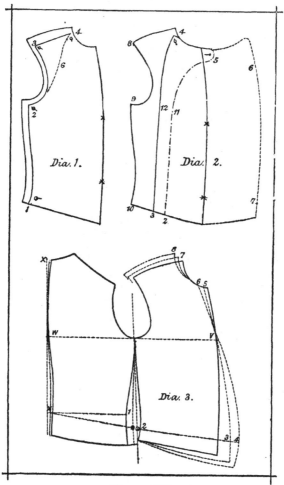

PLATE 113.

good guide by which to form the small side of vest
2 11 5 4, by telling the operator how much to allow
for underlap or catch, and showing how to form it,
almost as clearly as a teacher of cutting could tell
him how to do so.

VESTS FOR CORPULENT FIGURES.
Dia, 3, Plate 113.

In the absence of any other information than con-
veyed in the lengths, and breast and waist measures,
⅛in. for every inch of disproportion in the waist can
be distributed between the side and back seams and
the remainder allowed on the front ; and the shoulder crookened and lengthend ⅛in. for every inch of
disproportion. The waist meaeure should be applied
along the line X 2 4, and not straight across ; and it
should be taken round the most prominent part of
the tub, and not above it. There is no reason for
taking two waist measures.

CAPES AND CLOAKS.

INVERNESS CAPES.—Dias. 1 and 2, Plate 114.

The difference between a chesterfield and Inverness back is shown by dia. 1, in dots and inches,
unless the cutter chooses to have a high shoulder,
when the amount the back shoulderseam is risen
from 2 towards K, dia. 2, comes off front shoulderseam 1 towards K ; in short, what the one seam
goes up the other seam comes down, point K being
the highest point of the end of customer's shoulder.
The depth of scye may be carried 4in., 5in. or 6in.
below the level of a coat scye.   In drafting by system, the amount X top of sideseam passes over the
back is 3in. to 4in. The width of forepart at bottom
may be made the same as a chesterfield, ulster, or
more, according to the looseness wanted.

The wing always runs with the front shoulderseam
A 1, whether it is high or low.   The bottom of the
cape is swept from point A, by the measure of the
width of shoulder and length of sleeve from head to
hand, added together.   This measure may be taken
on the customer, or from his coat pattern. Of course
it may be longer if desired.

Dias. 3 and 4 give the form and dimensions of
what has been called the Irish constabulary cloak.
The 5½ at the bottom of dia. 3 is intended for 52,
being an engraver's error. Hooking-in at point F
should be carefully avoided, as it leads to fullness at
point 29—which bagginess is troublesome to get rid
of, once too much is taken off at F, without cutting
new wings.

Dia. 5 reveals the differences in style and widths

between a close-fitting chesterfield forepart and an
Inverness forepart, cut to go with the back dia. 1.
The 8 means from top of sideseam, and not the
level of scye.

Dia. 6 shows how sn Inverness cape with sleeves
is cut—viz., the scye is extended to measure the

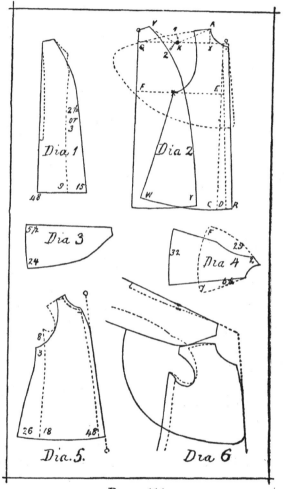

PLATE 114.

amount the back scye measures more than forepart
scye, and then the scye is formed into a hole in the
forepart in making, by jnining the top of sideseam
and end of shoulderseam together by a short seam
formed by blunting their ends as indicated.

SLEEVE INVERNESS.—Dias. 1 and 2, Plate 115,

Exnibit the manner in which an Inverness with sleeves is drawn from a chesterfield—viz., the scye is carried round to back pitch, and the shoulderseam

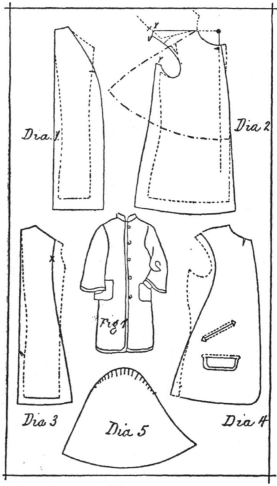

PLATE 115.

is on O X. Point Y is risen the amount the back scye is below pitch, and Y sews to V X.

A close-fitting wing has a V taken out near the end of shoulderseam, as shown by the wing on dia. 2, which wing is for inserting in a shoulderseam risen to the top of shoulder. A close-fitting wing

for dia. 2 would have the V taken out on line OX at
the same distance from neckpoint, and it would be
run from the V straight down to the same point as
the bottom of shoulderseam of wing, shown by dot
and dash lines

STANLEY CAPE.—Fig. 1, Dias. 3, 4, 5, Plate 115.

The figure shows what this cape is like, and the
drafts the form in which the garment is cut from a
chesterfield pattern. The form of the wing is got
by laying the shoulderseams of back and forepart
together, and running it from forearm pitch round
top of scye to any point of the back sideseam, such
as X, continuing the run of hinder part thence
on to full length required; and springing the front
forward from the front pitch almost to the front
edge of forepart. When made, this great front spring
falls or folds in over the front of the arm, as seen in
the illustration fig. 1. The head of the wing should
be rounded over the scye line, the same as the head
of a sleeve placed-to at the fore and back pitches of
a coat, and fulled-in in making.

THE RAIN CAPE.—Dia. 1, Plate 116.

This cape is formed by simply continuing the
sideseam in the run of a shoulderseam placed on the
top of a shoulder. It can be produced from a coat
pattern by shifting the shoulderseams so that they
will come on the top, as per solid lines. The spring
at points P and K may be as ample as desired, or
arranged to produce a less full garment. In any
case point Q should be sprung forward a bit. 2 1 is
the only line of the system that is shown, it being
superfluous to show the others.

THE RAGLAN.—Dias. 2, 3, 4, Plate 116.

Dia. 2 shows how the forepart draft of a chesterfield is altered into the forepart of a Raglan. In
order to get an easy, loose coat, the shoulder is
formed rather round between 1 and 2, and the scye
sunk below the scye line at 3. Dia. 3 shows how
the back draft of a chesterfield is altered into a
Raglan back, the shoulder and back scye as per the
solid line 1, 2, 3. An addition of from 2in. to 5in.
to the width is made at 3, and at least double the
same quantity from 4 to 5. Dia. 4 shows how the
sleeve is formed — viz., the shoulderseams of the

chesterfield are placed together, and the chesterfield sleeve patterns placed with tops of back and forearmseams at back and front pitches : this opens the scye end of the shoulderseam a bit. The front of the Raglan sleevehead is run from 2 to 1, and the back part of its head from 1 through X, to as far as

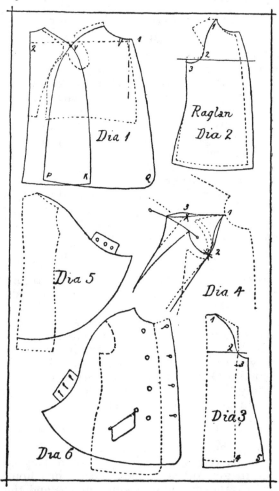

Dia 1

Raglan
Dia 2

Dia 5

Dia 4

Dia 6

Dia 3

PLATE 116.

top of sideseam of the back is below the back pitch. The hindarm is sprung out from the ordinary sleeve to this point, and underside hooked-in a corresponding quantity. The forearm may be without a seam, as solid line. In the old style Raglan, the only seam was under the arm, and joined to the top of under-armseam of coat, both starting at the armpit.

THE OLD GERMAN ARMY TALMA.
Diagrams 5 and 6, Plate 116.

These diagrams show how this ancient garment can be produced. The shoulderseam can be risen on to the top of the wearer's shoulder, as indicated by dia. 5, taking the same amount off the front shoulder slope. This garment forms a sort of shawl or dolman over the arms, the buttons and holes showing it.

THE ANCIENT BRITISH TALMA.
Diagrams 1 and 2, Plate 117.

The quantities shown on these diagrams are inches, and will produce a garment for any ordinary size. Readers will be able to discern in its formation the germs of the somewhat later Talma that went by the name of Raglan recently. The wing part forms a sort of open bell sleeve; and the old Raglan sleeve was bell-shaped too, only it went completely round the arm instead of only over it. It cannot be said that it had an underside, for it was all in one. It will be seen that this garment is very similar to the Stanley, which perhaps ought to have been named Talma.

A MODERN STANLEY.—Dia. 3, Plate 117.

Being somewhat similar to an Inverness, this garment is shown as produced from an Inverness pattern. The bottoms of sideseams are placed together, and the back scye is made to start from the measure of the forepart sideseam up from the bottom, and in form as per the solid line, in place of as per the Inverness dotted sideseam. The wing is all in one from the centre of back to front, its back shoulder being formed the same as the shoulder ot back, and its overarm part extending forward much after the form of the wing part of the Talma, without there being any side or backseam.

THE SYRIAN MANTLE.—Dia. 4, Plate 117.

Square 3 4 and 3 2 1. Mark 4½in. each way from 3, and curve the gorge. Find 2 at 31½in. from 3, and square down to 5. Find the centre of back at 64in. from 3, and square down to 6 say 52in. to 54in.; the length in front is about 3in. shorter, and at the side about 6in. shorter still. This cloak is for travelling, and has a Prussian collar and hood like dia 6.

Dia. 5 shows how an ordinary gents' hood is formed, the numerals being inches. A hood can be produced by the quantities shown.

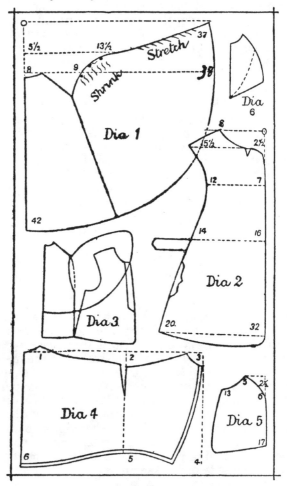

PLATE 117.

HALF-CIRCLE CAPE.—Dia. 1, Plate 118.

The system is applicable for these in practically the same manner as for coats, either by measure or division. By division ED is one-sixth waist length, DC one-third breast and from 3½in. to 4in. instead

of 3, because of its being worn over the coat or
the overcoat. E F is one-eighth the breast and
1in., or one-sixth the neck and ½in. The back
neckpoint is risen ¾in. above F and the shoulderseam drawn to C. D C is square with the back

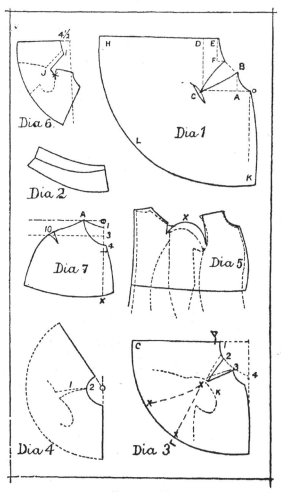

PLATE 118.

centre, and C A square with D C. C O is the same
width as DC. Angle C is the pivot from which FB
is swept, to make C B the same length as back
shoulderseam. OB is one-fourth the breast and ½in.,
or one-third the neck, A B the front shoulder slope
the same as the back shoulder slope, while the

excess of size to go round the neck comes out between the back and front neckpoints. The customer may be measured in E D, D C, and C O, or right round the shoulder-ends; and round the neck, and D C and C O, each made a quarter the all-round measure. A complete square of this measure can be drawn by continuing D E above E, and meeting it by line KO, as in the case of dia. 3. Length EH is of course to measure. F L is the same length and BK about ½in. longer.

Dia. 2. The Prussian form of collar is mostly used on these capes, but stand collars are used on policemen's and other capes.

DRAFTING CAPES FROM COATS.

Dia. 3, Plate 118.

Square the angle lines 4 and V; then humour the back and forepart of the coat so that they will lie within the angle as shown by the dotted lines, the back centre on the back line, and the front centre against the front line 4. Mark the cape shoulder-seams forward to solid lines from 2 and 3 to X. Lower the back top ½in., and sweep 2 3 either by pivot X or the angle point. The bottom can be swept by the angle point, or got as per dia. 1.

To make this cape without a backseam it is sometimes necessary to cut it through from X at shoulder to the bottom; to make it closer-fitting, as much or as little may be taken out between X and X at the bottom to nothing at X at shoulder-end as necessary —see dotted lines. It can also be made closer-fitting in the way shown by dia. 6.

Diagram 6 shows the forepart of coat swung backwards by pivot X, thus opening out a V to be cut out. By this means the width round the bottom is reduced, and the front shoulder brought back to meet the back shoulder. The shoulderseam is risen to I and J, and the forepart dropped if shoulder-end 3 X is to be fulled into scye side of V.

THREE-QUARTER CIRCLE CAPE.

Dia. 4, Plate 118.

These are produced by placing forepart and back as shown, open at the scye end, instead of neck end of shoulderseam. The bottom can be swept from O.

THE PUFFED SHOULDER-END CAPE.

Dia. 5, Block 118.

These capes have only been worn by females.
They can be cut by laying the sleeve between back
and forepart, as per dotted lines, and marking the

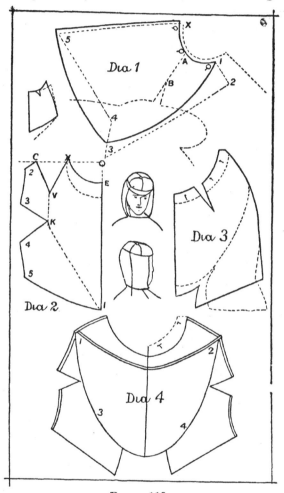

PLATE 119.

cape as per solid lines, high or low at X, according
to the amount the puffings are to stand up.

Dia. 7 shows practically the same system as dia.
1 in a condensed form—back under forepart—the
bottom width being reduced on the same principle

as shown in dia. 3, and a V taken out across the shoulder-end. O to 1 is ¾in., and then all points found as per dia. 1, A4 being one-third of neck, and O 4 about 3½in.

HOODS FROM COATS.—Dia. 1, Plate 119.

The easiest way to produce a hood is by the neck of coat. See back and forepart laid as per dotted lines, and form the hood as per the solid lines. The style of hood may be altered as per dotted lines 1, 2, 3, 4, 5, to enable it to be made up to look quite differently, and more fanciful. This hood can also be made up as small diagram, with a V out of neck, by closing the shoulderseam of coat at scye and opening it at neck ; and it can be cut more pointed as dots. A plain hood is like a monk's cowl. The dotted line hood is more for the lady.

HOODS BY SYSTEM.—Dia. 2, Plate 119.

O E one-third neck 5½, O X half neck 8, O C 11in. E1 the crease 17in. Turn the edge 5, 4, 3, 2, C, over on the underside, at the line X V K 1 ; and cut off, on the double, from X to V. Next form C2 as per dotted line below X, and take out the surplus length as per cut 3 and 4 to the crease at K ; when 4 5 will form the remainder of the dotted line, high or low at the centre of back according as point 5 is sprung more or less outwards before turning the piece that is bounded by the lines K 1 5 4 K over at line K 1.

Dia. 3, plate 119, shows how the one half of a hood with its bottom point cut off looks on the flat. Its bottom looks more like the line running round from 3 to 4, dia. 4, when made up. Cut square with the centre of back crease line, as per dotted line, with nothing taken out, this hood can be easily turned into a cap-hood, similar to the small back and front view ladies' heads with this new invention on them illustrate.

Dia. 4, shows how the hood is cut and looks laid on the flat before the bottom and the cuts are sewn up, and the elastic or drawing-string is put into the double line edges, which in the end become the line 1 2 continued up to the neck, and is more or less drawn according to fashion.

CLERICAL VESTMENTS.

THE system is applied to all these garments, which are of a plain-fitting or coat form, in the same manner as to coats.

CASSOCKS.—Figs, and Dias. Plate 120.

Dia, 1 shows the most general form of cassock. It is cut like a close-fitting, button-to-the-throat SB

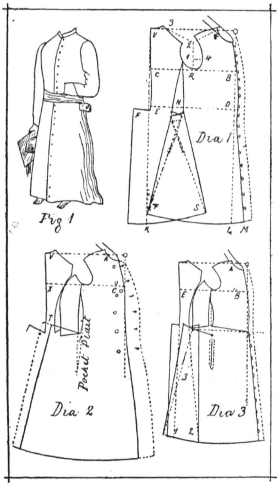

PLATE 120.

clerical lounge or chesterfield, skirts wide with big back centre plait, and heavy plaits from sideseams.

Pockets in the plaits. The back plait may be 4in.,
the width of side plait the same at top, the width at
bottom in K S and M F combined 36in. for the 36
breast figure, length about 50. As stated, the draft
down to the waist may be made by button-to-throat
lounge.

Fig. 1—a pen and ink sketch—delineates the style
of a High-church cassock.

Dia. 2 shows how the Broad-church DB cassock
is cut — viz., like an old-style Paletot, only DB
closing to the throat, and considerably wider in the
skirts. The pocket goes in the plait which is formed
at the bottom of underarmseam. The total width
at the bottom of a 50in. cassock, 36 breast, not
measuring plaits and lapel, 40in.

Dia. 3 shows how the frock cassock is cut. It is
made long and full in the skirts as indicated, and
can be cut from from a clerical frock coat, allowing
more width in skirts.

CARDINAL'S AND BISHOP'S CASSOCKS.

Figure and Diagrams, Plate 121.

The pen and ink sketch B depicts the style of a
cardinal's cymata. It is cut as per dias. 1, 2, 3, 4,
5, and 6. It is twice 26in. wide at the bottom, exclusive of back plait and amount in front of buttons.
The figures on these diagrams are inches, from
which the full-size pattern can be produced with the
aid of the system.

Bishops' cassocks are cut the same as cardinals',

It will be seen that a cassock is not always called
a cassock. When worn by Catholic orders, monks,
&c., it goes by the name of tala. It is true there is
some slight difference in the form, and so the difference of names may be justified; though from a cutter's standpoint, they are all one and the same
thing.

PRIESTS' SOUTANES.—Dias. 7 and 8, Plate 121.

Priests' soutanes, dias. 7 and 8, are cut like cassocks, and made in black cloth for street wear. In
the United Kingdom they usually have sidebodies.
The 20 width at the bottom of back includes the
back and sideseam plaits.

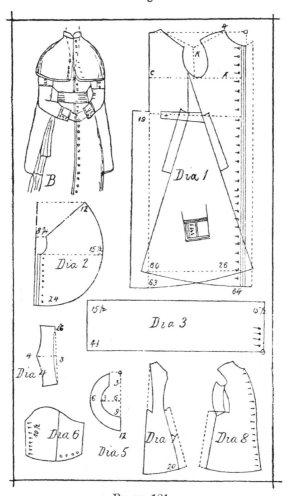

PLATE 121.

TALA FOR CATHOLIC ORDERS, MONKS, ETC.

Fig. C, and Dias. 1 and 2, Plate 122.

Sketch C shows what this garment is like made up, and dias 1 and 2 its shape flat on the cutting board. It is, in short, similar to an SB clerical full sac overcoat with cape. Numerals 47 and 24 give about its usual length and width at bottom of back, and 28 its width at bottom of forepart. It will be seen that the system can be used to produce it in the same way as an ordinary chester or ulster.

THE CONTINENTAL VERGER'S OR CHURCH SERVANTS' GOWN.—Dias. 3 to 6, Plate 123.

The total length is about 53. O 2 is square with OK. The slope of shoulder is $2\frac{1}{2}$, and depth of scye 12. The widths of back are, at top O 2 $16\frac{1}{2}$, across

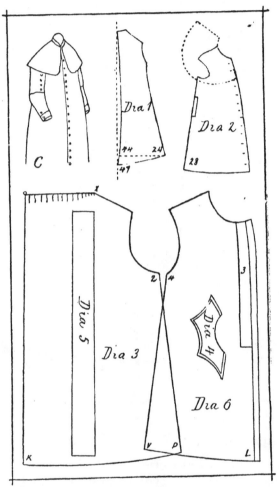

PLATE 122.

to shoulder point $21\frac{1}{2}$, across to top of sideseam 26, and to bottom of sideseam $29\frac{1}{2}$.

The widths of forepart are about $4\frac{1}{2}$ straightness, width to shoulderpoint $10\frac{3}{4}$, across to top of side-seam 14, and to bottom of ditto 22. The slope of front shoulder and depth of scye are 2½ and 12. The wing, dia. 5, is 53 long and 5½ wide. The collar is cut as per dia. 4, its top edge to fit the neck, and its bottom edge scolloped as shown. Its depth is about 4½in.

DALMATICA.—Fig. 1, Plate 123.

Fold the goods as if about to cut a shirt, or draw a line down right through its centre, and square a

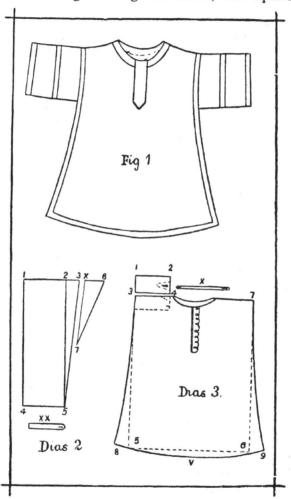

PLATE 123.

short line across the top. Mark across 4in. for side of neck, down 2in. and 4in for the back and front of

neck, and about 39 for full length. The shoulder-
ends are exactly level with the back of neck, and
hence 2in. below the level of neckpoints or side of
neck; the shoulder is 6in. wide, or 10 from centre
line. The depth of scye is 15½, and the width at
that level 11½ and at the bottom 15½. The sleeve is
about 14in. along its top, and about 13 under the
arm. 2in. taken from 15½ of course makes the armhole 13½ in depth. The opening comes about level
with the bottom of armhole. In fact, the whole
process is just like cutting a shirt or chemise, and
equally simple and primitive. The bottom is
rounded 2in.

ALUMNEN OR CATHOLIC CHORAL AND ALTAR BOYS' DRESS.—Dias, 2 and 3, Plate 123.

Choir boys in the Established Church wear what
is called the short round surplice. Catholic choir
boys' dress is much shorter. Dias. 2 and 3 delineate
the form or cut of vestment for alumnen, &c. The
whole width at the top of shoulders is about 24, and
at the bottom 3½ each side, or 7in. more. It can be
cut by folding the material down the centre, and
marking off 25in.; then forming the neck after the
manner of a sailor blouse neck, leaving the shoulders
7in. wide. 14 out of 24 leaves 10 neck opening, or
5 from the centre to side of neck. The shoulders
are quite square, and the whole garment merely a
straight piece of material, with the exception of the
3½in. of spring added outside of 5 and 6. The bottom is rounded a little as shown. The sleeve is
composed of a piece of straight goods 24 long and 20
wide, folded at line 1 4, from 1 to 2 and 4 to 5 being
10in. 2in. more adds the first gusset or spring 2 to
3; the gusset X to 6 is about 4in. wide at the top,
and 12 long. The opening and the etceteras being
all shown nothing more needs adding concerning it.

VARIOUS VESTMENTS.—Figs. 1 to 6, Plate 124.

Fig. 1 shows the vesper mantle, worn by priests
at the elevation of the Host; fig. 2 shows the dal-
matica in wear; fig. 3 shows casula on wearer;
fig. 4 the reverend with his white body-belt; fig. 5
the acolyte; fig. 6 the evangelical gown.

A vesper mantle is merely a piece of broad-cloth,
about 80in. long, opened out to its full extent;

then a neck dent made in the centre of the one side of it, about 4½ in depth by 13 in width; then the length made about 56in., and the bottom made circular in form by rounding off the two bottom corners of the oblong piece of cloth. Practically

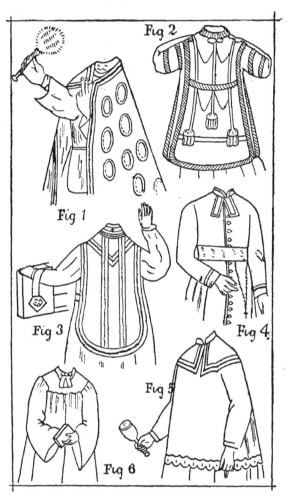

PLATE 124.

speaking, it is about the same thing as a full half-circle, with a 4½ by 13 half-circle neck-hole, in its straight edge; so that anyone who can cut what is called a circular cape can cut one of these without any difficulty or bother.

THE ALBA. — Dias, 1 and 2, Plate 125.

The back and front of the alba are cut as per dia.
2, about 44in. long, and 24in. wide from 4, 8, 3, to
2, 1, 5. The extra widths for gathering at 5, 6, and
8, 9, are about 4½in., widening out to about 6½in. at

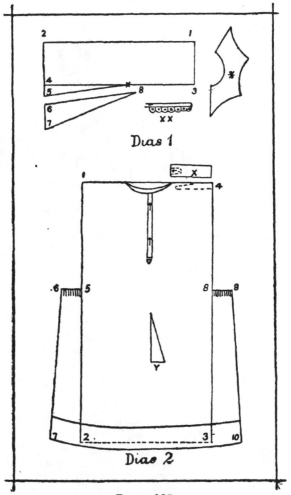

Dias 1

Dias 2

PLATE 125.

the bottom. There is an opening at centre of front
like a shirt, about 12in. deep, and the neck is formed
as shown, hollowed out about 2½in. in front and ¾in.
behind.

The alba can also be drafted out either by the shirt

·or sailor's blouse diagrams or systems.

The sleeve, dia. 1, is very much like a shirt or sailor's blouse sleeve, pieced out with gussets. The large piece is 24½ long by 9½ wide, exclusive of the gusset parts. The gusset part 5, 4, X, may extend in a straight line from 5 to 3, and be 3in. wide at 5; and the piece 6, 7, 8, be 12 to 13 inches long, and 4½ wide from 6 to 7. The cuff, dia. XX, is a needle-work affair, about 4½ on the half. The bottom of the sleeve is gathered into it, and the top into a scye of about 13in. in depth. As the sleevehead is 17½, this will about 4½ or 9in. in all, for fulling in over the shoulder.

MASS CLERK'S OR CHURCH BOY'S CASSOCK.
Dia. *, Plate 125.

This diagram represents the cape or collar, which is about 16in. deep, and cut in the form shown to fit the neck. The body and sleeve parts are like an ulster or dressing gown, but formed like a man's cassock in front, with a catch, extending to below the waist, and stand collar.

THE CHASUBLE.—Dias. 2 and 3, Plate 126.

The chasuble can be cut by the quantities marked on the diagrams. Before drafting fold the material down its centre to cut on the double.

Dia. 3, the back. O 53 represents the crease. Mark down and across the quantities shown. From O outwards to shoulder strap is 10½in.

Dia. 2, the front. Mark down the crease from X to V 20in., and to O 29in. From X outwards to side at top 4½in., and from V to 1 12in.

ANOTHER STYLE OF CASULA.
Dias. 1 and 4, Plate 127.

The back, dia. 1, can be produced by the quantities shown down the crease line O to 50½, and on the one side. The front, dia. 2, can be produced by the quantities marked down the crease line O to 29½, and on the one side of it. From the crease line to top of side is 6½in.

STOLES.—Dia. 4, Plate 126.

Stoles are cut straight, and about 3½in wide, except at the ends, which may be formed as diagram, or similar to the blade end of a scull—gradually expanded to 7in wide.   Its total length is about 2½yds, less for pulpit, baptizing, and the confessional. The trimming and colours of stoles correspond with those of other vestments.

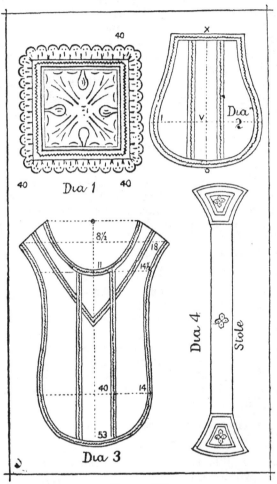

PLATE 126.

THE MANIPLE OR HAND-STOLE

Shown on the left arm of fig. 3 plate 124. is in form the same as the end of another stole ; and is held in place preferably by elastic.

THE VEIL, Dia 1 Plate 126,

Is of the form shown, 16 to 20 inches square, elaborately embroidered, or with cross in centre of the lower half.

THE BURSA, Dia 2 Plate 127,

A wallet-receptacle, of the form shown by the diagram, 8in square, with cross below its centre and opening left at the top.

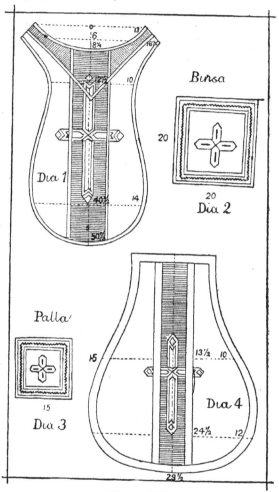

PLATE 127.

THE PALLA, Dia 3 Plate 127,

Is made of fine white linen, interlined with cardboard or stiff material, and is 6in square with cross below its centre.

The colours used for vestments are red, white, purple, green, old gold and black—the latter for requiem mass, and the others for feast days.

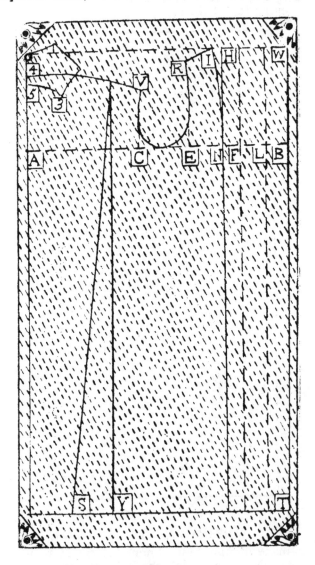

PLATE 128.

High mass Catholic vestments are always very elaborate and costly, and naturally more so in rich than in poorer churches.

MONK'S HOOD (Benedictine Order).
Plate 129.
This hood can be produced from the quantities
marked on the diagram. Facings and seams are all
indicated, also crease when hood is made. A stand
collar is sewn on the neck.

ROBES AND GOWNS.

COLLEGE OR CAMBRIDGE GOWN.—Plate 128.

Yoke 4in deep behind, point 5 another inch lower,
width of bottom 3 and of neck 3½, slope 2. OA half
breast and 3in, length 54 or to measure ; 5V and AC
one-third breast and 7in ; A E half breast and 13in ;
AB breast measure and 18in ; YS 6½in for spring.
The widths from back centre to VC, RE, HN, and
WB can each be increased 2, 4, 6 or more inches to
get a fuller back. Generally one width folded will
do for whole back, and one for each forepart, with a
quarter width sloped off from nothing to all, added
for spring. In making, B folds back to F, L to N,
and F back over N. The sleeve like barrister's,
preacher's, or municipal.

PREACHER'S GOWN. — Plate 129,

Take college gown pattern and cut off the front
shoulder from P to 8; and add the depth RP and the
width RI to back yoke as shoulder-strap extension.
To produce the sleeve, 8 to 9 is 2in, and 9 to O 1½in.
Line O through B to U is the front and crease. PO
and as dots from O to X is the head and fullness,
PXK the hole to fit the front part of scye, and XK4
the underside to sew to scye part X Q V. Spring
from 5 to 6 1oin at 24in down from K. In making,
the back is fluted into bottom of yoke, and sleevehead into over-shoulder end of yoke and strap, as
indicated by shading.

PROTESTANT OR EVANGELICAL GOWN.
Plate 130.

This gown is cut much after the manner of a long
shirt, only with a deeper yoke. It can be produced
from the quantities marked on dias. 1 and 3, except
the yoke, which can be marked out by the back and
front shoulders of a coat joined together at the
shoulderseam, making its depth in front reach to
about 1in. above the forearm pitch point, and its

depth behind to come level with front depth. See
dia 2.

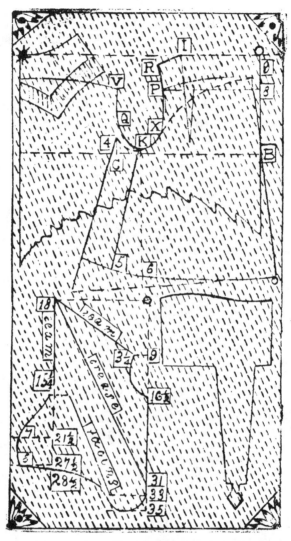

PLATE 129.

VERGER'S GOWNS

Can be cut like barrister's or Cambridge gown, with
sleeve like barrister's, cut square off just above the
elbow, from which depends a long tapering pendant.

with short neck and diamond-shape piece at the
lower end, reaching nearly to bottom of gown, as
the diagram on plate 129.

STUDENTS' GOWNS,
Worn at various institutions other than Oxford and
Cambridge, are cut similar to preacher's, Cambridge

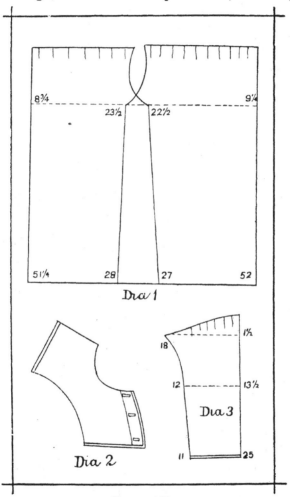

Dia 1

Dia 2

Dia 3

PLATE 130.

or barrister's gowns; with barrister's, preacher's,
municipal or other form of sleeve, according to the
custom of the college.

SACRISTANS' GOWNS
Are cut similar to verger's, only with round clerical

collarless neck, held together by cords and tassels. at neck. The sleeve can be cut like a barrister's or preacher's, only shorter and less voluminous.

BAPTIZING GOWNS

Are cut either like students' gowns, or with yoke in.

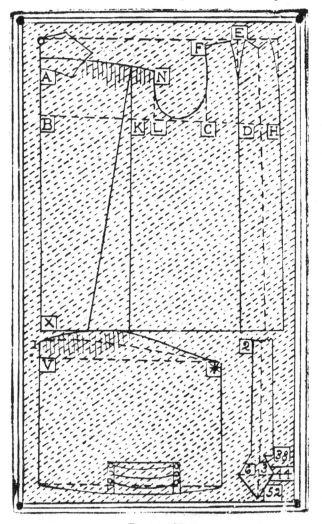

PLATE 131.

front as well as back, like a shirt, with stand collar, fastening down the front with twenty-four buttons. The sleeve is like a very full shirt sleeve gathered.

into wristband, a la bishop's or evangelical sleeve.

BAR GOWNS. — Plate 131.

K.C.'s silks and barrister's stuff gowns being the same in form, the same system answers for both. O A 3½, to B half breast and 3in, length to measure. Width of back neck 3¾, bottom of yoke 3½, shoulder 4 and slope 2. Width of AN and BL 24, BD 47, DC and EF 6in. 2in cut out at E. Spring 6½. The backward overlap or hem DH 5 or 6, or 2½ to 3 folded, can be cut on or sewn on. Seam E D must be arranged to come underneath hem.

The sleevehead is twice the scye measure in width, X V a fourth scye, X I an inch, length of sleeve 33 ; the scye being 33, X* is 33 and same at bottom

Of 27in Russell cord, one width cuts the whole back and 1¼ width for each forepart, the quarter-width being sloped off from nothing at top to 6½ at bottom. The purse can be produced by the amounts shown on the small diagram.

JUDGE'S ROBE. — Plate 132.

O V 3in, O D a fourth and 6in, length to measure. O I one-eighth breast and ½in, width of back to measure. Sideseam is got by half breast on scye line and 3in more on waist line. C X is 9in all the way down. Neckpoint 1½ above I.

D C half breast and 3in, D B the breast and 2in. B to line *P 2½in, * to A one-fourth breast. Depth of gorge 3½, and an inch off front of neck to nothing at breast. From line K B to N the waist or breast measure Front shoulder the same width as back ; shoulder sloped 1½. PQ one-fourth scye, PO whole scye, O R 1¼, the extra width for fulling into space of 3½ starting at 2in from shoulderseam. Underside hooked-in to the measure of underside of scye. Sleevehand 11. The collar, 38 by 55, can be cut by the quantities marked on its outline below bottom of scye line on the back.

MUNICIPAL ROBES. — Plate 133.

A robe that will do for almost any man can be cut from the quantities marked on diagrams. The three-cornered piece O to 5 and 5 forms part of the stole, when turned back to shoulderseam. The sleeve length is 40, width of head 15. A 3½in horizontal

cut across the crease, with a right-angled cut at
its end, is made to form a hole with over-lappet for
the arm to come out through. In making, after
seaming up the forearm, seam X X is flattened out
on to crease edge 40, and X becomes the sides; and

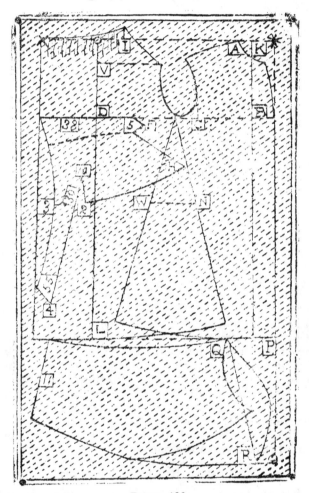

PLATE 132.

is seamed across the bottom in this position. For
yoke the back is shortened 2½, and the yoke cut 6in
deep, 9½ along bottom edge, 6 scye part, 7 shoulderseam and 3½ neck, the neckpoint rising 1in. In shape
it is similar to barrister's yoke, but its bottom edge
is horizontal.

LIST OF GOWN WEARERS.

Gowns are worn by clerics of the M.A. and B.A.
status; clerks and apparitors, graduates and under-
graduates at the Universities of Oxford, Cambridge,
Dublin, Durham, Edinburgh, Glasgow, London and

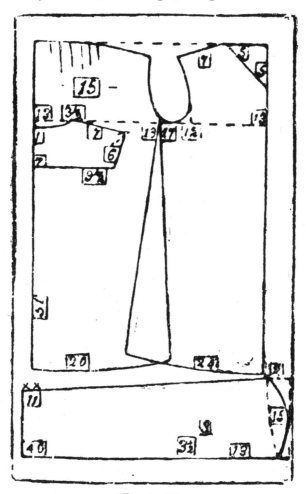

PLATE 133.

King's College; students or collegians, dignitaries
and heads of colleges; preachers, Protestant,
Evangelical. Geneva, Moravians, Scotch, sheriff's
chaplains, and by baptizing ministers; vergers, sacristans, sextons, beadles, &c.; K.C.'s and barristers,

Scotch advocates, town clerks, lawyers, sword and macebearers, &c.

Robes are worn by kings and queens, peers, judges, lord mayors, Scotch provosts, mayors, aldermen, councilmen, serjeants-at-arms, chancellors of universities, &c.

How to Form Pipings.

The thing to attain in the pipings is to give a full round appearance, which can be done by first baisting a piece or thin firm tweed on the backside; and then starting from the end of the piece to be gathered, with three needles each threaded with double thread, to take three rows, one with each needle, right across, of short stitches on the upper side and longer ones below, each exactly under one another, and almost $\frac{1}{2}$in. apart. Having run the threads, then draw them up, all at once. By this means nice round pipes are thrown up to the topside. Of course the threads must be fastened firmly at each end. Great care must be taken to produce the form of the sleevehead, while still keeping the pipings straight. These suggestions re the pipings will serve for all classes of piped gowns, both clerical and legal, professional, &c.

TROUSERS.

The Measures.—Dia. 1, Plate 134.

The measures to be taken are, the side lengths to knee and full length, the leg length the waist, seat, tight thigh, knee and bottom widths. The hip measure may also be taken, from a chalk mark at side of waist. through the fork to starting point, as indicated by dotted lines SC and SD, dia. 1, pl. 134.

The System of Drafting.—Dia. 1, Plate 134.

Draw lines O O and X X half the seat apart and parallel with each other. From 1 to 2 is the height above natural waistline, 1 to 4 the knee length, and 1 to 3 the side length Square all cross lines with the two perpendicular lines to the points of length marked. Apply the length of leg from V to I, and square I S. If the length to knee has not been taken, the knee line is 1in. to 2in. above half the leg length. The fork width may be adjusted to taste, or made equal to half the fork quantity ; the fork quantity is one-third of tight thigh measure and $1\frac{1}{2}$in. added to-

243

gether. In the case of a 21 tight thigh measure this would be 8½, and I S half of it. P C is half the waist. The sideseam is hollowed or not at knee. 4 to 5 is half the knee; 3 to N about 3½in. always. 3 to Q about 1in. less than half bottom in ordinary

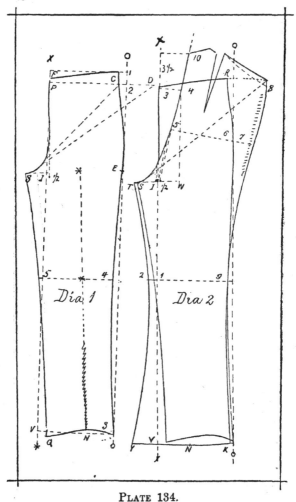

PLATE 134.

cases. 1* half diameter thigh, or one-sixth tight measure. In the case of large bottoms N Q to be ½in. less than X 5, to maintain the proper run of legseam. *N is the shrinking line, also knee width dividing guide. The top of fronts to be lowered from F to P, to taste or fashion.

THE UNDERSIDES.—Dia. 2, Plate 134.

I T is the remainder of the fork quantity, or half of it if I S of the topside was made half. Seams may be added. I W and 3 4 is the seat angle, and may range from $1\frac{1}{2}$ to 3, according to the amount of

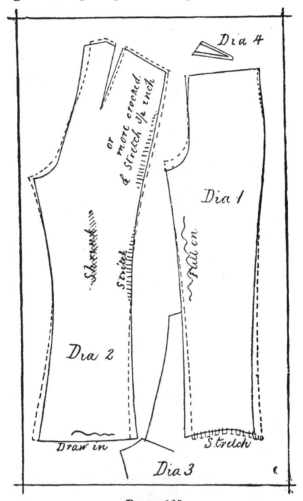

PLATE 135.

wedge intended to be let into seatseam, which should be less for loose and more for tight trousers. The bottom of seat line is found at half the fork back from fork point. The rise behind from 4 to 10 may be made anything from $3\frac{1}{2}$ up. The centre of the

bottom at N is from 2in. to 3in. nearer line XX than
N of the foreside ; the width of underside is divided
equally each side of N.   Seams are allowed at Y
and 2.   5 to 7 is half the seat and 1½ to 2in.   If the
hip measure is available, S C of the foreside is
measured and placed on T, and the full measure
carried out at the side point D, or 8 of the underside
if the trousers does not rise above the point marked
before measuring.   If the application of the hip
measure produces a lot of spring at sideseam, a cut
may be taken out well back where shown.

RIDING TROUSERS.—Dias. 1 and 2, Plate 135.

The dotted lines show the alterations for all kinds
of easy trousers ; the legseam is fulled on over the
prominence at inside of knee, and the top of underside legseam stretched up.   Such manipulations
dispose of the higher forkpoint of foreside, and the
process gives ease in the seat without having to bias
it more.   If biassed more, the sideseam ought to be
stretched up where marked.

SEAT BIASSING OR WEDGING.
Dias. 3 and 4, Plate 135.

By the usual method of cutting, a wedge. extending from seatseam to sideseam, gets let into trousers.
Practical trousers cutters are aware that this is unnecessary and is defect-engendering.   If customers
would be contented, a wedge like dia. 4, let into the
seat where shown by dia. 3, would be sufficient ; and
the closingseam might then be cut almost upright.

STRIPED GOODS AND BELL BOTTOMS.
Dias 1 and 2, Plate 136.

In the case of striped goods the sideseam is left
straight, and all sideseam hollowing taken out of the
sideseam of undersides.   If a sideseam, such as a
military trousers, is to be gold laced, a piece may
be put on at the bottom of foresideseam to nothing
at prominence of hip, and the same amount taken
off the undersideseam.   See dia. 1.

For bell bottoms the changes are shown by dotted
lines of dia. 2—viz., all extra width is divided equally
each side of underside, the width of foreside being
reduced if anything.   The bottom of foreside is
rounded, and the underside hollowed over heel.

The side and legseam of foreside should be hollowed where stretched, also the underside at knee.

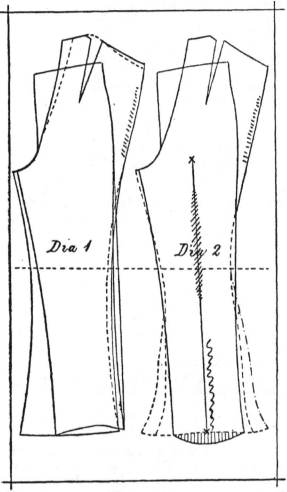

PLATE 136.

TIGHT-SLACKS AND SAILORS' TROUSERS.
Dias 2 and 3, Plate 137.

The small dia. 3 will be sufficient to show how tight-slacks are formed; they are a species of bell bottoms, only cut very tight-fitting at the knee.

As there is no sideseam in sailors' trousers, these have to be cut as shown by dia. 2. E 1 and 8 2 are half seat. 1 to 4 is half fork, and 4 to 5 the other

half of fork. The closingseam is drawn from 5
through 2, or so that 1½ or 2in. of material goes on
from flyseam to seatseam as shown, as an allowance
for making-up and ease. The extra width of bottom
goes on at legseam of underside as shown, point 3

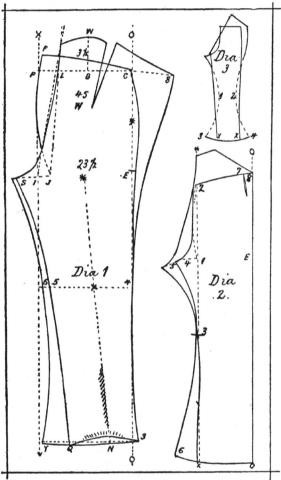

PLATE 137.

being the smallest part of the trousers leg. A cut
is taken out, in fish form, to reduce the waist, as
shown between 7 and 8.

TROUSERS FOR CORPULENT FIGURES.

Dia. 1, Plate 137.

For corpulent men the system is applied in the

same way as for others, only it is advisable to take
a measure frcm centre of fork to top of fronts, by
which to adjust the height to the customer's satis-
faction. Of course the fronts should be rounded
below P, as if an oval line were drawn from F
through P to J, and so that the fronts may be
hollowed or cleared out towards the bottom of fly.
The diagram indicates this, but the engraver made
a dent instead of a continuous run of front outline.

LADIES' RIDING TROUSERS.

In adapting the system to ladies' riding trousers,
the centre of leg line may be used or not. Actually
there is no necessity for it, as once the system is
understood the inch tape can be strained out from
the centre of thigh to point 3½ at the bottom to get
a chalk dot indicating the centre of knee, if the eye
cannot be depended on as regards the outline of leg.

MEASURING FOR LADIES' TROUSERS.

There are various methods of measuring, but the
best plan is to measure the side length, and the
waist, seat and bottom ; then ask the lady to sit
down, and measure from the height of sideseam or
waist to the seat of chair to ascertain the approximate depth of body part—which, deducted trom the
side length, will give the leg length near enough for
all practical purposes.

DRAFTING LADIES' TROUSERS.
Diagram 1, Plate 138.

After drawing the lines OO and XX parallel with
each other at half the seat apart, marking off the
side length, and squaring top and bottom, the leg
length is applied from Q to I, and the fork line
squared out to T. From line OO to Q is 1in. less
than half bottom. As there is no tight thigh measure
available, the fashion thigh must be regarded as
two-thirds of the entire seat measure, and one-third
of it and ½in. regarded as the diameter of fork quantity. Half of it is applicable from I to S. The
waist is suppressed to measure partly by taking out
cuts or fulling into waistband, and partly at the
sideseam, to avoid taking it all off at C.

As there is no knee width, straight lines drawn
from E and S to the bottom of side and legseams,
hollowed out equally from ½in. to 1in., or to taste or

what is thought necessary, will produce the leg part
about right.   A little round may be allowed outside
the sideline at hip, for ladies, in order to avoid
paucity of room.

The undersides are got in the same way as for
men, but the seat angle may be increased for riding.

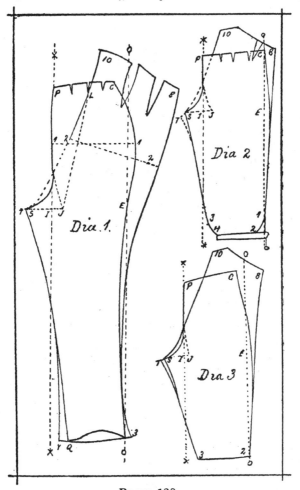

PLATE 138.

Two fair-sized cuts are taken out of the back of the
waist, as shown, and any other reduction or addition
needed made at side of waist.   2 2 is half the seat
and 2in. or 2½in., according to the amount of ease
allowed. Generally speaking, from 14 to 15 is about

250

the size the bottoms are cut. 3 Y is 1in. more than half bottom measure, exclusive of any allowance for seams. In allowing for making-up, the amount of stretching bottom (if any) must be taken into account

KNICKERBOCKERS.—Dia. 2, Plate 138.

C 2 is the side length and whatever is allowed for falling over—as for example, 3in. After squaring top and bottom, 4 I is made the leg length and the addition for falling over band ; I S found as usual ; and the waist suppressed by V's or else fulled into a shaped band. 1½in. to 2in. is allowed outside line O O, at E, to nothing at waist and 1, which is 1½in. to 2in. above bottom, from which point to 2 it is run in an inch or so, and 2 4 made half the garter size and a little for fullness and seams. Point 3, level with 1, is as much further out than 4 as 1 is than 2, and the legseam drawn by a straight line from 3 to S.

The undersides are got by the same process as the undersides of trousers. The bottoms can be finished with strap or cuff, according to taste ; and the width of knickers also depends upon individual taste. Practically speaking, there is hardly any cut in a pair of knickers, as they are merely "bags" with top and bottom openings, unless to be cut half breeches in style, and then they may be more appropriately called breeches.

SHORT TROUSERS.—Dia. 3, Plate 138.

Whether for runners or athletes or for boys, the system is applied in the same manner. C to 2 is the side length, and 3 I the leg length after the top and bottom have been squared. For boys there is no need to trouble about the tight thigh measure either for knickers or short trousers. I S may be made one-sixth seat, and 2 3 half bottom, after P C has been made half waist, and the sideseam shaped as shown, or less round. The legseam can be slightly rounded, also the bottom of foreside.

The underside can be got by first allowing 1in. or more from S to T, and coming back from T towards I one-sixth seat to find the bottom point of seat line. It is not necessary to go in from P for seat angle so much for short as long trousers ; and it is still less necessary to do so for the looser kinds, or for knickerbockers.

BREECHES.—Dia. 1, Plate 139.

All the measures requisite are the side length and
leg length to garter and bottom, the waist, seat,
tight thigh, tight knee, tight garter and tight bottom.
A lot of measures are not necessary; these are
sufficient.

The system is applied in a similar manner for

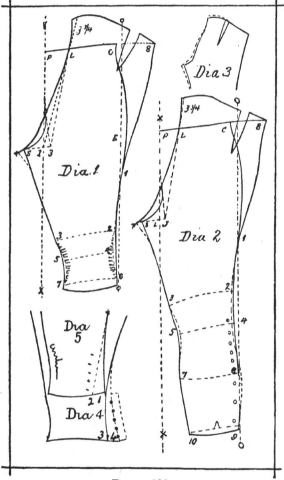

PLATE 139.

breeches as for trousers, the parallel lines being first
drawn, and the top and bottom lines squared; then
the leg length is applied from bottom square line or
7 to I, and the fork line squared. After finding C

by half waist from P, the sideseam is shaped after
the manner shown, with a little round on at E and
hollowed at 2 and 4 to 6.   I S is half the fork quantity or less, and the quantity made up at X.   S 5 is
the length of leg to garter, and on to 7 the full length.
Sweeps may be cast from the line X X by pivot S,
through points 5 and 7, and the half garter and bottom measures applied from sideseam to meet the
sweeps.   The centre of kneecap is near about 4in.
above the garter ; but the projection on inside of
knee is lower than cap centre ; and therefore point
3 is 3in. or 3½in. above garter, and so this quantity
will always find the knee line nearer than most people can find it by taking measures.   The undersides
are got as per system for trousers.   If more seat
room for riding is desired, it may be added on the
principle indicated by receding dotted line L 3
to dotted line L I, and adding the same amount to
forkpoint.   Waist fish is optional.

PANTALOONS.—Dia. 2, Plate 139.

As these are only extended breeches, or breeches
with continuations, the only extra measure required
is the size round the calf — the bottom measure of
breeches becoming the calf measure, and the bottom
measure transferring itself lower down.   It may be
understood that the position of the calf is 3½ lower
down than garter.

An inch or so extra length of foresides is allowed
in breeches and pants, for fulling-on over knees.

For baggy breeches allow 1½ or 2in. extra on the
sideseams, and 1½ to 2in. extra to all leg lengths, cutting the knee, small, and bottom to tight measures.

For buttoning forward, take off the foresides 1 to
2, and add to the undersides 3 to 4, after the manner
of dotted lines dias. 5 and 4, continuing the same
down to bottom for pants.

The dotted lines of dia. 3 show how to add extra
seat room in riding pants or breeches.

HOW TO MEASURE FOR LADIES' BREECHES.

Act in the same way as in taking the measures
for ladies' trousers as regards the sideseam, depth
of body part, waist and seat measures.   To find the
length of leg of breeches, add from 2½in. to 3in. to
half the length of trousers leg ; this gives the length
to garter.   Find the height of knee above and the

depth of calf below garter in the same way as laid down in the gentlemen's breeches system. Any additions for looseness, ease, or other purposes can be made from this basis. Most ladies who wear breeches very willingly allow their tailors to take the size of garter, knee or calf; but should a bashful customer have to be dealt with, either she herself, or her maid, will take the necessary measures.

I he lengths can be taken down the sideseam by feeling for knee and small, and body depth deducted to give leg length, if preferred.

LADIES' BREECHES.—Dia, 1, Plate 140.

Having drawn the lines O O and X X a fourth of the entire seat measure apart, make a mark at C, and from it measure off the full length, and back to E the leg length . Square top and bottom. Apply the leg measure to legseam, and square I to S, or square from E. Make I S half the fork quantity, or less; then apply the leg measure from S downwards, and, making S a pivot, sweep towards sideseam. Shape the sideseam, and apply the widths to meet the sweeps, and shape the legseam through the points given on the sweep lines which the width measures find. Reduce the waist to half measure and seams by taking out little cuts, or have the surplus fulled into the waistband. The front should be lowered from the square top line at D.

The underside is merely a repetition of the ladies' riding trousers, in the body part. In the leg part it is formed by that of the foreside, after allowing at T what IS was made less than half the fork quantity. As the dotted line indicates, it is advisable to hollow the undersides a bit behind knee.

DRAWERS FOR WOMEN OR CHILDREN.
Dia. 7, Plate 140.

These can be produced in the simplest manner. The length can be made to extend to any point below the knee, which can be taken by measure, and the depth of body found as for trousers. The sideseam is quite straight. E J is half the seat, and 2 3 half bottom. JS is swept from 3, and made one-sixth of seat and ½in. The legseam is straight from S to 3. No suppression is taken out at waist.

The underside is got by allowing from 4in. to 6in. from S to T, according to the amount of looseness required. The seat angle is drawn almost straight from T through front of waist point 4, and the rise square with it. As indicated, a drawing-tape is sewn into waist, and the waist drawn in to size when worn.

WHOLE-FALLS.—Dia. 2, Plate 140.

Cut the foreside to reach no higher than the natural waist, and make the top of the bearer form.

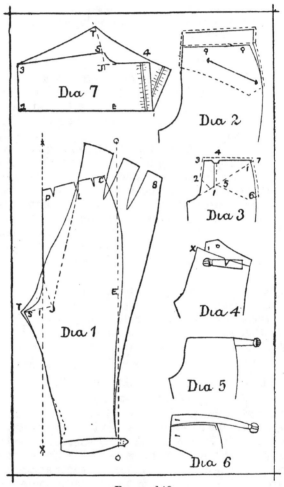

PLATE 140.

a sort of waist band or height above natural waist ; or else lay down the pattern of a fly-front foreside, as shown by diagram, and after forming a bearer by it as shown by dotted lines, cut off say 2in. of the fly-front pattern, as shown by the solid line over the buttons. The dotted line across above solid line shows that a waistband can be sewn on to the lower part of bearer if necessary. The depth of bearer below top of fall at sideseam should be about 5in., and in front about 2½in., or sufficient, with the waistband part, to take three brace-buttons and holes.

Split-Falls.—Dia. 3, Plate 140.

The fronts of split-falls are first cut lower than fly-fronts — or at least lower than fly-fronts having no waistband on them—as in the case of whole, old, or full-falls; then the bearers are cut as shown by the dotted lines, the back part as per 7, 6, 5, 4, 7, and the front part as per 4, 1, 2, 3, 4. A line drawn from 7 to forkpoint will generally define the depth of split-fall bearers at 5 and 1. 3 2 is about 2½in., and 7 6 about 5in. Line 7 to forkpoint finds the bottom of the split, the "dicky" being about 3in. at the bottom and 2½in. at the top.

Fulled Seats.—Dia. 3, Plate 140.

In order to produce the German or French style of trousers, the underside is cut wider than half waist measure, as from 1 to X, or partly at sideseam, and the extra width fulled into waistband, adding a back strap and buckle as shown.

Various Waist Straps,—Dias. 5 and 6, Plate 140.

Dias. 5 and 6 show how waistbands are sometimes put on, of various kinds. That on dia. 5 buckles at sides, and that on dia. 6 buckles at back of waist.

Gaiter-Bottom Trousers.—Dia. 1, Plate 141.

The fore and backsides of these are formed as shown, a piece being cut out of foresides from 5 to 1, spring allowed at 4, and a tongue formed as 1 2 3 4 sewn in from 1 to 4. 2 3 turns back to form the sideseam.

Footed Trousers.—Dias. 2, 3 and 5, Plate 141.

To put feet in trousers, the fronts are split up as per line 4, dia. 2, and a front-of-foot cover and sole-of-foot cover cut as per dias. 3 and 5. The quantities on these diagrams give the size and shape for an ordinary size man.

FRENCH AND ENGLISH STYLES OF TROUSERS
COMPARED.—Figs. 1 and 2, Plate 141.

Fig, 1 shows how a French trousers appears to
the critical expert, and fig. 2 how the ordinary
English style of trousers appears to the same individual. Each of these cuts and styles are far too

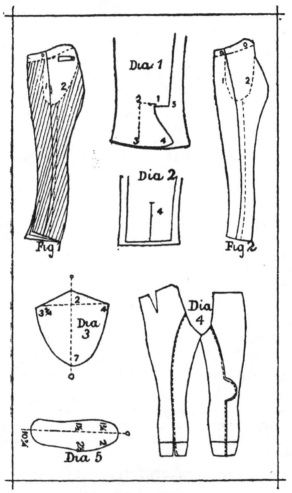

PLATE 141.

close between 1 and 2. In this respect the French
and Continental is the most faulty. Each requires
clearing out at and below point 2 in order to give the
figure its proper reception.

HOW TO MEASURE FOR LEGGINGS, GAITERS, &C.

Feel for the projection of bone below the front of
knee, and from below it measure the length to top
of foot for straight close leggings, and continue on
to the front of laceholes for the length of tongue of
gaiters; then take the size round top, calf and ankle
for leggings, and also the size round the bottom of
boot uppers for gaiters.

If a gaiter is to come below the boot upper, the
size of the part it is to reach to should be taken.
For a man whose foot is not large, the tongue of a
gaiter is 3½ to 4in. in length; and a gaiter should be
a little shorter round the side and back part than at
the tongue—i.e., should not reach down to the level
of the tongue.

HOW TO DRAFT LEGGINGS.—Dia. 2, Plate 142.

Line O O represents the front of the leg, upon
which the length is first marked off; and then the
front outline is shaped, and the measures of size
round top, calf and ankle applied backwards from
it, as from A to B, size of calf, and from C to D.
The sizes or widths give the shape of backseam;
and the top and bottom are run off to fashion, some
being lower over the heel than others.

The set of the buttons is as far from the exact
front of the leg as required, and can be ascertained
when measuring, by noting how far back from front
of leg the customer decides on; and this quantity
can then be taken off the outside and added to the
inside part of legging, as per lines 5 6 and 3 4. A
button catch can then be added to the outside, and
near about ⅛in. to project outside the ends of the
holes on the other side.

HOW TO DRAFT GAITERS.—Dia. 3, Plate 142.

For gaiters the process is the same, in the main,
as for leggings. The front length is applied 1in.
short to 7, and from 7 to 6 an inch longer, as the
tongue reaches a little higher than the top of foot,
as the hollowing indicates. A sweep is made through
6 by pivot 7; then the bottom width applied from 5
to 6, and the bottom shaped as shown.

7 8 of the half tongue, dia. X, is a seam wider
than 7 8 dia. 3. The half-tongue can be formed by
dia 3, as indicated, by the dotted line from 7 to line
2 4, down the line 2 4 to 4, from 4 to 6, and from 7

to 6. An addition of two seams must be made to the length of tongue, to compensate for those taken from 7 to 8. 8 6 and 8 7 of the tongue seam to 7 6 and 7 8 dia. 3. The buttons and holes on the tongue indicate it buttoned over on to outside part, and are

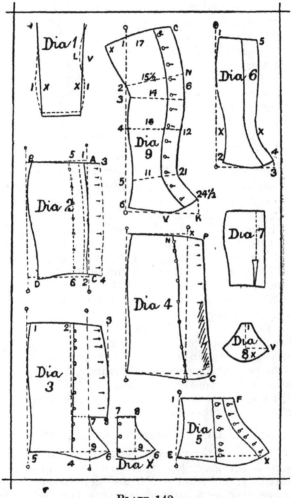

PLATE 142.

holes only when unbuttoned, running on from the other holes from point 8 dia. 3 to the bottom.

When the buttons are to run or twist round the leg from outside of foot towards front of knee, the top of line 2 4 is placed back the amount decided on,.

and the bottom of it from 2in. to 2½in. for the outside, and the buttonholes set forward the same amount as the buttons are set back ; this is like placing a piece on at 2 to nothing at 4, and taking a piece off at 3 to nothing at 8.

Whole-tongue gaiters can be produced by splitting up straight, close-fitting leggings about 4in. on the line OO, as indicated by dia. 7, taking a little out on each side of the line at the top of slit, so as to produce a space to sew the top of tongue to. Dia. 8 indicates the shape of a whole tongue. Its sewing-to edges and bottom must be well stretched, and its middle line IX well shrunk, in order to produce the same quality of fit as if there was a seam in front, after the manner of a half-tongue frontseam.

DRAFTING FARMER'S LEGGINGS.—Dia. 4, Plate 142

Spring-bottom leggings such as worn by farmers, are produced in the same way as close-fitters, the only difference being that they are cut what is called straight down behind—just shaped against the perpendicular back line (which is set back the width of the calf from line OO) as per dias. 3 and 4, and then sprung forward to the width of bottom required.

Draw lines O O and O O parallel with each other at the width of calf apart. Apply top width from X back to find top of backseam, and shape remainder of seam as shown. Apply half bottom width forward, make a mark, and draw a new front line from that point to X, behind which set the buttons as far back as desired, and add as much forward with ½in. added as in the case of close-fitters. In making, shrink well where trousers are shrunk, and stretch button-hole side where shown, also bottom, to help shrinking.

CLERICAL GAITERS.—Dia. 6, Plate 142.

Draw lines 5 X and O O parallel with each other at the width of calf apart. Make 5 1 the size of top, X X the width of small, and shape back as shown, springing out a little over heel. Apply the bottom measure 2 3 or 2 4. 4 is about an inch above 3, and 2 pretty nearly as much above O. The lapel is cut the same shape as the front, and seamed on up the front ; the distance it buttons over from the front of leg is a matter of taste, say 2in. or so. Cut as per solid line, and add a button-catch or hole-blind to the outside part. It can also be cut to button straight down, as shown by the hinder line of buttons on dia 5.

How to Draft Spats.—Dia. 5, Plate 142.

All the lengths can be taken from the height F down to top of foot and bottom of boot uppers, or down side or behind, and the width round top, ankle and bottom ; and in drafting applied as for gaiter bottoms, or from the back forward after shaping backseam as shown. If the lengths are applied from F down they are a lot shorter than from top of long gaiters—that is all the difference. Buttons may be straight down the side or slanting. A catch must be left on the button side to blind the holes.

OVERALLS.—Dia. 9, Plate 142.

Overalls were once much used for riding in, but are now mostly used as protections in altogether other pursuits. From iine 14 down they are drafted in the same way as clerical gaiters. only wide enough for wearing over trousers or breeches—over which the width measures should be taken. A set of width measures are marked on the diagram as a guide. The front can be run backwards more or less from 6 up through N to C, according to the particular service they are required for. The foot part of overalls can be produced by splitting up at the front of bottoms and letting-in whole-tongues as per dias. 7 and 8. All whole-tongues can be produced on the double, as indicated by dotted lines I X, treating that line as the crease and marking out to V half the amount required to make up the size of bottom.

Dia. 1, plate 142, shows how Germans form the legs of pants.

DRAWERS AND PANTS.—Dia. 3, Plate 143.

Measure for them as for breeches and pantaloons, and in drafting start at the sideline O O. Mark off the lengths and square the fork line. Make 1 4 half seat, and 4 5 near about a fourth ; 4 6 half seat, 2 H half garter, V W half calf, and 3 X half bottom. Draw and cut out forepart—which, if drawers, terminate at the garter.

Draft the undersides by the forsides, running the seatseam through 6 as shown. Flannels should have waistbands of cotton or linen sewn on them of the form shown, carrying two buttons in front for men, or buttonholes and catch behind for women. They can be cut wider than needed by the customer and gathered into waist measure, as indicated, to allow

for shrinkage from numerous washings. Allowance
for shrinkage should also be made in the lengths,

COMBINATIONS.—Dia. 4, Plate 143.

The easiest way to cut these is to join a waistcoat
to drawers or pants at their waist lines, after
the manner indicated by dia. 4. Little boys' trousers

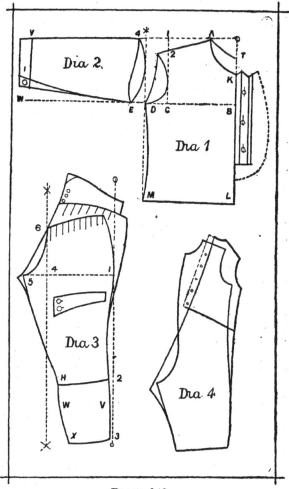

PLATE 143.

are sometimes held up in this way instead of by
braces; and these are producible in exactly the same
way. Combinations can be made to button up either
behind or in front, for boys, girls or women; and

loose or tight, long or short in the legs, and with or
without lace or open work at the bottom.   Knitted
ones, or those made of stockingette, are of course
skin-fitting, and generally made by hosiery manu-
facturers.   But flannels and linens are made by
ladies' costumiers and under-clothiers.

UNDERVESTS.—Dia. 1, Plate 143.

Square OL and OV.   Make O K 4in or 5in, or as
much deeper than an overshirt as required ; O A as
much more than one-sixth as necessary for height of
neck ; O B half the breast, and O L the full length.
Square B D W.   Make B C half breast, C D a good
sixth, and L M same width as B D.   Slope shoulder
1 2 about an inch, and curve front of scye as shown.
OO is the crease of material of the back as well as
forepart.   Come down from O to T 2in or 3in for
back of neck, and draw the back scye as shown.
Form the front buttonhole piece of cotton or linen
as shown, and the under catch as dots or otherwise.
The sleeve is drafted as shown, DE being one-eighth
breast and * 4 about an inch.   Its length is according to underarm length measure, and underarmseam
narrowed off towards the hand to width required at
wrist, as shown ; the wrist button being brought on
to the front of arm in the manner shown.

SHIRTS.

FLANNEL SHIRTS.—Dias. 1, 2, 5, Plate 144.

Square OE, OX.   Make OA one-sixth breast, O2
about 3½in , OB half breast, OX full length.   Square
BD and XN.   Make BC half breast, CD one-sixth.
N M half waist and one-sixth of breast.   X N half
seat and one-sixth breast.   Square line CE.   E to F
1in. for shoulderseam   Shape the scye as shown,
also sideseam and bottom.   V is where the small
gusset is inserted. or the tacking put in, below which
the sideseam is left open.

To get the back, lay the cut-out forepart on the
goods as shown by the dotted lines of dia 2. O to 1
1in., and run the back top from that point to neckpoint of forepart.   Shape the back scye and the
remainder of back as per solid lines, making it longer
than the front as below 4.   Cut straight across from
point 3 to form the yoke, or more fanciful in form.
If the back is to be fulled or pleated into yoke, add
as per dotted line outside 3 and 4, in cutting a pat-

tern. But the dotted line is the crease edge in
cutting from the goods, and the cutter must mark in
from dotted line to get the backseam of the yoke,
line 1 2.

If a yoke is wanted to come over on to the front
of the shoulder, cut the forepart off as line I H, and
add the same to the shoulderseam of yoke.

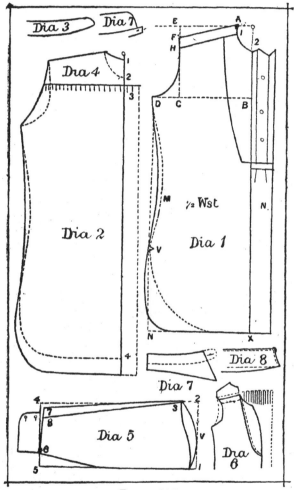

PLATE 144.

To produce the sleeve, dia. 5, square 1 5 and 1 2.
Make 1 2 half breast. Square 2 4, and make 2 3
one-eighth breast, 3 4 the length of forearm. Draw
forearmseams to 7 and 8. Allow for wristband, and

plait in the remainder 6 5 when making, 1 5 being
the crease. The head is formed as shown. Neck-
bands are formed as per dia. 3.

LINEN SHIRTS AND COLLARS.

To produce a linen shirt, all that is required is to
add material for forming a more or less plaited front
and for plaiting into bottom of front, as per piece N
and the outline of front shown on diagram, Plait-
ings are shown, leaving a button-hole piece on to
cover the opening of front. If not plaited in front,
the button-hole piece is sewn on in the case of flannels, as there is no overlaid front for it to grow to,
as in white shirts.

Dia. 6 indicates a considerably-gathered back,
and a different form of front, also a breast formed
for full-chested or erect men.

Collars can be formed as per dias. 7 and 8, the
double collar as a standing collar with square fronts
and fall over it. No systems are required for cutting
collars, as it can be done by the eye, to the length
of neck. A Shakespeare can be cut on the double-
double—i.e., by making the back centre the crease,
and cutting stand and fall together to half the size
of neck, thus cutting through four plies of material
at once, except at front and along the lower edge of
stand, which are formed after the top and bottom
edges are cut. Perhaps it takes from one-half to a
minute to cut a Shakespeare collar.

THE DIRECT MEASURE SYSTEM OF CUTTING.

By this system, all points are found by measures
taken, absolutely, without dividing them in any way,
or any form of guessing whatever.

THE DIRECT MEASURE SYSTEM OF MEASURING FOR COATS

Is as follows : Set the customer with his right side
toward you, facing the light ; and take the square in
the left and the chalk in the right hand. Slightly
lift the arm with the right hand, and place the square
close up under it with the left, quite level, as shown
by fig. 1, at the same time making a chalk mark
along its top edge both in front and behind scye, as
indicated by the dots.

Turn the customer's back towards the light, make
a chalk mark for intended height of shoulderseam,

and place the square across the back level with it, making a chalk mark along its top edge across back-seam. Slide the square down to on a level with the mark behind scye, and again make a chalk mark along its top edge on backseam, level with the mark

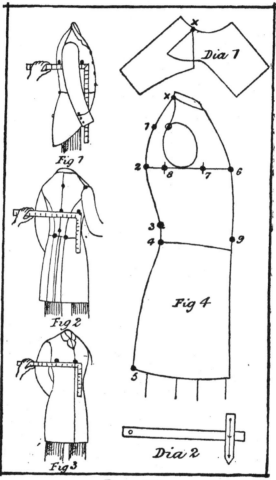

Dia 1

Fig 1

Fig 2

Fig 3

Fig 4

Dia 2

PLATE 145.

behind the scye. Next place the square round the waist to find the exact level of waist on backseam, making a chalk mark along its top edge to indicate it. All these marks on the back are indicated by black dots on fig. 2.

Turn the customer to face the light, and place the

:square across the front of chest level with the chalk mark in front of scye, and make a chalk mark along its top edge. See dot on front of breast, fig. 3.

Note, special care should be taken to place the square right on the front of breast, and no attempt made to make it touch point 7 shown on fig. 4, else point 6 will not be level with point 7. I he same applies to getting marks level on all round surfaces. The eye must be held level with top edge of square to tell whether it is level with the marks or not; it is the only sure guide.

Make the perpendicular chalk marks across the horizontal ones 6 and 8, the first to define exact centre of front of breast. Also place a square or straightedge against front of arm, and make one across horizontal mark 7. See fig. 4. A good way to do this is to place the square on fig. 1 over the shoulder-end, and draw it back by the left hand to front of arm. The width of square back from 7 gives exact front of scye.

Having placed all the chalk marks—which can be done in a few seconds—the measures are taken in positively the following order, and no other. See fig. 4. First the depths and lengths from X to 1, 2, 3, 4 and 5; the width of back and sleeve lengths; from 2 to 7 and 2 to 6; front shoulder length X 7, and straightness X 6; width across breast 6 7, on to 8, and centre of back for the breast measure over coat; the size of waist 3 9 over coat. This measure can be taken all round, and half of it entered in the order book, or from backseam to centre of front of waist, or vice versa, using the finger-end to send the backseam home to the centre of customer's back.

For waist suppressions, measures are taken from 8 to 3 and 6 to 3, fig. 4. For suppression 7, the measure from neckpoint to 8 is taken.

A measure can be taken from 6 up to neck for clerical coat, or as per our clerical vest measurement.

Dia. 2 is a small sketch of a plummet square for use in getting the chalk marks stationed level and correctly. It is made of white metal, 1in. or 1½in. wide and about 15in. long; the end piece is about 4in. or 5in., and has either a line down its centre or a point in centre of bottom. A small lead plumb-bob hangs from a rivet in its top, by a piece of coarse twist through a loop in centre, to save it from flying about. When the long arm of this square is held level the plumb-line or bob will show it. And as an instrument it is fifty times better than the best of erratic and fugitive spirit levels.

Dia. 7 shows a design in cloth which can be used to take off all the measures reliably. The two pieces are joined at X by any kind of swivel. Two eyelet-

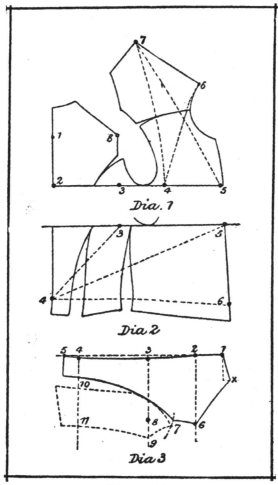

Dia. 1

Dia 2

Dia 3

PLATE 146.

holes, with a string through with knotted ends, makes a good swivel. The operator can take the measures off the cloth by means of the tape to enter in the book. In using this cloth measurer, only the chalk marks 7 and 8, fig. 4, need be put on the customer; the instrument will receive all the others.

THE SYSTEM OF DRAFTING.

IN drafting, the back is drawn out first, then the sidebody and forepart, or the sidebody, and lastly the forepart.

THE BACK.—Dia. 3, Plate 146.

The depth or length measures are applied in the same order as taken, from 1 to 2, 3, 4, and 5. Lines

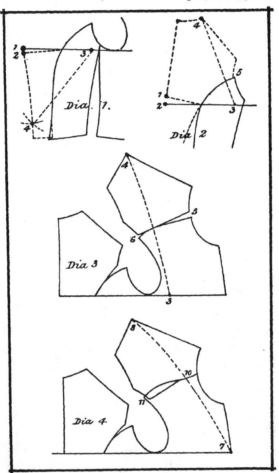

PLATE 147.

are squared from these points. The width of back top is made to taste, across to pitch to measure, and the remainder to taste, say 2¼ at waist and 4½ on the bottom of scye line.

Sidebodies separate from foreparts may be drawn
to taste in width to 9 and 11, after suppressions 5
and 10 have been taken out according to measures,
See dias. 1 and 2, plate 147.

THE FOREPART.—Dias. 1 and 2, Plate 146.

The first and only line to draw is that from 5 to 2.
The widths from 5 to 4 and on to 2 are adjusted to
the measures taken. The front of scye is the width
of square behind the chalk mark. The back is laid
down at 2, with its bottom of scye line on line 5 2,
and the top part of sideseam of sidebody run by it,
or suppressed as shown by dia. 2, plate 147. The
lower part of its sideseam is got by swinging the
back in until the measure 3 4, dia. 1, plate 147, agrees
with that taken; the sideseam of back thus finds
that of sidebody.

The shoulder is got by applying measure 4 6 and
5 6, then measures 4 7 and 5 7. The waist is got to
fit and measure by applying the measure 5 4; and
then, when 5 4 is right, the waist measure from 4 to 6.

Dias. 3 and 4, plate 147, show how to apply the
shoulder measures correctly. First 3 4 a little
on the curve, as the tape travelled in measuring;
then the measure 7 8 to get any hollowing out the
figure may require at 10.

Dia. 1, plate 148, shows how the measure 3 4 is
applied, after the back and sidedody have been correctly cut, including sideseam correctly suppressed.
After 3 4 is made correct, then the measure 4 5 will
find point 5 with absolute certainty, and 3 5 can be
connected with a proper run.

ANOTHER METHOD.—Dia. 2, Plate 148.

If preferred, measures may be taken from intended
end of back shoulderseam to 9, and from 12 to 10,
and used together with the front shoulder length and
straightness in drafting, instead of the measures 4 7
and 5 7, dia. 1, plate 146.

The length of forepart can be got by placing the
back as shown, or made say 1½ longer than back
from bottom of scye line downwards.

ANOTHER METHOD.—Dia. 1, Plate 149.

If preferred, measures may be taken as per 2, 3,
4, and 5, and sweeps cast by them from the black
dot pivots. 2 and 3 will get the back shoulder, and

4 and 5 establish the straightness and slope of front
shoulder, while its width and length are got from
the scye end and by the front shoulder length, thus
dispensing with the straightness and other shoulder
measures.

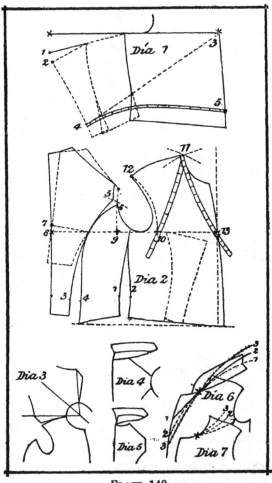

PLATE 148.

ANOTHER DIRECT MEASURE SYSTEM.
Fig. 1, Dias. 1 and 4, Plate 150.

Before measuring, chalk marks are put in at back
pitch, the highest point the shoulder touches the
square, by X, front of scye, point 1 in a line with
front of scye, and at 2. See fig. 1. Measures are

then taken as follows: 1, Length cf the back ; 2, the width of back and sleeve lengths ; 3, nape to back pitch, and on to the side of waist, point 1 ; 4, nape to side of waist ; 5, neck to front of scye and on to side of waist ; 6, neck to O and on to front of

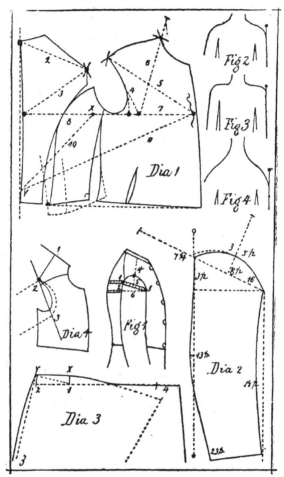

PLATE 149.

scye ; 7, O to back pitch ; or neck to O and on to front of scye and side of waist, and back pitch or back of waist to O and front of scye.

The breast measure is taken from 10 to 4 and on to 12, and the waist from 9 to * and on to 8, or vice versa.

To get point 7 the eye travels down in a line with

back scye to on a level with *. What 7 8 is less
than width of back is waist suppression, and what
* 8 is less than 4 12 is underarm suppression.

In drafting by these measures the system is as follows : The back is first delineated by the length and

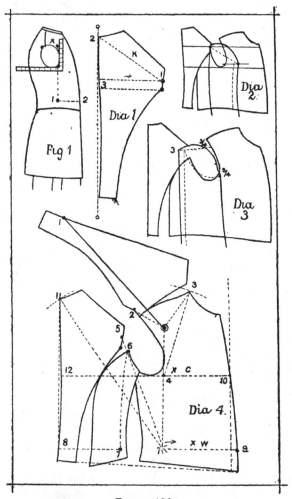

PLATE 150.

width measures, aided by the measure K which was
taken from 2 to 1. The shoulderseam and line 3 are
placeable to taste or fashion.

In drafting the forepart, the bottom of scye line
10 12 is first drawn, and the breast measures from

10 to 4 and on to 12 applied. Then the measure from 4 to *, and the measure from * to 11 to find out where to lay the cut-out back down—which is placed with its backseam on 12 and its top touching sweep 11. The measure * 5 is now applied to find point 6, and 7 8 to find out the amount of waist suppression of sideseam. The amount to take out under the arm is found out by applying the measure * 8 after the sideseam has been suppressed.

Point O is found by the measure o 4, point 3 by the measures 3 o and 3 4, and point 2 by the measure 2 o. If preferred, the measure 2 o can be omitted, and 1 o taken and applied instead. Point 9 is found by the waist measure after the waist suppressions have been taken out.

This great, if not the greatest of direct measure systems dispenses with all devices, means and necessity of finding a level line or points round the figure before measuring, to take the measures to or from, with the object of ensuring their correctness; thus entirely overcoming any difficulty anyone may find in getting the depth of scye point on backseam or on front of breast stationed correctly.

Any practitioner can take the measure * 9 as a separate measure, and use it to find point 9, if he chooses, as laid down in another of our direct measure systems.

DIRECT MEASURE SLEEVE SYSTEMS

Fig. 1, Dia. 2, Plate 149.

In marking up the job, so to speak, before measuring, or in making chalk marks to measure to before taking the direct measures for sleeves, point 3, dias. 1 and 2, plate 146, will answer for point 2, fig. 1, plate 149. This point is the same as point X, dia. 1, plate 149. Chalk marks may also be made at 1, 4, and 6. Point 6 is of course on the topside of sleeve on a level with the line from 3 to 4, dia. 1, plate 146. and points 1 and 4 where the operator may choose or thinks they ought to be in order to produce the style of cut wanted. In the absence of the chalk marks 4 and 3, dia. 1, plate 146, the inch tape can be used as shown on the figure to get the points by. It or a straightedge, held level with points 1 and 3, must be used to get the chalk mark at point 5.

How to Take the Measures.

The length of forearm is a better measure than the length of backarm; so the hindarm measure may either be dispensed with or taken. If taken, the first measurements are from 1 to 2 and backarm lengths; the second is from 1 to 3 only, or continued on to 2; and the third measure is from neck to 4, and on to 5 and 6, or on to 5 only; and the fourth measure is from 1 by 4 to 3, and on to the full length of forearm. The widths of elbow and hand are of course a separate matter, and left to the cutter's own discretion.

How to Draft the System.

Dia. 2, Plate 149.

Draw the line O to dot   Make a mark at $7\frac{1}{4}$, and apply the backarm measures—which we will suppose by way of example are $3\frac{1}{2}$, $13\frac{1}{2}$, and $23\frac{1}{2}$.   Square a line across from $3\frac{1}{2}$.   Then apply measure 1 3 from $7\frac{1}{4}$ to 16, square forearm and draw line 16, finding its centre as at $8\frac{1}{2}$, and square the line up through $5\frac{1}{2}$. Place the measure from neck to 5 on $8\frac{1}{2}$, and apply the measure from neck to 4 backwards.   Draw the sleevehead, and apply the measure 1 4 3 on to the full length of forearmseam.

Note that the distance of point 4 from 1 can be taken by measure, when taking the measure 1 by 4. to 3, and applied as indicated by the 3 on diagram, instead of finding the centre between $7\frac{1}{4}$ and 16. The quantities on the diagram give an example of one style of sleeve.   Naturally, as each cutter can design his own cut of coat and sleeve on the customer, each one's sleeve would be in form according to his own ideas as to what constitutes fit and style.

This is, by long chalks, the greatest sleeve system ever published.

Dia. 4, plate 149, shows not only what relationship a sleevetop bears to the shoulder, but also how to measure for sleeves in a new way—viz., the back width from 1 to 2, sleevehead width from 2 to 3, and forearm length from 3 to hand — a far more reliable method than the old plan.

Another Direct Sleeve System.

Fig. 1, Dia. 6, Plate 151.

Before measuring, place a chalk mark at O, fig. 1.

and others on back and forearmseams level with it.
Then take a measure from the backseam mark to 9,
on to 10 and top of forearm, or vice versa, and from
armpit to level with o under the arm.   In

DRAFTING, Dia. 6, Plate 151,

After drawing line o o o, and line o 9 square with it,
the section o9 of the first measure finds point 9, the

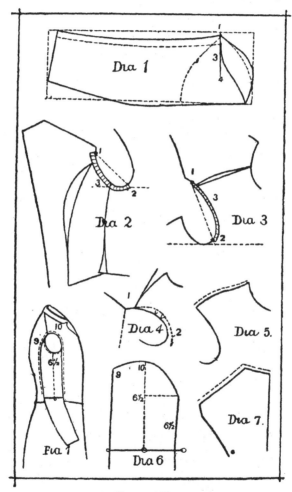

PLATE 151.

width 9 to 10 finds point 10, and line 10 to o is parallel with line o 9.   The measure o to 6½ finds point
6¼, and the measure o to 10 finds point 10.   A line is

squared from 6½ forward, and the two sections 9 to
10 and 10 to forearm of the first measurement finds
the top of forearmseam, in so far as width of sleeve
is concerned. The underarm or measure from the
top of forearm to the front mark finds its height, as
for example from the front 0 up to it 6½in. The
total lengths and widths of sleeve can be taken in
any way the cutter chooses. The length of forearm,
however, is sufficient, as the width of top will dictate
the width of elbow and cuff.

This is a very facile system; and the same may
be said of it as of the system on plate 149, as its
equal was never published in the whole history of
the art and science of cutting.

For quickness and expedition the scye measure
system, dia. 1, plate 151, may be used; the width of
topside being got by the measure 1 3 2, dia. 3, and
the width of the underside by the measure 1 3 2, dia.
2. A line can be squared across as per 1 3 4, and
the hooking-in done at forearmseam as shown, which
will of course necessitate that the topside be made
that much wider at elbow and hand.

Dia. 4. indicates the relationship of the sleeve to
the scye; the dotted line of dia. 5 what change from
normal balance necessitates more width of topside;
while dia. 4, plate 149, indicates how that measure
is the governing factor, whether taken from the cut-
out coat or on the customer; and the dotted line of
dia. 7 what change from the normal balance necessitates more width of underside.

Dias. 2 and 3, plate 150, indicate both how to
balance a sleeve in the scye, find the pitch points,
and whether the depth points of a sleeve are correct.

Figs. 2, 3 and 4, plate 149, delineate the normal,
high or square shoulder, and low or sloping shoulder
types of build. It is not these peculiarities that
affect the shape and size of a garment in the shoulders and sleeves, but changes in the dimensions over
which the different direct measures are taken.

Dia. 8, plate 152, indicates how a sleeve needs to
be enlarged when a scye is cleared out — viz., O 2
requires increasing to the extent of the clearing-out
enlargement, and OX to the extent the front shoulder
width is cut away.

Dia. 4, plate 152, shows that when closed at back

and forearmseams, the top of underside should run fair with the top of sleevehead.

Dia. 1, plate 152, indicates the safest method of reducing the width of a back, and dia. 2 the safest

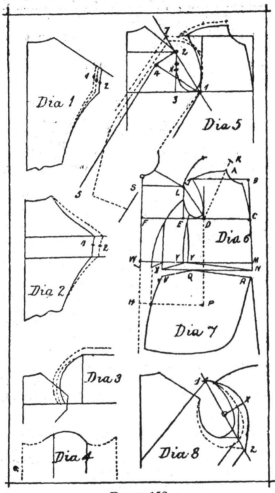

PLATE 152.

way of increasing it — in the absence of direct measure certainty.

Dia. 3, plate 152, shows how not to alter a sleeve for a scye cleared out in front, depth or back.

Dia. 5, plate 152, shows how to draft a sleeve in or by the scye. First, the back pitch is found

either by a quarter the scye, or otherwise; then a
line is drawn from 1 through 2 to 7. The front and
top of scye is measured from front pitch to back
pitch, and that amount applied from 1 to 7. A line
is squared from 2 to 4, in length the difference between 1 2 and 3 X. A line is drawn from 4 to 1, and
the straight back and forearm lines drawn square
with it to 5 and S. The head is drawn by the guidance of the front of scye, as shown. See dotted
lines for complete outline of topside.

SKIRTS.

THE SKIRT SYSTEM.—Dia. 3, Plate 149.

In this system the front edge is the line of depar-
ture for frocks, and the waist line for morning and
dress coat skirts.

For frocks the waist line 4 2 is drawn square with
front edge, and in length the width of lapel, forepart
and sidebody, and fullness. From 2 back to 1 is the
width of sidebody, or one-fourth breast. From 2 to
Y and 1 to X equals the amount of waistseam hollow
of body. The angle of square placed at Y, with one
leg on 1, will cause the other leg to give straight
plait line 3, which, rounded a little, will make it
right. The frock skirt is hollowed between 4 and
X, and is a close-fitter. For a wider skirt round
bottom, wedges can be let in to nothing at waist,
wherever extra width is required.

The morning and dress coat straight waist line is
from Y through 1 to front. Above this line the
waistseam is rounded from nothing at front through
X to Y.

THE SKIRT SYSTEM.—Dias. 1, 3, 4, Plate 153.

These diagrams show the easiest and simplest
way in which skirts can be produced.

To produce a frock skirt, the sidebody and forepart are laid down as shown by dia. 1. Spring is
got by drawing line O O and rounding the plait a
little; and the waistseam is got by the sidebody and
forepart, and the front edge by marking down ¼in.
and squaring by it and front of waistseam. Or the
front edge can be got by drawing a straight line
from the top to bottom of breast, continuing it downwards over the skirt as per dotted line, and allowing

the lapel width in front of it.

To produce a morning or dress coat skirt, the sidebody and forepart are laid as per dias. 3 and 4, and line OO drawn for spring, and the plait rounded

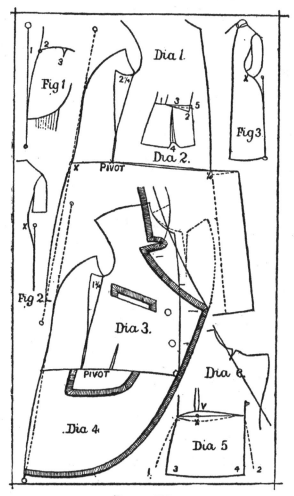

PLATE 153.

a little from it. The waistseam of body part gives the waistseam.

The $2\frac{1}{4}$ overlap, dia. I. can be either increased or decreased. Increasing it makes the skirt wider round the bottom, and vice versa.

The $1\frac{3}{4}$ overlap, dia. 3, can also be increased or decreased, even to none at all; and the less it is the closer will be the skirt round the bottom. The word pivot indicates the point on which the forepart is pivoted to get more or less width or drapery into a skirt bottom.

Dia. 2, plate 153, shows what the infusion of extra width or drapery into a skirt brings about — viz., when the underarmseam is closed, and the sidebody joined to the skirt as shown at 1, the forepart will drop down to 2; and the waistseam of skirt 3 5 also drops down to 2 when seamed to waistseam of forepart, thereby dropping loose material into the side of skirt, as shown by shading from waist to 4.

Dia. 5, plate 153, indicates that the more the waistseam of a skirt is hollowed, the more is needed on at 1 and 2. See dotted lines. The best way to understand this matter is to let wedges at all points into the bottom edge to nothing at waistseam of a skirt pattern.

Figs. 2 and 3, plate 153, clearly evidence the fact that the larger the hips the more width is taken up, and more fullness must be held on, else V's taken out of waistseam of skirt; also that the larger the dimensions at the bottom, as in the case of a ladies' skirt, the greater the amount of drapery required.

Fig. 1, plate 153, indicates that the back spring depends largely upon the amount of fall-in from the perpendicular line O O, from 1 to 2; and that large male hips need more width to cover them, and the waistseam reduced to size either by taking out V's or shrinking and fulling-on. In other words, the seat or hip width must be right, and the surplus width reduced sufficiently by cuts, shrinking, or fulling-on, to make it close in to the figure's waist as from O to X, figs. 2 and 3.

DIRECT MEASURE SKIRT SYSTEM.

Dia. 7, Plate 152.

It is probably more important to fully understand the principles involved in skirt cutting, or any more or less loose drapery, than to know how to cut such parts by direct measurements. Still, the extra trouble entailed when taking direct measures for the body of a coat, is but little. It need not be any more than one measure — that from P to H, or in a right

line from D to P, and on from P to H. Point D
would be point 4 on dia. 1, plate 146, and point 10 on
dia. 2, plate 148.

If a mark is made on posterior, and the point is
included in the back length measures, then a measure
can be taken from point 5, dia. 2, plate 146, to it, as
from C to H, plate 152.

For those who like simplicity, an easy method of
measuring for and drafting a coat is as follows:
Chalk marks are made at natural waist both under
arm and on backseam; then the lengths of back and
side are taken, and following in succession as set
down, the scye measure, width of back, width across
chest, front shoulder, waist and forearm. In drafting, dia. 7, plate 152, the waist length applied from
O finds point W. and the side length from W finds
F. The width of back from S and F find L and E.
Quarter the scye finds D; and after a line has been
squared up from E through L, half the scye less 1in.
applied from D finds L, wherever it reaches line EL.
Line SL is superfluous. The width across the chest
applied from D finds C. D J is the same as D L—
1in. less than half scye; and both can be swept from
D. Line JB may be drawn horizontal from J, but is
more or less superfluous· The front shoulder length
applied from D to A, less the width of back top KA,
intersected by the measure OD, finds the length and
straightness of the front shoulder. The waist can
be suppressed in the usual manner, or by measures
taken from points perpendicular with E and D.

In cutting skirts, VQ should run parallel with YZ.
From Q forward the run of waistseam is a matter of
drapery, as explained in connection with the other
skirt systems.

COLLARS, TURNS, GORGES, &C.
Plate 148.

When a V is taken out of a gorge, it should be
formed as per dia. 6, plate 153.

The form of neck is similar to dia. 3, plate 148. A
collar has to be cut and worked to fit one half of the
neck and to turn over on to shoulder.

Dia. 4, plate 148, represents a fair average form
of collar.

Dia. 5, plate 148, indicates that a collar hollowed
in that way, increases the length of crease and leaf

·edge. If hollowed above the back top, it causes the collar to stick out and away from the neck behind.

All collars need hollowing in from back top to back of crease, and the leaf sprung so that it will cover the stand comfortably.

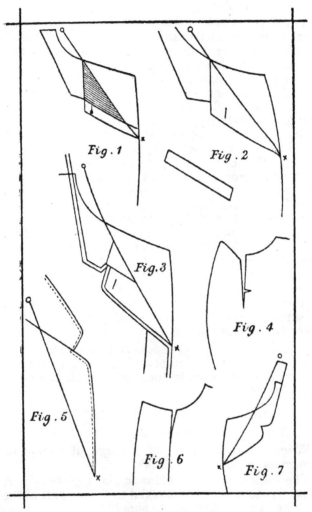

PLATE 154.

Dia. 6, plate 148, indicates the method by which thousands of tailors cut their collars. In practicing the method, it should be remembered that the deeper the leaf the longer its edge has to be, so as to cover the larger circumference of the figure the lower it reaches and is below the crease or collarseam.

The higher a coat buttons the longer the leaf edge should be, and vice versa.   Point X is the break,

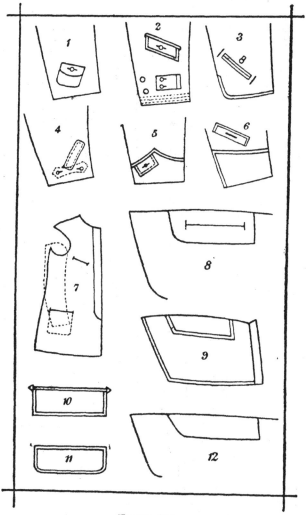

PLATE 155.

and 1, 2, 3, different heights of buttoning.   Crease lines 1, 2 and 3 indicate the nature of the variations in the crease line of collar that are necessary in order to make it suit turns 1, 2 and 3.   1 goes with 1, 2 with

2, and 3 with 3. 1 and 2 will not go well together, because it makes the leaf too short and necessitates too much working-up, and is apt to fly back to some extent through atmospheric influences.

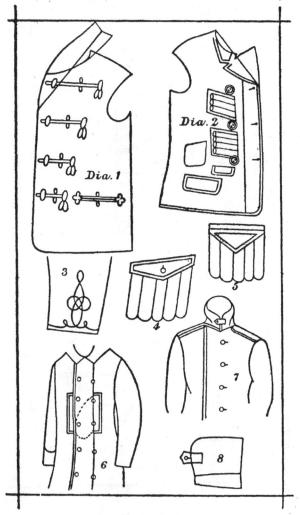

PLATE 156.

Dia. 7, plate 148, indicates how the width of leaf affects the run of stand edge. If line X 2 is the run for an ordinary width of leaf, X 3 may be taken as the run for the narrow leaf, and X 1 for a wide leaf.

285

STYLE DESIGNING.

Rolls (turns), collars, fronts, skirts, flaps, sleeves and pockets, offer a very wide field in which the cutter can exercise his talent in designing. Proof of this will be easily discerned in the examples shown on plates 154, 155, and 156.

Figs. 1 to 7, plate 154, exhibit immensely different styles of fronts, collars, turns. &c., and are highly suggestive to style-students.

Dias. 1 to 6, plate 155, represent the same number of entirely different styles of sleeves for gentlemen's coats, all brought about by very simple means.

Dia. 7, plate 155, indicates how to know or find out where a pocket mouth should be, whether horizontal, vertical, or diagonal.

Dias. 10 and 11, plate 155, represent different styles of flaps.

Dias. 8, 9, and 12, plate 155, show other styles of flaps on various styles of skirts, thereby indicating the formations most agreeable and suitable to each other.

Dias. 1 and 3, plate 156, represent a very striking design of lounge smoking jacket.

Dia. 2, plate 156, represents a most striking style of reefer, with no fewer than five pockets on one forepart. Pockets 4 and 5 are two other styles which can be put on any kind of three-seamer, civilian or military.

Fig. 6, plate 156, shows a most uncommon style of double-breasted fronts and pockets.

Fig. 7, plate 156, shows a still more uncommon style of chesterfield or ulster front, with a kind of deep Medici collar held together in front by a tab; and dia. 8 shows how this collar is formed. The entire style has the appearance of being military or semi-military.

APPENDIX.

MANUFACTURERS' MEASUREMENTS OF READY-MADE GARMENTS.

JUVENILE JACKETS AND TROUSERS.

Size	00	0	1	2	3	4
Breast	22½	23½	24	24¼	25½	26¼
Waist	23	23½	24	24½	25	25½
Sleeve	18½	19	19¾	21	22	23½
Leg	8¼	9	9¾	10½	11¼	12

JUVENILE JACKETS AND TROUSERS,

Size	00	0	1	2	3	4	5	6
Breast	22	22½	23	24	25	26	27	28
Waist	23	23½	24	24½	25	25½	26	27
Sleeve	17	18	19¼	20½	21¾	23	24½	25½
Leg	8	10	11	12	13	14	15	16

KNICKER SUITS.

	Size	00	0	1	2	3	4	5
JACKET	Breast	23	24	25	26	27	28	29
	Sleeve	18	18¾	19¾	21	22	23	24
	Back	14	14½	15½	16½	18	19	20
TROUSERS	Waist	23	24	24½	25	25½	26	27
	Leg	8	9	10	11	12	13½	15

Size	000	00	0	1	2	3	4	5	6
Breast	23	23	23½	24	24½	25	26	27	28
Sleeve	16½	17¼	18¼	19¼	20½	21¾	23	24¼	25½

JUVENILE JACKETS.

Size	3	4	5	6	7	8
Breast	25½	26¼	27	27¾	28½	29¼
Waist	25	25½	26	26½	27	27½
Sleeve	22	23½	24½	25¾	27	28¼
Length	20¼	21¼	22	23	24	25

BOYS' AND YOUTHS' JACKETS.

Size	4	5	6	7	8	9	10	11	12
Breast	26	27	28	29	30	31	32	32½	33½
Sleeve	23	24¼	25½	26½	27½	28½	29½	30	30½

BOYS' AND YOUTHS' TROUSERS.

Size	4	5	6	7	8	8	10	11	12
Waist	25½	26¼	27	27½	28	28½	29	29	31
Leg	22¼	24	25½	26½	27¾	28½	29¼	29¾	31

JUVENILE OVERCOATS.

Breast	26	27	28	29	30	31
Waist	26	27	28	29	29½	29¾
Sleeve	23	24	24½	25½	26½	27½
Length	34	35	36	37	38	39

JUVENILE OVERCOATS.

Size	00	0	1	2	3	4	5	6
Breast	21	21	22	23	24	24¾	25½	26
Back	5½	5½	5¾	6	6	6	6¼	6¼
Sleeve	19	20	21	21½	22	22½	23½	24½
Length	22	23	24	25¼	26½	28	30	32

Size	7	8	9	10	11	12	13
Breast	26½	27	27½	28	28½	29½	30½
Back	6¼	6½	6½	6½	6½	6¾	6¾
Sleeve	25½	26	26½	27	27¾	28¼	29
Length	34	36	38	40	42	44	46

BOYS' AND YOUTHS' JACKETS.

Size	5	6	7	8	9	10	11
Breast	28	28½	29½	30½	31½	32½	33½
Sleeve	18	19	20	21	22½	23½	24½
Length	21	22	23½	25	26	27	28½

BOYS' AND YOUTHS' VESTS.

Size	5	6	7	8	9	10	11
Breast	28	28½	29½	30½	31½	32½	33½
Waist	28	28½	29	30	31	31½	32½
Length	19½	20½	21	21½	22½	23½	24½

Boys' and Youths' Jackets.

Size	7	8	2	10	11	12	1	2
Breast	27	28	29	30	30	31	32	33
Sleeve	24	25	26	27	28	29	30	31
Length	22	23	24	25	26	27½	29	30½

Boys' and Youths' Vests.

Size	7	8	9	10	11	12	1	2
Length	20½	21	21½	22	22½	23	23½	24

Boys' and Youths' Trousers.

Size	4	6	7	8	9	10	11
Waist	26	26½	27½	28½	29½	30	31
Sideseam	35	36	37	38½	39½	40½	42
Leg	25	26	27	27½	28	29	30

Boys' and Youths' Trousers.

Size	7	8	9	10	11	12	1	2
Side	30½	32½	34½	36½	38½	40	41	42
Leg	20½	22	23½	25	26½	28	28	30
Waist	26	26½	27	27½	28	29	30	30½
Seat	28½	29	29¼	30	31	32	33	34
Knee	15	15½	15½	16	16½	17	17	17½
Bottom	15	15½	15½	16	16½	17	17½	18

Men's Coats.

Breast	33	34½	36	37½	39	40½	42
Waist	30	31½	33	34½	36	37½	39
Back	6¾	7	7¼	7½	8	8¼	8½
Length	17½	18	18½	19	19½	20	20¼

Men's Coats.

Size	2½	3	4	5	6	7
Breast	34	35½	37	38½	41	43
Sleeve	30¾	31½	32	32½	33½	34¼

Men's Trousers.

Size	2½	3	4	5	5	7
Waist	31	32	34	36	38	40
Leg	31	30½	31½	32	32	31½

Manufacturers' Measurements.

JUVENILE BLOUSES.

Size	000	00	0	1	2	3	4	5	6
Length	9	9½	10½	11	12	13	13½	14½	15
Breast	22	22	22½	23	24	25	26	27	28
Waistbelt	11¾	1 ¾	11¾	12¾	13¼	13¼	13¾	14¼	14¾
Sleeve	17½	18	18¾	19½	20¾	21¾	23¼	24¾	26

KNICKERS.

Side	16	16	17	18	19	21	22	24	25	26
Leg	8½	9	9½	10	10½	11½	12	14	15	
Waist	11	11	11	12	12½	12½	13	13½	14	
Seat	12	12	12	12½	13	13½	14	14½	15	

KNICKER SUITS.

Sizes	00	0	1	2	3	4	5	6
Length		16¼		18		20		
Chest	23	24	26	26	27	28	28	29
Sleeve	18	19	20	22	25	24	25	26
Legsm.	8	9	10	11	12	13	13	14

BOYS' AND YOUTHS' TROUSERS.

Size	1	2	3	4	5	6	7	8	9	10	11
Waist	24½	25	25¼	26	26½	27	27½	28	28½	29	29
Seat	25	25½	26½	27½	28½	29½	30	31	32	33	34
Leg	17	18½	20	21½	23	24½	26	27¼	28¼	29	30

BOYS' AND YOUTHS' REEFERS AND VESTS.

Size	3	4	5	9	7	8	9	10	11
Length	18½	19½	20½	22	24	25	26½	27½	28½
Breast	25	26	27	28	29	30	31	32	33
Waist	29	26	26	27	27	21	28	29	29½
Back	4¾	5	5¼	5½	5¾	5¾	6	6¼	6¼
Sleeve	21½	23	24¼	25¾	26¾	27¾	29	29	30
Vest length	18	18¾	19¾	20½	21	22	23	23½	26

KNICKER TROUSERS.

Sizes	0	1	2	3	4	5	6	7
Waist	23	23½	24	24½	25	26	26½	27
Legseam	9	10	11	12	13	14	15	16

Boys' and Youths' Trouser Suits

Sizes	1	2	3	4	5	6	7	8	9	10	11	12
Chest	26	26	27	28	28	29	30	30	31	32	33	34
Sleeve	21	22	23	24	25	26	27	28	29	30	31	32
Waist	25	25	26	27	27	28	28	29	30	31	31	32
L'gseam	23	24	25	26	27	28	29	29	30	31	31	30
Knee	14	14	14½	15	15	15½	16	16	16½	16½	16½	17

Boys' and Youths' Trousers

Sizes	1	2	3	4	5	6	7	7½
Waist	26	26½	27	28	29	30	31	31
Legseam	16	18	20	22	23½	25	27	28

MEN'S COATS.

Size	2½	3	4	5	6	7
Breast	33	34	36	38	40	42
Waist	31	32	33	34	36	38
Sleeve	30½	31	31¼	32¾	33¾	44½
N. waist	15	16	17	18	18	18

Full waist length 1½in. small, large sizes 2in. longer.

Vest lengths	24	24½	25	26	27	27½

Men's Trousers.

Sizes	2½	3	3½	4	4½	5	5½	6	6½	7	7½
Waist	30	32	32	33	34	36	36	38	38	40	40
Seat	34	36	38	38	38	40	40	42	42	44	44
Legseam	31	29	31	29	31	29	31	29	31	29	30

Other half-sizes are same waist, and 33 legseam all round.

Size	2	2½	3	3½	4	5	6	7
Side	40	41	42	46	42	44	45	46
Leg	28½	31½	29¼	33	30½	31¾	31	32
Waist	30	31	32	33	34	36	38	40
Seat	34	34½	36	36½	37½	39½	41	41
Knee	17½	18	18	18	18	18½	19	19
Bottom	17	17	17½	18	18	18	19	19

Men's Suits

Sizes	3	4	5	6	7
Chest	36	38	40	42	44
Sleeve	31½	32½	33½	34	35
Waist	33	34	37	39	43
Legseam	30½	31	31½	32	34

GIRLS AND MISSES.

Age	2	3	4	5	6	7	8	9	10	11	12
Breast	20½	21	22	23	24	25	26	27	28	29	30
Waist	20½	21	21¾	22	23	24½	25½	25½	26	26½	27
Hips	22½	23¾	24¼	25¼	26½	27¼	28	28¾	29½	30½	31
Length Skirt	20	21	22	23	24	25	26	27	28	29	30

LADIES' MEASURES.

Breast	32	34	36	38	40	42	44	46
Scye Depth	7½	7¾	8	8¼	8½	8¾	9	9¼
Waist Length	14½	14½	15	15½	16	16	15½	15

Small Womens, sizes from 35 to 37.

Womens or O's, sizes from 34 to 36.

O's's, sizes from 38 to 40.

MEN'S OVERCOATS.

Breast	49	50	51	52
Waist	48	49½	50	52
Sleeve	35	35	35	35
Length	50	50	50	51

Breast	30	32	34	36	38	40	42	44	46	48	50
Length	38	40	42	44	46	48	50	52	54	54	56

Military Clothing Measurements for Sergeant Major, Sergeant, Band Master, Piper Major, Drum Major and Rifle Instructor.

Height 6ft. and 6ft. 1in.

Breast	Waist	Lengths		Collar	Front
43·44	39·40				
41·42	37·38				
39·41	35·36	18½	28	17½	27½
37·38	33·34				
Height 5ft. 10in. and 5ft. 11in.					
43·44	39 49				
41·42	37·38	16¼	27		25½
39·40	35 36				
37·38	33·34	17	25¾	17⅓	25½
Height 5ft. 8in and 5ft. 9in.					
41·42	37·38				
39 40	35 36				
37·38	33·34	17½	18 26	17	25½
35·36	31·32				
Height 5ft. 6in. and 7ft.					
41·42	37·38				
39·40	35·36	16½	24½	16	24
37 38	33·34				
35·36	31·32				
41·42	37·38				
39 40	35 36				
37·38	33 34	16¼	23½	16	23¼
35·46	31·32				

TROUSERS

Sideseam	49¾	49¾	49¾	48½	49¾
Legseam	35	35	35	35	35
Width	38	36	34		32

Sideseam	48¼	49	48¼	47	48¼	46½	48¼
Legseam	34	34	34	34	34	33½	34
Width	38		36		34		32

Sideseam	46¾	46¾	46¾	46¾	45¾
Legseam	32¾	32¾	32¾	32¾	32
Width	36	34	32	30	
Sideseam	44¾	44¾	42	44¾	44¾
Legseam	31	31	30½	31	31
Width	36	34		32	30
Sideseam	42½	42½	42½	42½	41
Legseam	29	29	29	29	29
Width	36	34	32	30	

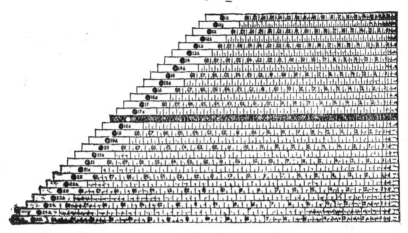

This diagram shows how graduated tapes are made, viz., strips of paper the length of every size breast measure from 12 to 24 are taken and divided into eighteen equal parts. The dark shaded one shows the eighteen size, which is of course the inch tape. And the spaces on this are already eighteen to the eighteen scye. Just 18 inches of it are taken and used for that graduated tape. The spaces may be formed by folding the strips of paper first into three, then each of these three spaces also into three equal parts, which will make nine. Then each of these nine equal parts can be divided into two equal parts, thus turning each strip of paper of every breast measure length into 18 equal parts, on the same principle as there are eighteen equal parts in eighteen inches. As a rule these parts are called units on all tapes but the inch tape, to distinguish them from inches; but inches are just as much units or part as the divisions on any other tapes.

———o———

How to Deviate for Baggy Breeches.

Dotted line on the foreside of the long breeches on this plate shows how to deviate from plain close fitting breeches so as to turn them into the baggy style. Amount put on at the sideseam is from one and half to two inches. In addition to this, care must be taken to add say two incs. each of the leg lengths, to knee, garter, calf and bottom ; the run of the dotted lines show how the deviation for buttoning in front is made. Extra length caused by this run must be allowed for at the bottom of the undersideseam. How the deviations to the undersides are effected is shown by means of laying the

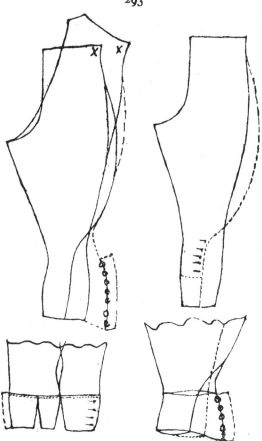

topsides on the undersides and altering as per
dotted line, adding the button catch. Solid lines
show both the unaltered and altered sideseams, and
the dotted line the alteration to the sideseam of
u derside to produce baggy breeches, with the exception of the extra length.

The dotted line across the altered forepart indicates the lengths of the breeches reaching the calf,
and the diagram below it how this style appears at
knee and bottom when a cross cut is taken out of
the underside behind the knee. Dotted lines of
this diagram shows the sideseam at the side of the
leg and solid lines the alterations for buttoning to
the front. The diagram under the long undersides
shows how to cut tight fitting continuations of a
breeches buttoning at the sideseam. This style of
continuations can be applied to breeches buttoning
forward. All that has to be done is to take from
the sideseam of foreside and add it to the sideseam
of underside.

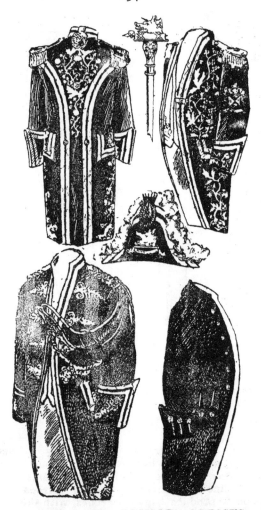

"JAMES" and " BUMBLE" DRESSES.

My Lord Mayor's 'James,' when a full dress is as gorgeously attired as a peacock-blue butterfly James and his carriage companion, the coachman and "Bumble" go out and in with the Lord Mayor, they only hold office like his Worship a year, Each Lord Mayor has to provide his servants with three suits, one for state functions, gold laced. In cut the regognised shapes are followed ; but the trimmings are according to his Worship's fancy ; Royal blue velvet is used for the state coat with gold epanelettes, worthy of a K.C.B. ; with which goes a white buckskin breeches, Vest and general's peaked hat as shown. The half state uniforms are of royal blue, coat with gold lacings, aigrettes and shoulder cords, vest fo match, and flesh coloured plush breeches and stockings, and silk hats with gold bands, There is a postilion

suit for grooms ; one for 'Bumble,' such a one as Dickens
pictured being still fashionable ; also a lovely suit for page
consisting of tail coat and breeches of black velvet, with
rose shaped steel buttons, lined with white silk. Each Lord
Mayor has also his private liveries of blue cloth, with drab
overcoats

Naval Uniforms

Fig. 1 of this group represents the Admiral in full dress.
Fig. 2 the Commander in Frock Coat and Epanelettes ; Fig
3 Colonial Mounted Rifles ; Figure 4 Lieutenant in Summer Dress ; Figure 5 Lieutenant over eight years in frock
coat ; Figure 6 Lieutenant in undress,

Fig. 1. Fig. 2.

PRIEST'S VESTMENT (Casula)
Gold Embroidered.

An embroidery executed on Bordeaux-red velvet
most effectively from a pale red silk brocade foundation. In the middle of the cross at the back of
vestment is seen the head of Christ surrounded by
elegantly curved arabesques, and along the length
and width are the heads of the seven Apostles ; the
other five being depicted on the border which orna-
ments the middle of the front part of the vestment.
The illustration shows the lower part of the border
on the cross, as far as where the design is continued
in the proper size; the small alteration taking
place in the arabesques in the middle of the cross,
are not difficult to make. The arabesques are edged
with gold cord, the inner part filled in with a few
shapes patterned with pieces of gold purl and close-
ly worked embroidery of gold thread, this being first
worked separately in a frame. Inside the contours
traced out on a grey linen ground, a thin piece of
string is led backwards and forwards in the width
and fastened down with short stitches ; the bars
thus formed give the foundation for a double gold
thread, always overcast and fastened at distances of
two bars and in reversed rows, with fine yellow
silk. When the embroidery is finished, the linen

stuff, which is still left in the frame, must be wetted at the back with paste and writing paper pasted under, the different figures are then cut out when the stuff is quite dry, leaving few lines round the contours afterwards pasted on the velvet ground of the border, also stretched in a frame, This is done before the gold cord is put on. The heads are also worked alone in gold brocade with the finest possible black and gold-brown silk, and the inner edge of the medallion margined with fine red silk cord. A narrow stripe answering to the arabesques, finishes the border on each side, yet can be replaced by gold braid, which must then be put round the whold vestment, lined with coloured silk.

Priest's Vestment (Surplice).

This robe is made of muslin, or French cambric, and edged with a broad border either worked in the material or set on to any kind of handsome lace with which the surplus is trimmed. The illustration conveys full information on these matters.

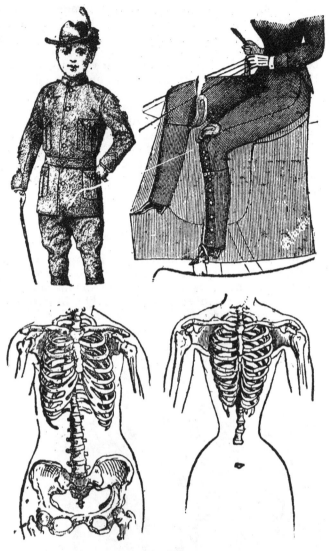

Block 1

Block 1. The anatomical figures show the difference between the natural and compressed female
figure. The lady's figure in saddle, attired in
breeches shows pretty clearly what is wanted in
garments of that class.

The Boy figure shows a Juvenile C.I.V Dress.

Block 2. The first figure shows how ladies

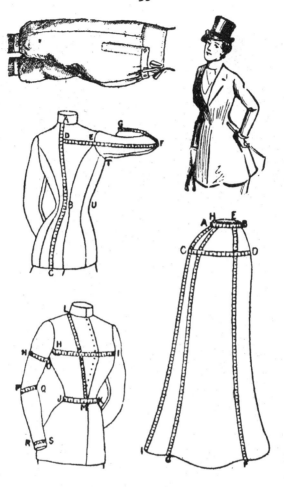

Block 2

knickers are frequently cut, namely with deep hip
waist band, and back fall-down. The second figure
the fashionable style of ladies' habit. Figure 3 how
measures for ladies jackets for breast measure cutting are taken. Fig 4, how measures are taken for
ladies' dress bodices, viz., over the dress bodice,
breast, waist and seat measures inclusive. The
length of front and opening are taken as for a vest,
and the sleeve widths as indicated. The waist
measure is taken as tightly as possible, so as to be
as correct as if taken under the bodice. Figure 5

Block 3

shows how the measures are taken for ladies' skirts, namely, front, side and back lengths. Tight waist and fair hip measure, and width round the bottom.

Block 3. These figures illustrate the manner in which the measures are usually taken for coat, vest and trousers— most clearly —for cutting by the breast measure or by patterns. Stereos or electros of any of these figures supplied for use on measure forms printed in any style required.

CPSIA information can be obtained
at www.ICGtesting.com
Printed in the USA
LVHW092244070421
683674LV00009BA/471